catalyst groupzine™
Volume 3: Courageous in Calling

Catalyst GroupZine™

Volume 3: **Courageous in Calling**

Published by Nelson Impact, a Division of Thomas Nelson, Inc., P.O. Box 141000, Nashville, Tennessee, 37214.

Scripture quotations marked NKJV are taken from the New King James Version®. Copyright © 1982 by Thomas Nelson, Inc. Used by permission. All rights reserved.

Scripture quotations marked NCV are taken from the New Century Version®. Copyright © 1987, 1988, 1991 by Thomas Nelson, Inc. Used by permission. All rights reserved.

Scripture quotations marked NIV are taken from the HOLY BIBLE, NEW INTERNATIONAL VERSION®. NIV®. Copyright©1973, 1978, 1984 by International Bible Society. Used by permission of Zondervan. All rights reserved.

Scripture quotations marked NLT are taken from the *Holy Bible*, New Living Translation, copyright © 1996. Used by permission of Tyndale House Publishers, Inc., Wheaton, Illinois 60189. All rights reserved.

Scripture quotations marked as MSG are taken from *THE MESSAGE.* Copyright © by Eugene H. Peterson, 1993, 1994, 1995. Used by permission of NavPress Publishing Group.

Scripture quotations marked ESV are from *The Holy Bible*, English Standard Version, copyright © 2001 by Crossway Bibles, a division of Good News Publishers. Used by permission. All rights reserved.

All book excerpts and articles used by permission.

Art Direction and Design:

FiveStone
Atlanta, Georgia
www.fivestone.com

Brad Lomenick would like to thank:
Tim Willard—you demonstrated your unique calling with great clarity on this project. Thanks.
Beth Nelson—the spreadsheet became a beautiful book, and credit goes to you.
Jason Locy—dude, your creativity amazes me, and your artistic design inspires me.

Tim Willard would like to thank:
Christine Willard for helping me understand the beauty in order. I love working with you.
Beth Nelson for conquering the insurmountable. And laughing with me.
Jason Locy "There's a trapdoor in the sun."
Brad Lomenick for committing to and shaping a new generation of leaders.
My Little Peanut for keeping me up late in anticipation. Can't wait to meet you!

Special thanks also to:
Kerry Priest, Jayme Stevens, Anne Alexander, Cindy Gould, Craig Canfield, Cathy Leeke, Melissa Kruse, Chad Johnson, Jennifer Hundley, Whitney Allison, Jesse Phillips, Jayson Teagle, Jeremie Kubicek, Brent Cole, Ben Ortlip, the Fire Family, the FiveStone Crew, Jason Bourne, Gabe's red book, Four AM, Taco Mac, and all our contributors.

For more information on the Catalyst Conference or to order additional copies of the **Catalyst GroupZine™**, call 888.334.6569 or visit **www.catalystspace.com**.

To find out how to exhibit or be a sponsor at the Catalyst Conference, contact Stacy Coleman (**stacy.coleman@injoy.com**).

ISBN-10: 1-4185-0327-4
ISBN-13: 978-1-4185-0327-7

Printed in the United States of America.

07 08 09 CJK 9 8 7 6 5 4 3 2 1

HOW TO USE A GROUPZINE

Welcome to *Courageous in Calling*—the next volume in the *Catalyst GroupZine* series. Pursuing the call that God has placed on your life is difficult enough on its own, let alone leading a group in doing the same thing. With that in mind, let this be a guide to help you effectively use the GroupZine with your community.

As you browse through this study you'll notice six sessions, representing each of the Elements of a Catalyst Leader: Courageous in Calling, Engaged in Culture, Authentic in Influence, Uncompromising in Integrity, Passionate about God, and Intentional about Community. Within each session you'll find:

Catalyst Study: The first article and primary curriculum for each session.

Group Discussion: Questions and journal space to reflect and prepare for group discussion.

Articles: Writings and stories from some of our favorite speakers and authors discussing the Elements.

Catalyst Features: Check out the True Story profiles, read interviews from the Global Perspective, and hear other young Catalysts' Perspectives.

Engage Journal: Reflect and respond to the entire session and engage in the challenge.

As a leader, you are often expected to have all the answers, but let's be honest, you don't. Understanding that from the start and sharing that is a great way to begin. However, you do have a lot of questions, sincere commitment, and the confidence to speak up and communicate your thoughts. So lead that way: Bring your questions to the group and explore the ideas together. Conversation is a starting point to form true community, and the group will grow through your dialogue.

Some discussion points are provided throughout the GroupZine, but you'll notice there is also plenty of white space to doodle, dream, and create your own questions. Always have a few personal ideas and questions prepared to share with your group.

Challenge each person to bring a question, a new thought, or a conviction to discuss every time you meet.

Gather your group at a coffee shop, over dinner, in a museum, or in some other beautiful space in your community. Pursue creative environments that spur your thinking and drive your conversations. Mix up the location of your meeting to inspire and be a catalyst for the conversation.

For those of you who prefer specific instructions for group dynamics, you can download a more detailed leader's guide from the *Catalyst GroupZine*™ website, **www.catalystgroupzine.com**.

Catalyst GroupZine™
Volume 3: **Courageous in Calling**

TABLE OF ELEMENTS

catalyst **5**
A Study for Next Generation Leaders

THE CATALYST STORY

CATALYST: THE LEADERSHIP FILTER FOR WHAT'S NEXT IN THE CHURCH
Catalyst exists to ignite passion for Christ and develop the leadership potential of the next generation, equipping them to engage and impact their world. Catalyst is a brand of GiANT Impact dedicated to serve, connect, and develop men and women of faith through innovative resources, events, and training, creating forward thinking church leaders that will serve as change agents in our churches, communities, and culture.

THE CATALYST STORY

In 2000, Catalyst was birthed out of a handful of young leaders who imagined a new experience—a leadership awakening that would revolutionize Next Generation Leaders for the Kingdom of God. What began as only a vision caught fire, and over the past eight years, more than 60,000 young leaders have gathered for the annual Catalyst Conference.

Today, Catalyst is much more than a conference—it's a creative community of young leaders who are passionate about their generation and eager to learn from wise communicators, mentors, and teachers in order to increase their influence. Catalyst continually serves as a leadership filter for hundreds of thousands of next generation leaders, providing relevant training, innovative events, and cutting edge resources that will shape the next generation of Church leaders. Learn more about our podcasts, online magazines, new media, and unique gatherings by visiting **www.catalystspace.com**.

THE ELEMENTS

We believe that a Catalyst leader is:

Courageous in Calling

Engaged in Culture

Authentic in Influence

Uncompromising in Integrity

Passionate about God

Intentional about Community

LETTER FROM THE EDITOR

Calling. Purpose. Meaning. If you are like me you wonder at and even struggle with these words and their significance in your life. Working on this issue of the GroupZine allowed me to study these concepts on a new level. I was able to talk to others who were sacrificing everything to heed God's call on their life. This moved me.

My conversations with leaders like Catherine Rohr, Jon Tyson, and Blake Mycoskie uncovered gems of wisdom and affirmation. Their singular vision, obedience to the call, and outright courage in the face of the unknown are not only inspiring, they're challenging—even convicting.

Their stories remind me that in order to hear God's call I must spend more time listening in His presence than talking. I must be willing to go without, so He can build me within. I must give myself to God's call, like Christ gave Himself to His Father's call. I must serve with my gift, so Christ's message remains untainted. And I must pursue with confidence, so that I feel God's pleasure when I pursue my calling.

As I sat reflecting on these conversations, Francis Chan's article hit my inbox. It's one of those articles that after you read it, all you can do is stare at the wall. What Francis does from the stage, he does in this article. He is transparent, brutally honest, and whimsical all at once. His piece reminded me that my pride is often the obstacle I like to ignore. How quickly I can forget the Voice behind the call.

My wife and I moved to Atlanta—away from the security of family and deep friendships—to pursue God's call; writing. Along the way I have had opportunities to veer from this path in favor of a more stable income. I have also been thrown from the path by a company layoff. Yet the God-prompting in my spirit continues to urge me in a direction I can't always decipher.

Though I do not always understand this path, I feel called to venture down it. At times it feels nonsensical, but I've learned that God is not bound by our syllogisms. I am only to follow, which demands that I concede "self" and serve God with acts of faithful living. At times this tastes bitter, but beauty works from the bitter roots to blossoms sweet. The glory comes from the process, and we all are called to a process—unique, bitter, and sweet. This is calling.

And so I pose the question to you, the Catalyst Leader: What is your calling—and do you have the courage to pursue it? Our intent with this issue is to prod and poke, to spur and stimulate you to think about the calling God has placed on your life—the God-whispers. Furthermore, we are honored to offer you a resource that, we pray, will assist you and your team in your ministry context. It is our hope that these words will penetrate both personally and corporately as you consider God's call to the Church universal and how your role plays out in His beautiful story.

Tim Willard
Editor

catalyst
GROUPZINE ™

Catalyst
PO Box 7700
Atlanta, GA 30357
www.catalystspace.com

Executive Editor
Brad Lomenick

Editor
Tim Willard

Managing Editor
Beth Nelson

Art Direction and Design
FiveStone
Jason Locy
Patricio Juarez
Samuel Lober
Andy Watt

Contributors:

Thomas Addington	Rick McKinley
David Batstone	Erwin McManus
Mark Batterson	Reggie McNeal
John Brandon	Brenda Salter McNeil
Mark Buchanan	Sally Morgenthaler
Marcus Buckingham	Blake Mycoskie
Francis Chan	Nancy Ortberg
Jim Collins	Dave Ramsey
Andy Crouch	Tri Robinson
Sarah Cunningham	Catherine Rohr
Tim Elmore	Chris Seay
Margaret Feinberg	Jeff Shinabarger
Mark Foreman	Priscilla Shirer
Mike Foster	Andy Stanley
Stephen Graves	Ed Stetzer
Craig Groeschel	Leonard Sweet
Os Guinness	Trish Teves
Gary Haugen	Jon Tyson
Chris Heuertz	James Emery White
Bill Hybels	Joshua White
David Kinnaman	Jud Wilhite
Patrick Lencioni	Christine Willard
Gabe Lyons	Tim Willard
Mel McGowan	

If you have a story idea, question, or feedback, email us at **info@catalystgroupzine.com**. For information on the Catalyst Conference or to purchase other Catalyst resources, visit us online at **www.catalystspace.com** or call 888.334.6569.

DRIVING ON ICE

BY ANDY STANLEY

THE LANDSCAPE OF LEADERSHIP MAKES COURAGE AN ESSENTIAL IN-GREDIENT. IT TAKES COURAGE TO CHALLENGE THE STATUS QUO, TO EMBRACE OUR FEARS, TO SAY NO TO THE GOOD TO MAKE ROOM FOR THE BEST, TO FACE CURRENT REALITY, AND TO DREAM. THESE FIVE EXPRESSIONS OF COURAGE OFTEN ELUDE YOUNG LEADERS, BUT ARE NECESSARY FOR THOSE WHO ASPIRE TO BE LEADERS WORTH FOLLOW-ING. I'M SURE THERE ARE MORE THAN FIVE, BUT THESE ARE THE ONES I KNOW A LITTLE ABOUT.

THE COURAGE TO CHALLENGE THE STATUS QUO ...

Leaders love progress. Nothing is more discouraging to a leader than the prospect of being stuck in an environment where progress is impossible. If an organization, ministry, business, or relationship is going to make progress, it must change. It must become better, more relevant, more disciplined, better aligned, more strategic.

But organizations, like people, resist change. Organizations seek equilibrium. People in organizations seek stability. Both are deterrents to progress. Change is viewed as the enemy of stability. To suggest change is to suggest that your predecessors lacked insight. Or worse, that your current supervisor doesn't get it! Consequently, you decide it is just easier to leave things as they are, to accept the status quo and learn to live with it.

While that may be easier, it is not an option for a leader. So leaders find themselves in the precarious and often career-jeopardizing position of being the ones to draw attention to the need for change. Consequently, courage is not a negotiable quality for the next generation leader.

Simply *recognizing* the need for change doesn't define leadership. Leaders are the ones who have the courage to *act* on what they see. Every church, business, and non-profit organization in need of change has within it a group of insiders who are keenly aware of the transformations that need to take place. They don't lack insight into what needs to happen, they simply lack the courage to do anything about it. In their minds, the risk is too great.

A leader says publicly what everybody else is whispering privately. It is not his insight that sets the leader apart from the crowd. It is his courage to act on what he sees, to speak up when everyone else is silent. Courageous leaders are those who would rather challenge what needs to change and pay the price than remain silent and slowly die inside.

Beyond the need to spotlight what needs to be changed, leaders must take people to places they have never been before. Leaders provide mental pictures of a preferred future and then ask people to follow them there. As leaders, we are not only asking men and women to follow us to places *they* have never been before, we are asking them to follow us to places *we* have never been before.

COURAGEOUS LEADERS ARE THOSE WHO WOULD RATHER CHALLENGE WHAT NEEDS TO CHANGE AND PAY THE PRICE THAN REMAIN SILENT AND SLOWLY DIE INSIDE.

THE COURAGE TO EMBRACE YOUR FEAR ...

We all know the fear associated with walking into a dark room or down an un-lit path. Leading into the future conjures many of the same feelings. The darkness is the uncertainty that always accompanies change; the mystery of what's at the end of the dark tunnel; the angst everyone feels when a new idea is introduced; the risk of being wrong.

When my children retreat from the darkness of the basement, I am quick to remind them that although they are afraid, they are not in danger. As true as that might be, it never helps. Fear defies logic. Information only goes so far. Even when armed with all the reasons why we should not be afraid, the fear remains.

For this reason, it is the darkness that provides leaders with their greatest opportunities. It is your response to the darkness that determines in a large part whether or not you will be called to lead. Many who lack the courage to forge ahead alone yearn for someone to take the first step—to go first—to show the way. After all, if the pathways to the future were well lit, it would be crowded.

Leaders are not always the first to *see* opportunities. They are simply the first to *seize* opportunities. But fear has kept many would–be leaders on the sidelines, while good opportunities paraded by. Think for a moment about some of the life experiences you would have missed out on if you had given in to your fears. Chances are you would have never learned to swim or ride a bicycle. You never would have asked any-one out on a date. Most of us men would never have gotten married. Unbridled fear results in missed opportunities.

Courage is not the *absence* of fear. Courage *assumes* fear. Leaders who refuse to move until their fear is gone will never move. Consequently, they will never lead. What could be and should be will not be ... at least not under their watches. Fear, not a lack of good ideas, is usually what keeps a man or woman standing on the sidelines.

Fear of failure is common to man, but leaders worth following view failure differently. Failure to move things forward is the type of failure most feared by the leader. Failure in any particular enterprise is something a leader can live with. Even laugh about. Leaders can live with the prospects of having tried and failed much easier than they can with not having tried at all.

Failure is a part of success. Veteran leaders view failure as simply a necessary chapter in their stories: lessons learned, lessons that are essential to future success. Leaders know that failure looks and feels completely different in the rear-view mirror than it does when it is staring at them through the windshield.

Leaders know that the best way to ensure success is to take chances. While the average man or woman fears *stepping out* into a new opportunity, the leader fears *missing out* on a new opportunity.

Tom Watson, Sr., founder of IBM, understood this principle. A junior executive with the company once managed to lose over $10 million in a venture that was considered risky even by company insiders. When Watson found out about the disaster, he called the young man to his office. Upon entering, the young man blurted out, "I guess you want my resignation?" Watson allegedly responded, "You can't be serious. We've just spent $10 million educating you." [1]

You can't lead without taking risks. You won't take risks without courage.

THE COURAGE TO SAY NO ...

Early in our development as leaders, we assume that when opportunity knocks, we must answer the door and embrace whoever or whatever is standing there. The ability to identify and focus on the few necessary things is a hallmark of great leadership.

Don't allow the many good opportunities to divert your attention from the one opportunity that has the greatest potential. Learn to say no. The complaint I hear most about young leaders is their inability to focus. A lack of focus eventually translates into a loss of vision. When the vision is fuzzy, people can't follow.

Leaders and organizations that entangle themselves in an array of unrelated "opportunities" dilute their effectiveness in every area. Often the reason we won't say no is that we are afraid. We fear disappointing people. We fear being passed by. We fear missing out on a good opportunity. But at some point, every leader must come to grips with the fact that there will always be more opportunities than there is time to pursue them. If we don't choose our opportunities carefully, we will dilute

IF YOU ALLOW FEAR TO OVERSHADOW YOUR DREAMS, YOU WILL NEVER TRY ANYTHING NEW OR CREATE ANYTHING NEW.

our efforts in every endeavor. Refusing to say no eventually robs leaders of their ultimate opportunity: the opportunity to play to their strengths.

Choose your opportunities carefully. Many opportunities are worth missing.

THE COURAGE TO FACE CURRENT REALITY ...

Leaders must be willing to face current reality. When someone refuses to face reality, we call it denial. We say that person is sick. The same is true of organizations. To state the obvious, organizations in denial are usually led by leaders who are in denial. They refuse to face the facts.

As leaders, we want to believe things are good. Our egos are inexorably intertwined with our ability to lead. So the tendency, as Peter Senge points out in his book *The Fifth Discipline*, is to put a positive spin on everything and ignore evidence to the contrary. [2] The danger, of course, is that over time we lose sight of what is actually happening around us.

As I said, leaders worth following are willing to face and embrace current reality, regardless of how discouraging or embarrassing it might be. To be that kind of leader, you must be relentless in your quest to know the truth about what is happening around you. You must make it your habit to root out misinformation and refuse to reward those who deliver it. In doing so, you will create a culture that is healthily transparent about what is and what is not taking place.

It is impossible to generate sustained growth if your plan for the future is not rooted in reality. When time after time your grand strategies don't work out, it is evidence that there is either low capacity or no interest. In other words, there was something about current reality that you overlooked. Jim Collins says, "Leadership does not begin just with vision. It begins with getting people to confront the brutal facts and to act on the implications." [3] If we are not careful, we will ignore the brutal facts and act instead on what we have convinced ourselves to be true.

Facing current reality is often nasty, but always necessary. Nasty, because it may entail acknowledging that you aren't as far along as you thought you were. Necessary, because you can't get where you need to be if you don't know where you are. This is why every successful organizational turnaround begins with an intense fact-finding mission. To ensure that we are leading with our feet firmly planted on the soil of what is, we must live by the seven commandments of current reality:

1. Thou shalt not pretend.
2. Thou shalt not turn a blind eye.
3. Thou shalt not exaggerate.
4. Thou shalt not shoot the bearer of bad news.
5. Thou shalt not hide behind the numbers.
6. Thou shalt not ignore constructive criticism.
7. Thou shalt not isolate thyself.

Attempting to lead while turning a blind eye to the truth is like treading water. That can only go on for so long. Eventually you are going to sink. As a leader, be

willing to face the truth regardless of how painful it might be. And when you don't like what you see, change it.

THE COURAGE TO DREAM ...

Every great accomplishment began as a dream. As Stephen Covey put it, "All things are created twice. There's a mental or first creation, and a physical or second creation to all things." [4] As a next generation leader, you must dream about what could be and should be. You must allow your mind to wander outside the boundaries of what *is* and begin to create a mental picture of what *could be.*

But dreaming requires courage. For on the heels of every dream is the demon of doubt. No sooner have we latched on to a preferred future than our minds are filled with all the reasons it won't work. We find ourselves wondering if we are really up to the task. And if we are courageous (or foolish) enough to share our dreams with others, they are generally quick to confirm our suspicions.

If you allow fear to overshadow your dreams, you will never try anything new or create anything new. Worst of all, if fear causes you to retreat from your dreams, you will never give the world anything new.

I keep a little card on my desk that reads, *"Dream no small dreams, for they stir not the hearts of men."* More than once that simple statement has kept me from retreating from my dreams. I know from experience that it is impossible to lead without a dream. When leaders are no longer willing to dream, it is only a short time until followers will be unwilling to follow.

So dream! Dream big. Dream often. Somewhere in all those random ideas that flood your mind will be one that captures your heart and imagination. And that seemingly random idea may very well evolve into a vision for your life and leadership.

As a leader, you have no idea what hangs in the balance of your decision to act courageously. When I look back over the last twelve years, I shudder when I realize what would have happened if our team had been unwilling to challenge what *was* for the sake of what *could be*. We would have missed out on being a part of what God has done through North Point Ministries. But understand that we were often afraid. Many, many times we had to say no to good ideas in order to stay focused on what we believed God had called us to do. With our success came the tendency to accept the status quo, to not continue to dream and ask, "What's next?" But, as I said, too much hangs in the balance.

So let's continue to ask ourselves these questions as we go forward:

Am I willing to challenge the status quo?

Do I have the courage to embrace my fears?

Am I willing to say no to the good opportunity for the sake of the one with the greatest potential?

Do I have the courage to face and embrace current reality?

Am I willing to allow my mind to wander outside the boundaries of what is and begin to create a mental picture of what could be … to dream?

If you embrace and digest these five expressions, you will have the foundation you need to leverage the opportunities God brings your way. Ignore any one of these five, and you will expend an inordinate measure of energy with little progress to show for it. If you have ever driven on ice, you know that horsepower is worthless without traction. These expressions of courage will provide you with the traction you need to maximize your leadership potential. **C**

Andy Stanley is the lead pastor of North Point Community Church in Atlanta, Georgia. (**www.northpoint.org**) He is the bestselling author of *Visioneering, The Next Generation Leader, The Best Question Ever,* and the recent *It Came from Within.* Andy and his wife, Sandra, live in Atlanta with their two sons and daughter.

I. COURAGEOUS IN CALLING

God has a unique purpose that He desires to carry out in me. To know this purpose
I must first know Him. To fulfill this purpose, I must trust Him and have the courage to act
on it, which may feel like a risk. My talents and heart converge to create my calling and
purpose. I am competent in my calling because I am committed to further developing and
honing my talents and skills. My foundational understanding of how God is working during
my current season of life determines the specific way I apply this calling vocationally.

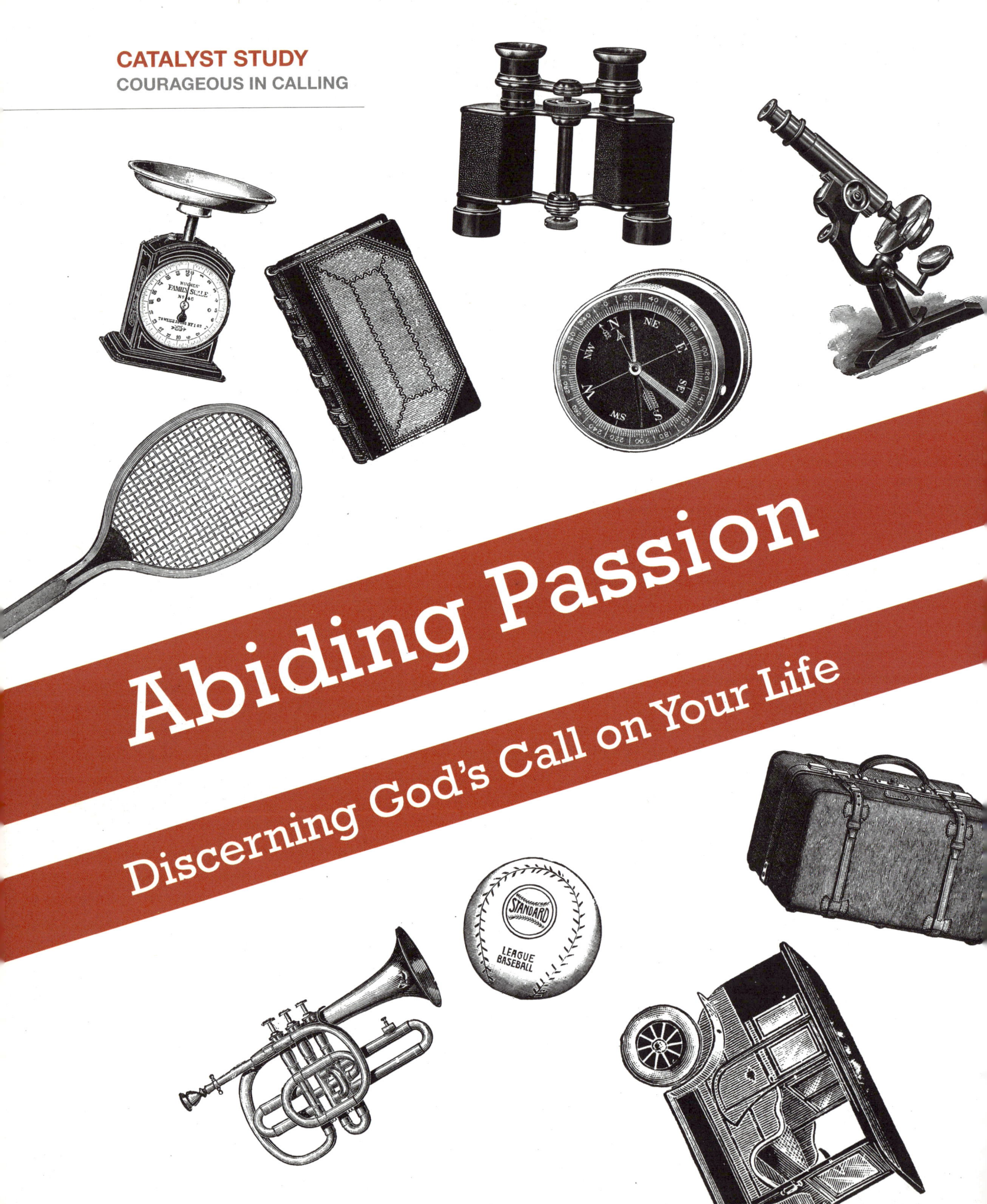

Abiding Passion

Discerning God's Call on Your Life

By Stephen R. Graves and Thomas G. Addington

THE BIBLE INCLUDES MANY VERSES THAT SPEAK OF A CALLING CONNECTED TO OUR WORK. BUT CALLING, IN ITS FULLNESS, IS AN IDEA TOO GOOD TO BE TRUE—UNLESS AND UNTIL JESUS IS INVOLVED IN THE CONVERSATION. WHEN HE CALLS, HE DOES SO WITH GREAT PRECISION. NOT ONLY DOES HE KNOW WHAT NEEDS TO BE ACCOMPLISHED AND HOW THAT TASK FITS WITHIN ETERNAL BOUNDARIES, HE ALSO KNOWS THE ONE HE IS CALLING. AFTER ALL, HE MADE THAT PERSON *SPECIFICALLY* TO DO WHAT HE OR SHE IS BEING CALLED TO DO.

In his book, *The Rest of God*, Mark Buchanan writes, "Virtually any job, no matter how grueling or tedious—any job that is not criminal or sinful—can be a gift from God, through God, and to God. The work of our hands, by the alchemy of our devotion, becomes the worship of our hearts."

So how does your view of calling match up to that standard?

On Purpose

The rat race. The treadmill. The old grind. Surely God has something better in mind for your life than the futility and tedium implied by some of our most familiar synonyms for the workaday life. We human beings weren't designed to go around in circles, as on a treadmill. We were made to move toward a purpose. We were made to grow. The thought of purposelessness strikes horror in us. The huge appeal of books like Rick Warren's *The Purpose Driven Life* should come as no surprise. We need to know we're a part of something larger than ourselves. We need to know there's more to our work than "another day, another dollar." God has a grand design for the universe He created. The work we do from 9 to 5 is—or should be—one of the most important ways we take part in that grand design. That's what calling means. The knowledge that we are working out a calling imbues our work with a dignity and joy that go well beyond the goods we produce and the services we render.

What is Scripture's definition of calling? Calling is **God's personal invitation for me to work on *His* agenda, using the talents I have been given in ways that are eternally significant.**

To be called means I know that what I am doing is what God wants me to do. God calls every one of us to a specific work assignment at any given time. When Paul was speaking to philosophers in Athens, he made it clear that God had a very precise plan for individual lives: "From one man He made every nation of men, that they should inhabit the whole earth; and *He determined the times set for them and the exact places where they should live.*" (Acts 17:26, NIV emphasis added) God designed *me* to do something for *Him*.

We are men and women who do consulting, banking, truck driving, plumbing, doctoring, full-time parenting, teaching, pastoring, and a host of other things. God calls individuals to all kinds of careers. The common factor that we all share, however, is the One who has called us all. Our work involves the implementation of God's agenda in history.

Looking Outside Ourselves

It's true that knowing yourself—your skill set, your limitations, your passions—is an important part of pursuing your calling. But ultimately, calling isn't about getting in touch with yourself so much as it's about letting God touch you. This is an important point. There's nothing wrong with looking deep inside. But calling is about being part of something that's a whole lot bigger than you: God's purposes—and not just His purposes for your life, but His purposes for everything else, too. Your calling reaches beyond you, and pursuing your calling means responding to a big God in ways that always expand your boundaries.

Let's look at two of the most dramatic cases of calling in the Bible: Moses and Paul. When Moses encountered God in the burning bush, his career had been in a 40-year freefall. He had once been a prince of Egypt, but a moment of violent anger destroyed all that and sent him running to the desert. In the desert, it had been his job to take care of his father-in-law's sheep. Talk about going nowhere! Then came the unmistakable call of God: "I will send you to Pharaoh that you may bring My people, the children of Israel, out of Egypt." (Exodus 3:10 NKJV)

Moses was doubtful that God had the right man. Years of working for his father-in-law, far from the privilege and honor of his old station in life, had done a number on his self-confidence. But he answered the call anyway, and as time went on, it became obvious that this kind of leadership was what he was born for. He had all the advantages of being raised and educated in the house of Pharaoh. He had a heart for the sufferings of the Hebrew

people—as evidenced by his rash killing of an Egyptian overseer who was oppressing them. And his 40-year banishment to the desert was vital training for the 40 years he would spend leading his people in a similar desert.

Paul—or Saul, as he was known at the time—was on a much different career path when he heard God's call. He was a rising star among Jewish religious professionals. He had all the qualifications of birth and had been trained by some of the greatest scholars of the Jewish faith. He had ambition, drive, smarts, and single-minded commitment to the cause. He had become the Pharisees' go-to guy for stomping out the latest threat to their religious hegemony: the Christians.

He was on his way, in fact, to stomp out more Christians when he saw the light—or more precisely, he was blinded by it. His call from God was as specific as Moses':

We human beings weren't designed to go around in circles, as on a treadmill. We were made to move toward a purpose. We were made to grow.

I have appeared to you for this purpose, to make you a minister and a witness both of the things which you have seen and of the things which I will yet reveal to you. I will deliver you from the Jewish people, as well as from the Gentiles, to whom I now send you, to open their eyes, in order to turn them from darkness to light, and from the power of Satan to God, that they may receive forgiveness of sins and an inheritance among those who are sanctified by faith in Me. (Acts 26:16-20 NKJV)

Once Paul responded to God's call, it became obvious that everything in his life up to that point had been preparing him for this work. The drive and energy and focus that had made him such a formidable enemy of the early Church made him an even more formidable force in the growth of the Church during extremely difficult times. In Paul's epistles, which are so important in the definition of the truths of Christianity, you can see the logic and rhetorical skill that had been sharpened during his training under Judaism's leading lights.

One thing to note: the word *calling* isn't just Christian-ese for *career*. No career counselor would have looked over Moses' resume and said, "Have you ever thought about facing down the most powerful ruler in the world and leading three million slaves to freedom?" No corporate headhunter would have thought to take Saul out to lunch and recruit him to take the lead in shaping the Christian Church as we know it.

In retrospect, it's obvious that Moses and Paul were the men for the jobs God gave them. But they could have filled out personality profiles and self-evaluations until the cows came home, and they would have never found inside themselves the incredible things God would do through them. One looked like an abject failure and one looked like a wild success, but for Moses and Paul alike, the act of responding to God's call focused a lifetime of misdirected energy into a career of mind-boggling significance.

Settled Calling

So what does life look like when you're pursuing your calling? There's no single answer to that question, but there are at least a few guidelines. There's a certain settled-ness about a person who is pursuing his or her calling. You've seen people who are always looking over the fence, people who get a little too excited about every new possibility, whose interest is piqued a little too much by every conversation. That's not a person who has settled into his or her calling. When you've answered God's call, you're able to live in the now. You can enjoy what God is doing in the present; you can look forward to the future too, but in a way that rests in God's sovereignty. You don't have that luxury if you don't feel settled.

Living out your calling involves obeying Christ's command to "abide" in Him. In the Greek, "abide" is related to the idea of a bowstring when it's not pulled tight. To abide in Christ is to be released from the constant tension of being unsettled and

When you're pursuing your calling, you're not constantly trying to convince God to go along with your plan.

discontent. That doesn't mean your life will be struggle-free. Of course there still will be challenges to be met. Sometimes you've got to pull back the bowstring and let fly. But you always return to a state of rest. Max Lucado calls it living in your sweet spot: "A zone, a region, a life precinct in which you were made to dwell. He tailored the curves of your life to fit an empty space in His jigsaw puzzle."

When you're pursuing your calling, you're not constantly trying to convince God to go along with your plan. Instead, you find out what God is doing, and you join Him. A sense of calling gives you a relaxed view of God's sovereignty. You're in your spot, doing your part, but you realize there's a lot more going on than your one-person drama. It's your job to grow and go, to be sure you're who you ought to be as a person. It's God's job to weave your life into the larger tapestry of His purpose. If God sees fit to make you the next Warren Buffett or Bill Gates or Rick Warren or Michael Jordan, that's great. If He chooses to use your talents on a smaller stage, that's great too. There's real rest in that realization.

Another important means of discerning your calling is to *listen to your desires.* What is it that you want out of life? What truly matters to you? If you're seeking God's calling for your life, those desires might be your next clue.

Christians are often suspicious of desire. Misguided desires, after all, are the cause of all kinds of trouble. Yet just as wrong desires can lead you down the wrong path, right desires are signposts to the right path. "Delight yourself also in the LORD," said the psalmist, "and He shall give you the desires of your heart." (Psalm 37:4 NKJV) Saint Augustine said the same thing in a different way: "Love God, and do as you please." If your desires are in harmony with God's desires for you, why wouldn't He give you the desires of your heart?

C.S. Lewis is frequently quoted on the subject of desire. His remarks in the sermon "The Weight of Glory" are worth repeating:

It would seem that our Lord finds our desires not too strong, but too weak. We are half-hearted creatures, fooling about with drink and sex and ambition, when infinite joy is offered to us, like an ignorant child who wants to go on making mud pies in the slum because he cannot imagine what is meant by the offer of a holiday at the sea. We are far too easily pleased.

Our desires and longings are homing signals, calling us back to the One who alone can fulfill every desire. True, we often get off track, settling for things that fall well short of our true desire. Nevertheless, desire is one of the chief ways God calls His people to the work He would have them do. That longing you feel for something more in your work—perhaps it's not simple (and sinful) discontent. Perhaps it's the call of God on your life, to do your part in God's grand design of building His Kingdom.

The Agitation of Calling

Consider the case of Nehemiah. Nehemiah enjoyed tremendous career success at the court of Artaxerxes, the Persian king. Nehemiah rose all the way to the position of cupbearer to Artaxerxes. He seemed pretty well set as far as his career went. He had direct access to the world's most powerful ruler, which gave him tremendous influence.

But Nehemiah's career trajectory was changed completely by a conversation with his brother, who brought news from the land of their ancestors:

Hanani, one of my brothers, came from Judah with some other men, and I questioned them about the Jewish remnant that survived the exile, and also about Jerusalem. They said to me, "Those who survived the exile and are back in the province are in great trouble and disgrace. The wall of Jerusalem is broken down, and its gates have

been burned with fire." When I heard these things, I sat down and wept. (Nehemiah 1:2–4 NKJV)

A new variable rocked Nehemiah's world. His status quo was shattered by news from his homeland that tore at his heartstrings. That is to say, his desires changed completely when he heard what was happening in Judah. For over four months he fasted and prayed. This was no "here today, gone tomorrow" burden. Nehemiah was affected to the core of his being.

Noted nineteenth-century French writer Honore de Balzac commented on such heartfelt callings: "Vocations which we wanted to pursue, but didn't, bleed, like colors, on the whole of our existence."

At work, Nehemiah had every reason to put on his game face. But he could not hide his heavy heart. And his heart must have skipped a beat when the king asked what was the matter. However, he had such a firm sense of his calling by then even the potential threat of a king's wrath could not stand in the way of pursuing his mission:

I was very much afraid, but I said to the king, "May the king live forever! Why should my face not look sad when the city where my fathers are buried lies in ruins, and its gates have been destroyed by fire?"

The king said to me, "What is it you want?"

Then I prayed to the God of heaven, and I answered the king, "If it pleases the king and if your servant has found favor in his sight, let him send me to the city in Judah where my fathers are buried so that I can rebuild it."

Then the king, with the queen sitting beside him, asked me, "How long will your journey take, and when will you get back?" It pleased the king to send me. (Nehemiah 2:1–6 NKJV)

It is obvious that Nehemiah was truly following the call of God when he went to Jerusalem to rebuild the wall. The same natural talents that attracted the attention of Artaxerxes, sharpened by years of service in the palace—not to mention the goodwill of the world's most powerful man—qualified Nehemiah for the challenges of managing a massive building project in the dangerous setting that was Jerusalem. The burden Nehemiah felt was God's undeniable call to a very specific task.

How Do I Know I'm Called by Desire?

Calling is a process of definition, identifying both what you are and what you are not. To determine if a desire is a genuine, God-given direction, here are some filters:

It might be calling by desire if the sense of urgency is persistent and relatively longstanding. A calling is more than a passing fancy. Life always has its zigs and zags. We are not talking here about a "passion of the moment." No, a calling is an abiding passion of your soul. When God places a desire on your heart and then uses that desire to call you to do something specific, it is usually something that builds and is seasoned over time,

not something that just shows up on your doorstep today for you to do tomorrow.

It is probably *not* calling by desire if I am completely unequipped to get the job done. God equips whom He calls and calls whom He equips. If I feel called to do something that is outside the bounds of who God has made me, then it probably is not a calling after all. Calling is more about doing than it is about thinking. Calling requires that I take action that results in accomplishing something. It is not primarily about ideas that I just roll through my mind. Many people have dreams that they equate with God's call; but calling is about doing, not dreaming.

J. K. Rowling had a dream to write a book. In that regard, she is not particularly unique. One day she sat down at a keyboard and began to write. The difference is that she had what it takes to do it, and she sat down and did it. Of her own journey, she said, "It does not do to dwell on dreams and forget to live." A calling is not something you just dream; it is something you must be capable of bringing to fruition.

It is probably *not* calling by desire if I quit when I encounter significant hurdles. Life is seldom a cakewalk for one who hears God call by desire. A calling is tenacious. It works itself out despite the obstacles. Robert Morrison, the first Protestant missionary to China, was a man called by desire. He was 25 years old when he arrived in China in 1807. He was filled with a driving passion to see the Chinese people come to know Jesus. He died 27 years later, a very discouraged man. Over his entire career he had only baptized ten Chinese. He considered his work a failure. Yet his influence continues on in the Chinese church to this day. Why? Because Robert Morrison translated the Bible into Chinese, and the Chinese Bible is a testament to his persistent pursuit of calling despite all odds.

When you answer God's call on your life, you have bigger dreams than a big paycheck or success as the world defines it. You want to be a part of what God is doing in the world. Your deepest desire is to respond to God's invitation to work on His agenda, using the talents you have been given in ways that are eternally significant. **C**

Stephen R. Graves is a highly sought business coach and life guide for entrepreneurs and leaders desiring to successfully make it to the finish line of life. In 1991, he co-founded the Cornerstone Group, a company built to integrate biblical wisdom and business excellence. He and his wife Karen have three children.

Thomas G. Addington is the co-founder of Cornerstone Consulting Group and WellSpring Group. He advises senior corporate leaders, helps organizations and their boards formulate strategic solutions, and assists leadership as they chart the future and navigate new realities. He and his wife Susan have three children.

This article is based on concepts drawn from Life@Work *by John C. Maxwell, Stephen R. Graves, and Thomas G. Addington, published by Thomas Nelson, Inc.*

GROUP STUDY QUESTIONS
FOR DISCUSSION

1. How are you planting eternal seeds in the ground of the everyday through your calling?

2. As you listen to your desires, what are they telling you about your calling?

3. How are you letting God touch you through your calling?

4. As you pursue your calling, is there evidence of being settled? If so, what evidence?

5. How does abiding in Christ relate to being settled in your calling?

{ THE CALL }

By Os Guinness

CALLING IS THE TRUTH THAT GOD CALLS US TO HIMSELF SO DECISIVELY THAT EVERYTHING WE ARE, EVERYTHING WE DO, AND EVERYTHING WE HAVE IS INVESTED WITH A SPECIAL DEVOTION, DYNAMISM, AND DIRECTION LIVED OUT AS A RESPONSE TO HIS SUMMONS AND SERVICE.

Our primary calling as followers of Christ is by Him, to Him, and for Him. First and foremost we are called to Someone (God), not to something (such as motherhood, politics, or teaching) or to somewhere (such as the inner city or Outer Mongolia).

Our secondary calling, considering who God is as sovereign, is that everyone, everywhere, and in everything we should think, speak, live, and act entirely for Him. We can therefore properly say as a matter of secondary calling that we are called to home-making or to the practice of law or to art history. But these and other things are always the secondary, never the primary calling. They are "callings" rather than the "calling." They are our personal answer to God's address, our response to God's summons. Secondary callings matter, but only because the primary calling matters most.

This vital distinction between primary and secondary calling carries with it two challenges—first, to hold the two together and, second, to ensure that they are kept in the right order. In other words, if we understand calling, we must make sure that first things remain first and the primary calling always comes before the secondary calling. But we must also make sure that the primary calling leads without fail to the secondary calling. The church's failure to meet these challenges has led to the two grand distortions that have crippled the truth of calling. We may call them the "Catholic distortion" and the "Protestant distortion."

The first distortion may be called the "Catholic distortion" because it rose in the Catholic area and is the majority position in the Catholic tradition. The early writings of Eusebius argues that Christ gave "two ways of life" to his church. One is the "perfect life"—dedicated to contemplation and reserved for priests, monks, and nuns. The other is "permitted"—a secular life dedicated to action and open tasks such as soldiering, governing, farming, trading, and raising families. Sadly, this "two-tier" or "double life" view of calling flagrantly perverted biblical teaching by narrowing the sphere of calling and excluding most Christians from its scope.

Whereas the Catholic distortion is a spiritual form of dualism, elevating the spiritual the expense of the secular, the Protestant distortion is a secular form of dualism, elevating the secular at the expense of the spiritual.

Under the pressure of the modern world, the "Protestant distortion" serves to sever the secular from the spiritual altogether and reduces vocation to an alternative word for work. The seeds can be traced back to the Puritans themselves as words such as work, trade, employment, and occupation came to be used interchangeably with calling and vocation. As this happened, the guidelines for calling shifted; instead of being directed by the commands of God, they were seen as directed by duties and roles in society. Eventually the day came when faith and calling were separated completely. The original demand that each Christian should have a calling was boiled down to the demand that each citizen should have a job.

At least two things are required to overcome the Protestant distortion: 1) We must refuse to play the word games that pretend calling means anything without a Caller, and 2) We must restore the primary calling to its primary place by restoring the worship that is its setting and the dedication to Jesus that is its heart.

In sum, we must avoid the two distortions by keeping the two callings together, stressing the primary calling to counter the Protestant distortion and secondary callings to counter the Catholic distortion. Whereas dualism cripples calling, a holistic understanding releases its power—the passion to be God's concentrates the energy of all who answer the call. **C**

Os Guinness is an internationally renowned speaker and the author of numerous books, including *The Call*, *Journey Home*, and *Time for Truth*. He is the co-founder and regular moderator of The Trinity Forum (**www.ttf.org**).

Reprinted by permission. Rising To The Call, *Os Guinness, 2003, Thomas Nelson Inc., Nashville, Tennessee.* *All rights reserved.*

CHASE THE LION

BY MARK BATTERSON

A FEW YEARS AGO I WAS PART OF A MISSION TEAM THAT HELPED BUILD A TEEN CHALLENGE CENTER IN OCHO RIOS, JAMAICA. AFTER A LONG WEEK OF HARD WORK, OUR FAMILY STAYED FOR A FEW DAYS TO RELAX AND ENJOY THE ISLAND. WHEN WE CHECKED INTO OUR HOTEL, I HAPPENED TO PICK UP A TOURIST BROCHURE ABOUT CLIFF JUMPING IN NEGRIL. THE SECOND I SAW IT I KNEW I NEEDED TO GO JUMP OFF A CLIFF. BUT A FEW DAYS AND A FEW EXCUSES LATER, WE WERE ON AN AIRPLANE HEADED BACK TO WASHINGTON, DC. AT ABOUT THIRTY THOUSAND FEET, I REMEMBER HAVING THIS THOUGHT: *I MIGHT NEVER GET BACK HERE.* I FELT LIKE I HAD FORFEITED A ONCE-IN-A-LIFETIME EXPERIENCE. AND I STILL REGRET IT.

In the grand scheme of things, I know that regret is rather benign. But that experience taught me a valuable lesson: at the end of our lives, we'll regret *opportunities missed* a lot more than *mistakes made.*

My conviction is backed up by the research of two Cornell sociologists, Tom Gilovich and Vicki Medvec. According to their study, time is a key factor in what we regret. Over the short-term, we tend to regret our *actions*. But over the long haul, we tend to regret *inactions*. Their study found that over the course of an average week, action regrets outnumber inaction regrets 53 percent to 47 percent. But when people look at their lives as a whole, *inaction regrets outnumber action regrets 84 percent to 16 percent.*

I have my fair share of action regrets. I've said and done some things that I wish I could unsay and undo. Who hasn't secretly wished that they could fly counter-rotational around the earth at supersonic speeds and reverse time like Superman? But I'm convinced that our deepest regrets at the end of our lives will be the risks not taken, the opportunities not seized, and the dreams not pursued.

THE GREAT OMISSION

Is anybody else tired of reactive Christianity that is known more for *what it's against* than *what it's for?*

The Church has fixated on sins of commission for far too long. It seems like our modus operandi has been to avoid action regrets so we have a laundry list of *don'ts*. Think of it as *holiness by subtraction*. So holiness becomes the byproduct of subtracting something from our lives that shouldn't be there instead of maximizing our God-given potential. Don't get me wrong. Holiness certainly involves subtraction. But I think God is far more concerned about sins of omission—those things we could have and should have done. Could it be that holiness has as much or more to do with seizing opportunities than it does with resisting temptation? Those who simply run away from sin are half-Christians—you can do nothing wrong and still do nothing right. Our calling is much higher than simply running away from what's wrong.

Maybe we've measured spiritual maturity the wrong way? Maybe following Christ isn't supposed to be as *safe* or as *civilized* as we've been led to believe? Maybe Christ was more *dangerous* and *uncivilized* than our Sunday school Flannelgraphs portrayed? Maybe God wants to raise up a generation of lion chasers?

CHASING LIONS

II Samuel 23:20 highlights one of the most obscure yet courageous acts recorded in Scripture, but it's more than that. It's a microcosm of how God calls us to approach life.

Benaiah chased a lion down into a pit. Then, despite the snow and slippery ground, he caught the lion and killed it.

Scripture doesn't tell us what Benaiah was doing or where he was going when he en-

I'M CONVINCED THAT OUR DEEPEST REGRETS AT THE END OF OUR LIVES WILL BE THE RISKS NOT TAKEN, THE OPPORTUNITIES NOT SEIZED, AND THE DREAMS NOT PURSUED.

countered this lion. We don't know Benaiah's frame of mind, but Scripture does reveal his gut reaction. And it was gutsy. It ranks as one of the most improbable reactions recorded in Scripture. When the image of a man-eating beast travels through the optical nerve and registers in the visual cortex, the brain has one overarching message: *run away.*

That is what normal people do, but lion chasers are wired differently. They don't see five-hundred pound problems. They see God-ordained opportunities.

For most of us, finding ourselves in a pit with a lion on a snowy day would pose a substantial problem, but you've got to admit something: *I killed a lion in a pit on a snowy day* looks pretty impressive on your résumé if you're applying for a bodyguard position with the King of Israel! Not only does Benaiah land a job as David's chief bodyguard, he climbs all the way up the military chain-of-command to become Commander-in-Chief of Israel's army. Benaiah was the second most powerful person in the kingdom of Israel, but his genealogy of success can be traced all the way back to a life-and-death encounter with a man-eating lion. It was fight or flight. Benaiah was faced with a choice that would determine his destiny: *run away* or *give chase.*

If you run away, you'll always wonder, *what if?*

FACE YOUR FEARS

It was two years ago that I was part of a team that went on a mission trip to Ethiopia. Before going on the trip, everybody on the team was a little nervous. It was during a time of political unrest; we were subjecting ourselves to a variety of third world diseases; and even drinking the water and eating the food was done conscientiously.

Understandably, everybody was a little nervous, but one team member was downright fearful. Especially when she learned that we were going to camp out in Awash National Park on our free day. Somehow, knowing that armed guards would keep watch all night didn't ease her mind. Neither did the crocodiles we saw in the river or the lions we heard around the campfire! But I was so proud of Sarah because she faced her fear. And because she pushed through her fears, she experienced some of the most amazing memories of her life.

We drove through the Ethiopian outback and went swimming in a natural spring that was heated by a volcano. You don't get to do that every day. We visited a tribal village that looked like it came right out of the pages of a *National Geographic* magazine. And none of us will forget our game drive on top of Land Rovers.

In retrospect, it's hard to imagine how many memories Sarah would have forfeited if she had run away from her fears. One of the greatest tragedies in life is the stories that go untold because we don't face our fears. But Sarah decided to live her life in a way that was worth telling stories about!

For what it's worth, none of the things that she was afraid of happened. The plane didn't crash. She didn't get sick. And she wasn't eaten alive by wild animals. The only bad thing that happened to her was when she got pooped on by a baboon. I'm not sure if the baboon was aiming or not, but what a shot. I know that is a nasty memory, but what a story. That is living life to the fullest!

So here is my advice: don't let mental lions keep you from experiencing everything God has to offer. The greatest experiences will often double as the scariest experiences. The defining moments will often double as the scariest decisions.

In the words of David Whyte, "The price of our vitality is the sum of our fears."

Benaiah must have been scared spitless when he encountered that lion. But he didn't run away. In fact, it was the fear he felt that made his "in a pit with a lion on a snowy day" story all the more fun to tell, ex post facto.

Imagine the bedtime stories Benaiah must have told his children! I can hear his kids, "Please, tell us the lion story one more time." I think we owe it to our kids and grandkids to live our lives in a way that is worth telling stories about. And more importantly, we owe it to God. So here is my question: *are you living your life in a way that is worth telling stories about?*

Maybe it is time to quit running and start chasing.

OPPORTUNITY ROARS

Nestled into Colossians 4 there is a great definition of spiritual maturity. If all of us obeyed this verse, it would revolutionize our lives. Colossians 4:5 says:

Make the most of every opportunity.

This Scripture doesn't specify how many or how few opportunities. It doesn't quantify how small or how large the opportunity. We simply need to make the most of every opportunity.

The word translated "opportunity" in Colossians 4:5 is the Greek word *kairos*. It refers to a serendipitous window of opportunity.

The English word, opportunity, comes from the Latin phrase *ob portu*. In the days before modern harbors, ships had to wait until flood tide to make it into port. The Latin phrase "ob portu" referred to that moment in time when the tide would turn. The captain and crew would wait for that one moment, and they knew that if they missed it, they would have to wait for another tide to come in.

Shakespeare borrowed the idea in one of his famous verses from *Julius Caesar*:

There is a tide in the affairs of men,
Which, taken at the flood, leads on to fortune;
Omitted, all the voyage of their life
Is bound in shallows and in miseries.
On such a full sea we are now afloat;
And we must take the current when it serves,
Or lose our ventures.

Seeing and seizing opportunities is an underappreciated dimension of spiritual maturity. We are surrounded by God-ordained opportunities—opportunities to love, opportunities to laugh, opportunities to give, opportunities to learn, opportunities to serve. Seeing and seizing those opportunities is at the heart of what it means to follow Christ and be filled with the Spirit.

Now here's the catch. The old aphorism is wrong. *Opportunity doesn't knock.* The giant Egyptian that Benaiah later did battle with didn't knock on the door. He knocked down the door. And the lion didn't roll over and play dead. *Opportunity roars!*

Most of us want our opportunities gift wrapped. We want our lions stuffed or caged or cooked medium well and served on a silver platter. But opportunities typically present themselves at the most inopportune times in the most inopportune places. Opportunities often come disguised as big, hairy, audacious problems, but lion chasers don't see problems. They see five-hundred pound opportunities!

A LION CHASER'S MANIFESTO

When opportunity roars, you have a choice to make: run away like a scaredy-cat or grab life by the mane.

Quit living as if the purpose of life is to arrive safely at death. Set God-sized goals. Pursue God-ordained passions. Go after a dream that is destined to fail without divine intervention. Stop pointing out problems and become part of the solution. Stop criticizing and start creating. Stop playing it safe and start taking risks. Expand your horizons. Accumulate experiences. Consider the lilacs. Find every excuse you can to celebrate everything you can. Don't let what's wrong with you keep you from worshipping what's right with God. Burn sinful bridges. Laugh at yourself. Keep making mistakes. Worry less about what people think and more about what God thinks. Don't try to be who you're not. Be yourself. Quit holding out. Quit holding back. Quit running away. And remember: if God is for us, who can be against us?

Unleash the lion chaser within!

So here is the question you need to ask and answer: *What lion is God calling you chase?*

Maybe it's time to apply for your dream job; admit your addiction; reconcile the relationship; ask her out; take the test; go on a mission trip; mentor someone; stop attending church and start serving; add a stamp to your passport; take a night class; start a business; write the manuscript.

There is an old aphorism: *no guts, no glory.*

When we don't have the guts to step out in faith and chase lions, then God is robbed of the glory that rightfully belongs to Him!

Chase the lion! **C**

Mark Batterson serves as lead pastor of National Community Church (**www.theaterchurch. com**) in Washington, DC. He is the author of *In a Pit with a Lion on a Snowy Day* and blogs at **www.markbatterson.com**. Mark lives on Capitol Hill with his wife, Lora, and their three children.

Beautiful is What Redemption Looks Like

Interview with Eduardo Verastegui by Trish Teves

EDUARDO VERASTEGUI HAS BEEN CALLED MANY THINGS. *PEOPLE EN ES-PAÑOL MAGAZINE* CALLED HIM ONE OF THE "50 MOST BEAUTIFUL" PEOPLE IN THEIR 2006 ISSUE. HE'S BEEN CALLED THE "BRAD PITT OF LATIN AMER-ICA." BUT MOST RECENTLY HE'S BEEN CALLED TO INFUSE THE AMERICAN FILM INDUSTRY WITH A LITTLE BIT OF HIS INNER BEAUTY.

Born in a small Mexican town to a sugar cane farmer, Verastegui led a quiet life until he left law school to pursue a career in Hollywood. After an extraordinary rise to fame in the boy band Kairo, hailed as one of the most successful music groups in Latin America, Verastegui was on his way to celebrity status as a musician. He then broke into the film industry and starred in five highly rated *telenovelas* and the American film, *Chasing Papi*. Verastegui was preparing to catapult to international stardom with a new talent agency, but as success came, emptiness consumed him. "All the things that I thought were important to me meant nothing. I was involved with projects that spread lies," he told me.

Consequently, Verastegui vowed never to sell his soul to another meaningless project—and he kept his word. It was four years later, with no money in his bank account, when he co-founded Metanoia Films and began to work again. His goal was to make movies that matter.

Enter *Bella*. Filmed in just twenty-four days on location in New York City, *Bella* is a story about sacrificial love ... the rare kind. As Verastegui explained the independent film to me. With his intense sapphire eyes and thick accent, I began to see why *Bella* has garnered so much attention. It snatched up the People's Choice Award at the Toronto International Film Festival, an early indicator of Academy Award nods.

Eduardo and his business partners are passionate men—so passionate they were willing to forgo their own dreams to follow "God's destiny." A decision, they say, that has led to peace, contentment, and, ultimately, "beautiful redemption."

This article is taken from an interview originally conducted for RISEN *Magazine.*

RISEN MAGAZINE: *What message do you want people to take away from Bella?*

EDUARDO VERASTEGUI: I hope that when people leave the theater after watching *Bella*, they will want to love more and judge less. I hope they leave with hope in their hearts, and they are inspired to use their talents and gifts to do something positive.

RM: *Bella seems to challenge the common definition of love.*

EV: It's a unique project. It's a love story, but beyond romance. It's a sacrificial love story. When someone is going to die and sacrifice everything for the benefit of the other, it shows that there is a time in everyone's life when one moment will change your life forever. If it hasn't happened to you yet, it will.

RM: *What does the name of your company, Metanoia Films, mean?*

EV: It means transformation; turning to God, conversion, repentance. To once live in darkness, corruption, and perversity, and then to dive into the crystal blue waters. It's beautiful to experience the serenity, joy, and peace of repentance. It doesn't mean that you aren't going to have challenges anymore. You are always going to have adversity and tribulations. But everything has a new meaning. Even suffering has a new meaning.

RM: *Is suffering good?*

EV: Pain is a universal language. Is pain good or bad? It depends on what pain does to your soul. When I look back on the mo-

ments in my life when I was going through a lot of pain and suffering and I thought it was the end of the world, then I realize that those moments were my biggest teachers. That's what made me a man—spiritually, mentally, and professionally. But I only understand that now, after the moment has passed. Pain can be beautiful and redemptive and can shape your soul.

RM: *Has your definition of success changed over the course of making this movie?*

EV: Well, it was actually the opposite. *Bella* is the result of the change that my business partners and I had in our lives. We realized life was not about us. It's not about just being a successful person. Mother Teresa said, "We are not called to be successful. We are called to be faithful." That's our success. If by being faithful to God success comes, then it's a blessing.

RM: *Is it easy to become addicted to what fame offers?*

EV: I was seduced by what this career offered me. Envy, ambition, and lust made me a slave. After I achieved many of my goals that I thought were going to give me happiness, I realized I still felt empty. All the things that I thought were once important to me meant nothing. I was involved with projects that spread lies to the audience. It was very sad, because I was twenty-eight years old and realized, What am I doing with my life? It was a very painful moment in my life. I was struggling and I was confused.

RM: *Was that the one moment in your life when everything changed?*

EV: Yeah, I'm a different person today. I completely changed the path I was on before and all by the grace of God. I didn't know

the good news before that. I didn't know about His mercy and His forgiveness. When you repent and ask for forgiveness, He gives you a new heart. He gives you new clothes like the prodigal son. He embraces you and changes you. He cleanses you. He makes you a new man. My focus in life now is to know and to love and to serve Him. By doing that, everything comes together. It was the greatest moment in my life when I completely changed my path to abandon myself and to follow Him.

RM: *You said you were a slave. Are you free from what enslaved you?*

EV: Before, my heart was corrupted and full of cancer. Then God came and purified it. It's the same heart, but it's pure now. To be free is not to do whatever you want, but to do what is right. And that is going to make you free.

RM: *Do you ever regret things you did or said in public before?*

EV: I look at some of my old interviews and I'm like, "Oh my gosh! What was I thinking?" I can't believe some of the things I was saying. But I was living a corrupt life. I was living those words. I'm a changed man now. It's like day and night.

RM: *But many people don't believe in transformation through faith.*

EV: Yes, but God *promises* to transform you. If someone like me can change, anyone can. The great news is that no matter how depressed you are, or how many horrible things you have done, or how far away you feel from God, you were created for a purpose. There is a mission here on life you are supposed to accomplish. As long as we're still alive, it's never too late to change.

"When I look back on the moments in my life when I was going through a lot of pain and suffering and I thought it was the end of the world, then I realize that those moments were my biggest teachers."

RM: *How do you balance being virtuous and having a career in Hollywood?*

EV: There is no way to balance anything between evil and good. You are either a virtuous person or you are not. So, as I said before, we are not called to be successful, we are called to be faithful. I knew that by following God it could mean that I would never work in Hollywood again. And I was OK with that.

RM: *You were willing to give up your dreams to follow God?*

EV: Sometimes our dreams can be our worst enemies. Especially if our dreams are not in line with God's will. When I realized it was not about what *I* want anymore but what *God* wanted me to do, a tremendous peace came over me.

I made a commitment to only do positive projects, and that one moment of conviction turned into four years of turning down numerous roles until I was completely broke. My bank account was at zero. But only if you are willing to die to yourself will you be free. For me, the end is not success in Hollywood. I was not born to be an actor or a rich and powerful man. I was born to love and serve God.

RM: *Is there a place for religion in Hollywood?*

EV: I believe that's why I was called to be in the media. Not to judge anybody, but to be a light in the dark world and to inspire others to do positive projects. It's possible to utilize the media to be a bridge in the community where everybody comes together to make this world a better place.

Pope John Paul II wrote in a letter before he died to not be afraid to use the media to speak the truth. It's a very powerful tool.

RM: *Is it hard to stay humble?*

EV: It's very easy to get prideful when the spotlight is on you. But I have to stay humble. There is this beautiful prayer in Spanish that I quote that reminds me to die to myself and to my vanity and to my ego.

RM: *Do you ever wish you could go back to life without the fame?*

EV: Fame can be a very powerful tool if you use it as a microphone to speak the truth and to help others. It becomes dangerous when one would do anything to become famous. That's what gets people in trouble, from celebrities to politicians. I wish I could go back and have faith and passion for doing the right thing, because I hurt a lot of people along the path to fame.

RM: *What's been one of your proudest moments?*

EV: One of the most beautiful moments in my life was when I made the promise to God that I would never ever do anything that would separate me from my faith. It was a beautiful moment of communion when I realized all I had to do was follow Him. All the directions I needed were in the Bible. It's a map for your life that is so clear. If you follow it, you're in a safe place. I was also very proud when *Bella* won the People's Choice Award at the Toronto Film Festival. It was a miracle. **C**

Visit **www.bellathemovie.com** for more information.

Reprinted with permission of RISEN *Magazine, originally published in* RISEN's *Oct/Nov 2007 issue.*

Catherine Rohr

THE LAST TWO CENTS

REAL STORIES OF CALLING

Jon Tyson

Blake Mycoskie

An Interview with Catherine Rohr,
Jon Tyson and Blake Mycoskie

By Tim Willard

SO THERE YOU ARE, IN YOUR FAVORITE CHAIR, BREEZING THROUGH THE GOSPEL OF MATTHEW, WHEN YOU FIND JESUS LAYING OUT AN ABUNDANTLY CLEAR MESSAGE TO PETER, TELLING HIM THAT THE CHURCH WOULD BE BUILT ON HIS SHOULDERS AND THE FOUNDATION OF HIS GREAT CONFESSION. [1] THEN IT OCCURS TO YOU—WAIT A MINUTE, I'VE HEARD A STORY LIKE THIS BEFORE. YOU FLIP LEFT TOWARD GENESIS TO FIND GOD SPEAKING (AUDIBLY, NO LESS) TO ABRAM, IN REMARKABLY SIMPLE TERMS, TELLING HIM THAT IT'S HIS TURN TO MOVE, TO TAKE HIS FAMILY TO AN UNDISCLOSED LOCATION SO THAT GOD CAN USE HIM TO BUILD A GREAT NATION. [2] BRILLIANT.

So why can't it be that easy for you? Why doesn't God hand-deliver calling anymore?

Discovering your life's calling isn't always a dramatic encounter with God, but it's not always a mysterious journey to the abyss, either. When you're not operating within your calling it can feel like you're just treading water—your passion for God can wane because you don't feel His pleasure in what you do. Your cultural engagement may feel forced or hindered because you're not maximizing your skills and abilities. You feel like your whole existence is an exercise in treading water, just waiting to be hit by that current of purpose.

We could give you Twelve Easy Steps To Discover Your Calling, or a thesis that charts the Bible's perspective through exegesis, but you may have tried that already. Sometimes it's better to hear how your contemporaries are discovering their calling, so we tracked down some Catalyst leaders who are making major waves in their respective fields and asked them about their experiences.

MEET JON TYSON

He's a passionate Aussie who, with two of his best friends, started a church planting movement called Origins that will cast anchor in the strategic cities of New York, Los Angeles, and Rome,

Italy. From his base at Origins Church in New York City, Jon explains, "We're just trying to follow the direction and narrative of the New Testament movement. The Christians basically conquered the Roman Empire and they did it through setting up and modelling the Kingdom of God in the culture-shaping centers of their world."

Clearly, Jon and his friends aren't short on dreams and aspirations. But where did their call come from, and what moves them from calling toward action? Jon says, "Our goals are ambitious, but I think that's the basic call that Jesus offered the disciples. I think God's call is the fulfilment of the Great Commission."

But perhaps that sounds more like a corporate calling to you, the calling of all believers. We asked, isn't there a difference between your personal calling and the corporate calling in the Great Commission?

Jon puts it this way: "I think they're very similar. It doesn't matter where you look in Scripture, God always calls people out of one small thing and into something that is bigger, whether it's Abraham being called out of a pagan city to go and found a new nation, or the disciples being called out of fishing and tax collecting into a better story."

He concludes, "I think what we're trying to do corporately is an overflow of my personal response to God's calling. God's always calling us into something bigger."

THE CAVEAT

But you probably know that God's calling doesn't necessarily mean a gentle, cushy, no-risk endeavour. Jon went from being a highly successful twentysomethings pastor to founding a church plant ministry in New York City. For those who are out where few others venture, stepping out of the familiar and comfortable seems to be a theme.

"One of the obstacles to any true calling is the element of risk," Jon says. "The only guarantee we had was that seventy percent of all church plants in New York City fail in their first year. So, the risk of selling our house, selling our possessions, and moving into a 580-square foot apartment with two roommates and two kids gave us no guarantee that it was going to work. That was a massive risk. My wife is an absolute hero for just saying, 'Let's do it.'"

The "let's do it" attitude is a prerequisite for pursuing that God-whisper in your ear—the one that beckons you out into the unknown. If you are committed to your call because God has placed it in you, no amount of risk or adversarial statistics can hold you back.

Jon concludes, "I asked myself, 'If I keep living like I'm living, what's going to be the outcome of my life? What was possible if we took a risk and we did this?' We started to see small signs early on—they were glimmers of hope."

The power of hope is often underestimated. But Jon realized, "If I can endure ninety percent of the pains for the shared beauty of the ten percent of redemptions, then it's worth it." He got to the point where the only thing that mattered was God transforming people, and once you arrive at that point, it doesn't matter what the naysayers are whining about.

"I had such absolute clarity on God's call on my life that if everybody else packed up and left, we'd still be here. Worldly success isn't the measuring line—it's the internal peace that what we are doing means something to God."

THE UNLIKELY MINISTRY

A successful ministry doesn't have to be stamped with a fish or doves. In fact, those Christian clichés are nowhere to be found in Catherine Rohr's Prison Entrepreneurship Program (PEP). PEP is the only program in America that offers values-based entrepreneurial training for current and former prison inmates.

Catherine was still working in venture capital and private equity in 2004 when she became involved with the idea of building successful entrepreneurs from inmates. She accompanied Chuck Colson on a tour of a Texas prison, saying, "That was an eye-opening experience for me."

Eye-opening? More like a revelation. Catherine essentially started PEP on the spot during that prison tour. The backstory reveals that God was working in Catherine's life in profound ways.

"Leading up to the Chuck Colson prison tour, I felt a calling from God to use my skills, my network, and my resources for something other than myself. I gave generously to ministries, but I knew that God was calling me into something bigger. I just didn't know what."

Catherine's promptings continued, shrouded in the unknown but becoming more and more clear. She remembers, "A couple of weeks before my prison visit I knew that God was telling me to leave my job, and I had never had such a clear sense before of God saying, 'Do this.' I didn't want to leave my job right then, because I didn't know what I was going to do. So I decided I wouldn't leave my job immediately."

For two weeks following that visit, Catherine suffered from extraordinarily painful ocular migraines. "I was almost blind. I couldn't see for two weeks. I knew it was because I was being disobedient."

The migraines prompted Catherine to resign from her job—a job where she made $200,000 a year as a venture capitalist. "My boss asked me what I was going to do, and I said that God was calling me to something else. I wasn't sure what it was, but I knew I had to go do it."

INTO THE DESERT

After leaving her job and operating PEP from California for a short time, Catherine and her husband, Steve, felt called to move

to Houston where PEP was headquartered. As Steve stayed behind to sell their house, Catherine made the journey to Houston penniless and with nowhere to live.

"One of the biggest steps for me was swallowing my pride," she says. "Steve and I loved to help others by giving generously, so I went from that to basically being homeless."

Often we don't see this side of the strongest leaders, the times of struggle, self-doubt, and pain. But often God takes us to the desert for a while to train—to be totally dependent upon Him. "I was humbled," Catherine says, "and my faith grew so much because I learned the meaning of thanking God for my daily bread."

Catherine explains that these times of brokenness were the impetus that left her with a distinct understanding of the past and its role in her future. "I truly believe that God has put me on this earth so that I could be in prisons today. It's clear to me that where I am now is the culmination of all of my experiences."

HUMBLE SURRENDER

But this kind of clarity requires action. In Catherine's case, as more clarity came, she gave more things up to God. "When I became a Christian one of my first prayers was, 'Bring it on, God. What do you want me to lose today?' He was taking at least one valued thing away from me every day. I was dying. I felt so stripped. But it was also incredible to be stripped and to be with God, knowing that I was doing what I should."

Catherine has found that God works with her mostly when she is totally willing to surrender every little department. "That doesn't mean He will necessarily take it from me, but usually He does." Catherine is influencing the greater culture because she has stripped off the hindrances, grabbed on to God, and answered the call.

Catherine puts an exclamation point on our conversation. "Without action, it just doesn't matter. You have to be a true disciple—able to live out what He's called you to do with excellence. Commitment is vital to living out any vision. A true disciple will realize that obstacles will come on the way to the vision, but sometimes the only way to deal with them is to put your head down, say a prayer, and plow through them."

THE CONTINENT WALKER
If Blake Mycoskie is not in Argentina dropping off shoes, he's catching a flight to Turkey, stopping off in London, and making it back to California to catch up on emails. He's all over the world. And for good reason.

Since its inception just over a year ago, TOMS Shoes (with "TOMS" signifying "shoes for tomorrow") has exploded all over the world. What makes TOMS so special?

Blake will tell you that he's selling more than shoes; he's selling a story. A story of hope that is simple and beautiful. For every pair of TOMS shoes sold, a pair is given to a shoeless child. Blake recently returned from Argentina, leaving behind more than 8,000 children wearing new shoes. Blake says, "If you have TOMS-itis, you want to give a child a pair of shoes." There's no doubt Blake is infected; hopefully TOMS-itis will continue to spread into a global epidemic.

For Blake, TOMS Shoes has become more than a career. "God's calling in my life is to demonstrate how service can be easy, cool, and very rewarding at any age." He continues, "For so long I believed you could only give back and serve *after* you were successful and established, which limited my experience and thus, the intimacy I had in my relationship with Christ. Now, after starting TOMS Shoes, I see that giving can be a part of your everyday life, and with each day, you can see God's love and grace manifested through such service. It doesn't matter what your age or economic status is—all can participate."

With TOMS' unprecedented success, Blake sees a window of opportunity to spread hope to people all over the globe. As his business grows, so does his calling. "My calling, besides serving, is to share what I have learned so that more young people will incorporate giving and service into their daily lives."

FROM THE ROOTS UP
Blake is aware, however, that this success extends far beyond the work he alone can do. TOMS is an endeavor that relies heavily on community. "Community is key, and no message, cause, or movement can spread without it. I can only do so much, but the community we are constantly building around us can move mountains."

Blake has learned that a calling without community is bound to fail. "The key is to surround yourself, and in our case, our cause, with others who are authentic, passionate, and supportive so that our message can be shared with as many people as possible."

WHAT'S YOUR CALLING?
The danger is that many people read stories like that of Blake, Catherine, and Jon and then spend time racking their brains to find a big idea or cause they can call their own—as if all callings require a high profile or public stage. When asked about this concept, Blake remarked, "A 'higher' calling does not mean 'public' to me, but it means authentic and pure. I believe God has a calling for each of us, but often times it is not something public or overly grand. I think of the woman in the Gospels who put her last two cents in the offering plate. That is 'higher' to me, and I think we must be open to these opportunities to truly serve by humbling ourselves." ■

Tim Willard is a full-time freelance writer and graduate student (Gordon-Conwell) who serves as editor for the Catalyst GroupZine, and as Creative Content writer for the Prison Entrepreneurship Program. He and his wife, Chris, live somewhere north of Atlanta. Tim exclusively rides Kona mountain bikes and prefers French pressed to filter-drip coffee. To read more from Tim, visit **www.flickernail.com**.

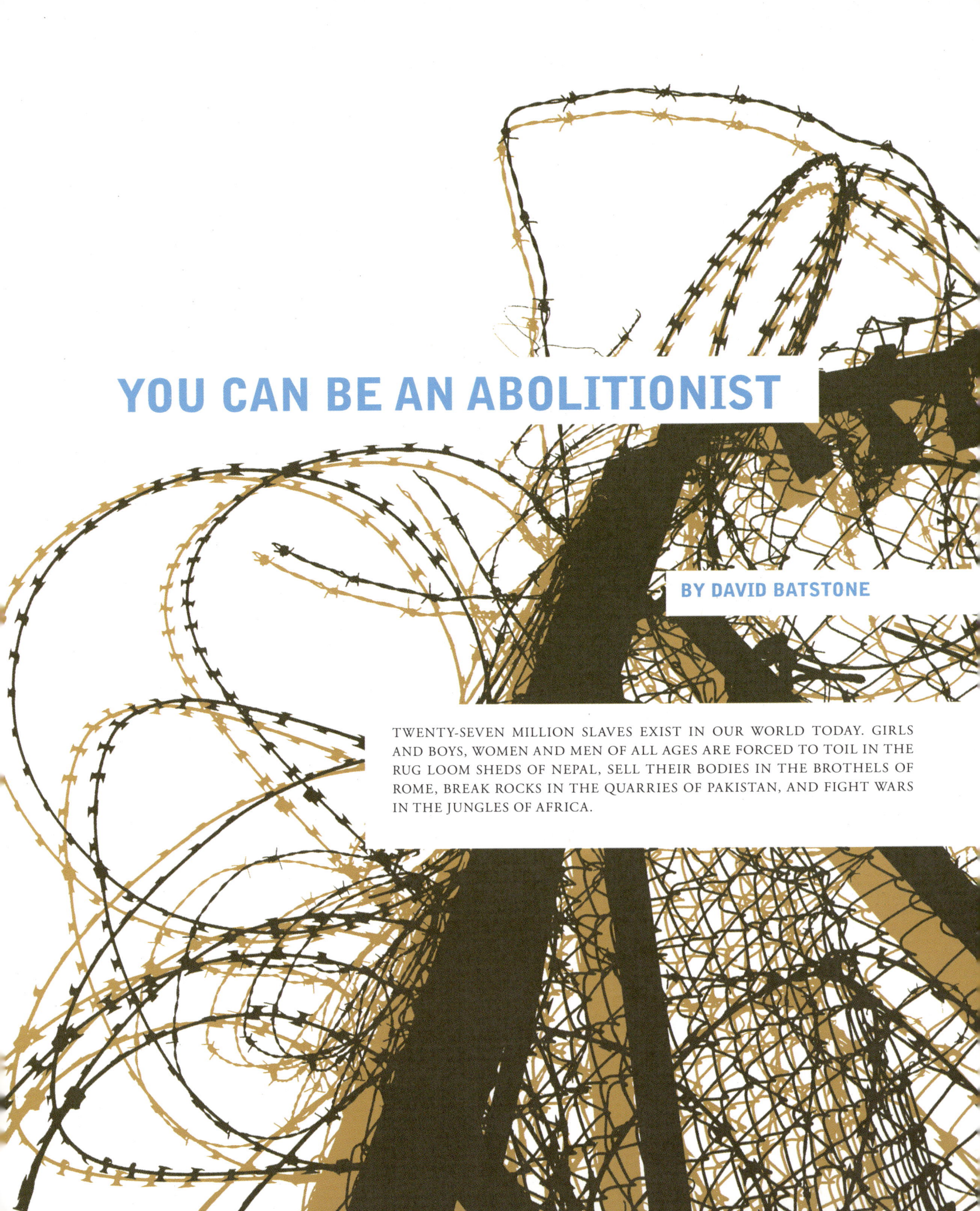

YOU CAN BE AN ABOLITIONIST

BY DAVID BATSTONE

TWENTY-SEVEN MILLION SLAVES EXIST IN OUR WORLD TODAY. GIRLS AND BOYS, WOMEN AND MEN OF ALL AGES ARE FORCED TO TOIL IN THE RUG LOOM SHEDS OF NEPAL, SELL THEIR BODIES IN THE BROTHELS OF ROME, BREAK ROCKS IN THE QUARRIES OF PAKISTAN, AND FIGHT WARS IN THE JUNGLES OF AFRICA.

Go behind the façade in any major town or city in the world today and you are likely to find a thriving commerce in human beings. You may even find slavery in your own backyard.

NOT FOR SALE

To write *Not for Sale*, I conducted hundreds of interviews with young girls from Cambodia, Thailand, Peru, India, Uganda, South Africa, Eastern Europe, and even the United States. I met a common storyline time and time again. Of those individuals extracted out of impoverished countries and trafficked across international borders, 80 percent are female and 50 percent are children. They are taken to unfamiliar destinations where in the absence of legal protections and family networks they can be kept in slavery. The consistency of

the storyline in fact suggests overarching mechanisms of a global industry.

Like any other commercial market, the slave trade is driven by the dynamics of supply and demand. Criminal agents make handsome profits off unpaid labor—using slaves it is cheaper to produce goods or, in the case of sex slavery or domestic servitude, to offer valued human services. Due to these financial advantages, slaveholders can compete successfully in most any market. The profit margins will rise as high as the demand will bear.

We may not even realize how each one of us drives the demand during the course of a normal day. Kevin Bales, a pioneer in the fight against modern slavery, expresses well those commercial connections: "Slaves in Pakistan may have made

the shoes you are wearing and the carpet you stand on. Slaves in the Caribbean may have put sugar in your kitchen and toys in the hands of your children. In India, they may have sewn the shirt on your back and polished the ring on your finger." [1]

Widespread poverty and social inequality ensure a pool of recruits as deep as the ocean. Parents in desperate straits may sell a child, or at least be susceptible to scams that will allow the slave trader to take control over the lives of their sons and daughters. Young women in vulnerable communities will be more likely to take a risk on a job offer in a far-away destination. The poor are apt to accept a loan that the slave trader later can manipulate to steal away their freedom. All of these paths carry unsuspecting recruits into the supply chains of slavery.

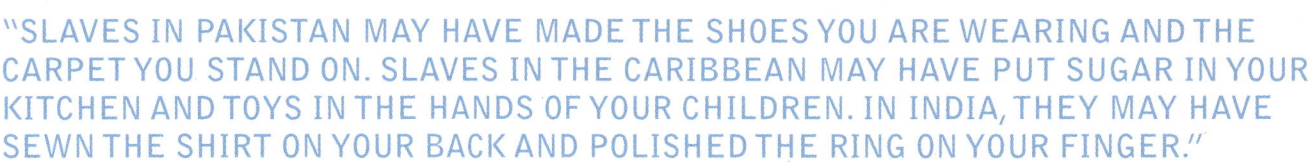

"SLAVES IN PAKISTAN MAY HAVE MADE THE SHOES YOU ARE WEARING AND THE CARPET YOU STAND ON. SLAVES IN THE CARIBBEAN MAY HAVE PUT SUGAR IN YOUR KITCHEN AND TOYS IN THE HANDS OF YOUR CHILDREN. IN INDIA, THEY MAY HAVE SEWN THE SHIRT ON YOUR BACK AND POLISHED THE RING ON YOUR FINGER."

Many of these victims end up in the United States. As many as 150,000 individuals live enslaved at this moment in our country, and an additional 17,500 new victims are trafficked into our borders each year.

ENSLAVED MARKET

During the era of the American plantation economy, the slaveholder considered slave ownership an investment. The supply of new recruits was limited—the cost of extracting and transporting the slave, and ensuring that they would be serviceable by the time they reached their destination, would be considerable. Though the slave owner usually treated the slave like a beast, it would be equal to the treatment of a prized bull. The slave owner aimed to extract the value of his investment over the course of the slave's lifetime. Proof of legal ownership therefore served an important purpose.

In the modern slave trade, the glut of slaves and the capacity to move them great distances in a relatively short period of time drastically alters the economics. As relative costs plummet, slaves cease to be a long-term investment. The fact that slave ownership is almost universally illegal today is of little consequence. The owner need not even be too concerned about maintaining the health of the slave. Kevin Bales' description of modern slaves as "disposable people" profoundly fits—just like used batteries, once the slave exhausts its usefulness, another can be procured at no great expense.

Notwithstanding these emerging trends in global markets, traditional modes of slavery also persist. Bonded labor has existed for centuries and continues to be the most common form of slavery in the world today. In a typical scenario, an individual falls under the control of a wealthy patron after taking a small loan. The patron adds egregious rates of interest and inflated expenses to the original principal so that the laborer finds it impossible to repay. Debt slaves may spend their entire life in service to a single slaveholder, and their "obligation" may be passed on to their children. Of the 27 million people worldwide held captive and exploited for profit today, the Free The Slaves organization estimates that at least 15 million are bonded slaves in India, Pakistan, Bangladesh, and Nepal.

PLIGHT OF THE BONDED LABORER

The tale of Simran, a slave I met during my travels in India, graphically illustrates the plight of a bonded laborer. The owner of a rice mill used small loans to enslave Simran's entire village. The villagers labored eighteen hours daily and were banned from passing beyond the walls of the rice mill without supervision. After years of relentless oppression, Simran's wife broke down one day and killed herself. Disconsolate over his loss, Simran threw caution to the wind. He saw a gate in the rice mill left open one day and bolted.

The owner did not treat insubordination lightly. He sent bounty hunters after Simran and they captured him without much trouble. Once they brought Simran back to the rice mill, the owner gathered all the slaves into an assembly in the center of the compound. For their edification, he used a cane to beat Simran within an inch of his life. The owner then chained the unconscious Simran to a wall in the slaves' living quarters. And that became his bed for the rest of his days at the rice mill. He did his daily chores and then was ushered back to his chains.

I am pleased to report that Simran's tale ends on a happy note. An abolitionist agency instigated a raid on the rice mill and emancipated him along with his entire village. Local police arrested the owner and put him on trial for his crimes.

Such rescues were the unexpected surprise of my journey. I had steeled myself emotionally to end up in the depths of depression and despair. To be honest, I made some unpleasant stops there. The day I went undercover to investigate a brothel in Phnom Penh, for instance, broke my heart. A brothel owner invited me to take my pick of any one of the thirteen-year-old girls that crowded the sofas in front of me. A few extra bucks and I could have two of them for the night, he offered. I could not bear to think of these little girls passing through this ritual a dozen times each night.

But my journey did not end at the station of despair. The prime reason: I met a heroic ensemble of abolitionists who simply refuse to relent. I felt like I had gone back in time and had the great privilege of sharing a meal with a Harriet Tubman or a William Wilberforce or a Fredrick Douglass. Like the abolitionists of old, these modern heroes do not expend their energies handicapping the odds stacked against an anti-slavery movement. They simply refuse to accept a world where one individual can be held as the property of another.

The abolitionists I met were truly extraordinary, but they cannot win the fight alone. They are overwhelmed and beleaguered. The size and scope of their project is about the norm for abolitionist organizations. They sorely need reinforcements, a new wave of abolitionists, to join them in the struggle. ◼

David Batstone is an award-winning journalist and professor of ethics at the University of San Francisco. After spending a year researching the slave trade for his book *Not for Sale*, he launched an international campaign to fight it. To join, go to **NotforSaleCampaign.org.**

A COMMUNITY OF THE BROKEN

CHRIS HEUERTZ

SEVERAL YEARS AGO, I MADE MY FIRST TRIP TO FREETOWN, SIERRA LE-ONE, JUST AS THAT COUNTRY'S CIVIL WAR WAS WINDING DOWN. ONE OF MY FIRST STOPS WAS A CAMP FOR THE WAR WOUNDED. LATE IN THE DAY, I FOUND MYSELF ON THE FRONT STEP OF A YOUNG WOMAN'S SLUM-LIKE CAMP HOME. SHE LOOKED ABLE-BODIED AND HEALTHY. YET HER STO-RY WAS AS TERRIBLE AS EACH OF THE OTHERS'—HER HOME HAD BEEN BURNED TO THE GROUND, HER HUSBAND WAS KILLED BEFORE HER EYES, AND SHE HAD BEEN BRUTALLY RAPED.

I looked over my shoulder to see her 3-year-old daughter, Grace, picking up a handful of peanuts with one hand. As a 2-month-old baby, Grace had lost her left arm to the same men who had already taken everything from her young mother. Grace was biting on the shell of a peanut, pressing it against what was left of her arm, to no avail. As a full-grown man with all my limbs, I still have trouble opening a peanut. Grace was trying to do the same without an arm.

That moment with Grace and her mother is seared into my memory—not just for what it taught me about human suffering and perseverance, but also for what it taught me about the plight of the Church.

OUR BROKEN BODY

An essential Christian conviction is that the Church is the community that anticipates and seeks to express the Kingdom of God. To explain the healthy functioning of the Church, Paul twice used the metaphor of the human body—a symbol of what it looks like for many parts working in unison, glorifying the Lord in a broken world.

But the body of Christ, far from being a healthy body with the capacity to respond to the world's needs, is more like a child who is missing a limb. We are fragmented, divided, and ineffective at even simple tasks. Yet, like Grace, some of us are young, foolish, or brave enough to try to overcome these limitations. That has been the goal of Word Made Flesh (WMF).

For many Christians today, mission can seem to be little more than sanctified tourism. WMF is working with those who are intelligent yet doctrinally confused, cause-driven yet commitment-averse, and over-educated yet deep in debt—to challenge them to establish community with and among the oppressed of the world.

THE VOICES OF FRIENDS

Western Christians are often isolated from people who are poor. This is all the more troubling given the centrality of the poor in the Bible.

As our Africa-Europe regional coordinator, David Chronic, wrote, "The poor do not need to be integrated into our community. God is calling us, rather, to identify with theirs." At WMF, ministry is not so much to "the poor" as "with friends." It is a simple verbal change that attempts to honor and humanize those we minister to.

Many in WMF have found that it is hardly a sacrifice to give up the freedom that comes with the developed world in order to offer the freedom that comes with knowing Christ.

A GLOBAL MOSAIC

Much of my early exposure to mission work was centered in missional communities that lived together creating a transplanted microcosm of their culture and society. I began to fear that this model of missions hindered the message of the Church and undermined genuine community.

This is a challenge for a ministry like WMF that draws its members largely from college and university campuses. As Michael Emerson and Christian Smith observe in *Divided by Faith*, the highly educated are less likely to express overt racism or prejudice—yet in North America, it is the university educated who live in the most segregated neighborhoods and whose churches seem least likely to have culturally diverse memberships.

WMF strives to cultivate a mosaic of diverse Christian community. The staff at its Omaha office includes middle-class alumni of Christian colleges, but there are also immigrants from Mexico and Vietnam. Finding a way to sustain a truly multiethnic U.S. office is an ongoing challenge.

WOMEN AND MEN AS PARTNERS

Not long ago, I was at a conference that boasted delegates from more than 100 nations in an effort to represent the global body of Christ. Just under a quarter of the participants were women. The gathering was far from an accurate picture of who is providing leadership to the global Church.

As Philip Jenkins points out, today's "typical" Christian is much more likely to be a young Nigerian or Brazilian woman than a Western white male. Women are the numerical majority of Christians around the world. And it is only when women and men work together that we demonstrate the wholeness of Christ's body.

MISSING OUR BROTHERS AND SISTERS

For many North American evangelicals, ecumenism has come to imply compromise. But in WMF, ecumenical partnership is seen as moving toward the center, Christ Himself. When Catholic, Orthodox, and Protestant Christians come together, the body of Christ regains some of its fullness.

But when we come together for the meal that is at the center of the Church's life, we encounter the persistent brokenness of Christ's body. Two Catholic priests serve on the U.S. board. But at the Communion table, they are unable to serve the elements or partake of them. Those experiences compel us to pray for the restoration of the unity of the Church.

At times like these, I especially feel like Grace, intensely aware of the brokenness of our body and the ways we are handicapped in our witness in the world. Calling the poor our friends, making partners of those from very different cultural backgrounds, advancing the calling of women as well as men—all of these more often reveal our disabilities than our abilities.

For me, Grace has become a symbol of hope. After all, she and her mother survived. Paradoxically yet wonderfully, even with their broken hearts and a missing limb, they had something to offer me.

Community with those like Grace is a community of the broken and incomplete—but I believe it is also the beginning of the Kingdom arriving in all of its wholeness, for Grace and for us. **C**

For more from the Christian Vision Project and Chris Heuertz, visit **www.christianvisionproject.com**.

MINDY BOYD

SINGER, SONGWRITER
Age 33, Strasburg, Pennsylvania, www.mindyboyd.com

FOR TEN YEARS MINDY BOYD HAS PLAYED HER SONGS IN COFFEE SHOPS, CONFERENCES, AND RETREATS ALL OVER THE COUNTRY; AND SHE'S GOOD AT IT. HOWEVER, IN THE THROES OF PURSUING HER MINISTRY CALLING, MINDY FELL INTO A RELATIONSHIP WITH ANOTHER WOMAN. THEIR RELATIONSHIP DEEPENED, AND IT WAS THEN THAT MINDY'S SONGS WERE SILENCED.

NOW, THROUGH HER INVOLVEMENT WITH EXODUS INTERNATIONAL, MINDY HAS RESURFACED IN HER MINISTRY WITH A RENEWED SENSE OF GOD'S GRACE. HERE SHE COMMENTS ON HER JOURNEY.

A HIGHER CALL

My desire is to steward my gifts to bring attention to God's endless grace and love for all people. I want to share this through my music and songwriting and the relationships I build along the way. I don't necessarily need a record contract to accomplish this. I communicate best by providing an intimate setting for smaller groups—connecting directly with them.

The end goal is to encourage people to enter into an intimate relationship with Jesus Christ. Apart from the music—and yet somehow connected—my own journey through sexual brokenness has given me the privilege of walking alongside other women who struggle with sexual and relational issues.

COURAGE IN TRUTH

I never want my music to be anything other than authentic and vulnerable. I'd rather be honest about the struggles that we face in this life and point people to the redemption that is offered in the midst of them. We forget that beauty comes from ashes.

For me, it was walking away from homosexuality. Was it easy? No. Was it fun? No. Was it painful? Extremely. But my journey through all of that gives me the confidence to stand before an audience and speak about the redemption of Christ and His power to heal us at the core of our being—even when the world screams that it is impossible.

IGNITING CULTURE

We are called to be lights—not isolating ourselves from darkness, but being in it. Our culture is being influenced by opinions and beliefs that are contrary to Biblical truth. We, as Christians, have the opportunity to offer a redeemed, intelligent, and more complete perspective—not in a way that separates and divides, but rather in offering love and respect to those who differ in opinion and in maintaining relationships with them. It's about examining our culture and exposing the enemy's lies. It's about finding God's redemption and His light in the midst of a culture filled with darkness.

A BASIN AND A TOWEL

I'm surprised that God even chooses to use me at all. He is able to accomplish His plans without me, but He chooses to use broken vessels to spread His truth. That's true for everyone. God chooses the "weak things of the world to shame the strong ... so that no one may boast before him." (1 Corinthians 1:27, 29 NIV)

Allow that understanding to keep you in a place where you are quick to reach for a "towel and basin of water." Be ready to serve the people God has placed in your life—even those who might disagree with you or hold a different opinion or worldview. Use your gifts with excellence and integrity to influence the world around you, to display the redemption of Christ. Shed light on it. Draw attention to it. And never dismiss anyone as unredeemable. God recycles it all ... for His glory. 🅲

Courage of the Nonsensical

By Bill Hybels

Jesus consistently made decisions that took courage, often leaving Him alone and misunderstood by His family and His disciples. Yet a call to ministry demands that we walk as Jesus walked.

Imagine my surprise recently when I decided to read through the New Testament book of Mark and noticed several occasions when Jesus seems willfully to violate well-known, widely accepted laws of leadership. My observations were more than a little shocking.

The first place I noticed the greatest leader in human history breaking a fundamental law of leadership is in the very first chapter of Mark. Jesus has just lost His strongest ally, John the Baptist, who has been thrown in prison for taking the leaders of the day to task on their sinful behavior. Losing John to a jail cell is a huge hit to Jesus, and the pressing question on His mind must be, "Who in the world do I recruit to replace a superstar like John?"

Perhaps Jesus should add a rabbi, or a highly trained Pharisee—possibly some brilliant students of the Torah?

No, Jesus goes out and instead gathers a rather motley crew of commercial fishermen. The majority of them are untrained, uncouth, and underage. Some have hot tempers, others have questionable business practices, and not one has evangelistic experience.

The next place I noticed Jesus breaking a law of leadership is found later in the first chapter of Mark. Jesus' popularity is building. The crowds are getting larger everywhere He goes. People see Jesus driving out evil spirits, healing sick people, preaching the Kingdom of God, and they wonder if He might actually be the long-awaited Messiah. Right in the middle of this "Nielsen-rating" upswing, Mark 1:35 records that Jesus actually *withdraws* from all the action; He goes off alone to a solitary place to reflect and spend some quality time in prayer.

Obviously, this is in clear violation of the well-known law of momentum. Every leader knows how hard it is to establish momentum. And every leader knows that once you get it established, you should do whatever it takes to keep it going. Momentum is one of a leader's closest allies. When the energy's high and the team is strong and people are buzzing, the last thing you want to do is pull the momentum plug.

But Jesus walks away from it all, a decision that really miffs His disciples, who are still flying high on the buzz of effective ministry. They quickly pull together a search party and, upon finding their fearless leader, reprimand Him for leaving: "Jesus, everyone is looking for you!" Which is simply code for, "What's up with this? We've all been busting our backsides to get this Kingdom dream realized for You, and now that we're on a roll, You want time off for a spiritual retreat?!"

From a leadership perspective, Jesus' seclusion makes zero sense, and the disciples know it. The greatest leader of all time violates a Leadership 101–level law, to the great shock of His followers ... and me. **C**

Bill Hybels is the founding and senior pastor of Willow Creek Community Church in South Barrington, Illinois. Hybels has authored over twenty books, including *Rediscovering Church* (with his wife Lynne), *Too Busy Not to Pray*, and *Courageous Leadership*. This excerpt is taken from *When Leadership and Discipleship Collide* (Zondervan, 2007).

COURAGEOUS IN CALLING

Find a quiet place to reflect on your life's calling. Are you operating in your "sweet spot"? Have you first answered the call of discipleship and allowed God to work in you? Have you been interrupted in pursuing your calling because of fear or what others have said? Write out some action steps that will move you closer to what God is whispering in your heart.

II. ENGAGED IN CULTURE

As a leader, I must understand the context God has placed me in. I must know the audience I am connecting with to have any opportunity of relevance. Because God desires that Christ-followers engage and influence their surroundings, I will be a source of hope, redemption, justice, and peace in my community, demonstrating a piece of the Kingdom of God in a fallen world.

The Horizons of the Possible
Why Changing Culture Requires Courage

By Andy Crouch

THE WORD *CULTURE* IS HUGE AND VAGUE AT THE SAME TIME, AND IT'S EASY TO MISUSE. PEOPLE USE *CULTURE* TO REFER TO A NEBULOUS SET OF BELIEFS AND VALUES THAT SURROUND US LIKE THE ATMOSPHERE, OMNIPRESENT AND INVISIBLE. IT'S LIKE THE WATER FISHES SWIM IN: ALL AROUND THEM, BUT TAKEN FOR GRANTED.

When we think of culture in this vague way, our engagement with culture is also vague. We make sweeping statements like, "The culture is becoming more family-friendly," or, "The culture is becoming more and more anti-Christian every day." Or we use the word in a more limited way, reserving it for the "finer things": art, music, literature, and the like. We think of a beautiful symphony or a provocative work of art in a museum. They contain powerful ideas and images, perhaps, but they don't seem to do anything real, anything tangible, to the world outside the walls. Or we can be thinking of the prof-

it-driven production of accessible music, films, and television shows—popular culture. This kind of culture comes closer to home, streaming in to our lives through iPods and widescreen TVs, but it is still immaterial—images and ideas that float our way through the ether.

But while all these ways of understanding culture have some truth to them, they miss one of the most important things about culture. This core idea is the key to understanding how culture changes us, and how we might change it. It's also the key to understanding just why changing

culture is so amazingly difficult—why cultural change requires so much courage, and why none of us are likely to change culture by ourselves.

Culture is concrete

Culture is not just beliefs, values, ideas, or images. It's actual, concrete stuff—material, corporeal, physical. It is the very tangible product of human activity. In the words of commentator Ken Myers, culture is "what we make of the world." That wonderful phrase suggests that while culture is indeed an expression of our beliefs and values, the way we express those values is to make particular things.

So to remind myself of just how tangible and concrete culture is—and to remind myself of how tangible and concrete its effects are on the world I live in—I like to think about, well, concrete itself. Specifically, the 47,000 miles of asphalt concrete that make up the United States' Interstate Highway System.

The Interstate Highway System, which celebrated its fiftieth birthday in 2006, is possibly the most significant cultural endeavor of the second half of the twentieth century. Does that sound farfetched? Well, ask yourself whether you, or anyone you know in the United States, has *not* traveled on a part of the interstate system in the last month. Then ask yourself whether the clothes you are wearing, the technological devices you are using, and the food you are eating today traveled on the interstate. Without a doubt, the answer is yes.

And then consider where you live, where you work, where you go to church, and the last restaurant you visited. Chances are every single one of those places are where they are because an interstate highway is where it is.

There were highways before the interstates, of course, but the creation of a nationwide network of well-maintained, uniform, limited-access roadways allowed America's transportation-intensive culture to flourish. We wouldn't have our car culture without the interstates. We wouldn't have green-lawned suburbs without the interstates—which means we wouldn't have the abandoned-lot "inner cities," created when middle-class families moved to the suburbs, without the interstates either. In fact, when the Fannie Mae Foundation asked urban planners to name the top ten factors in the way American cities developed (and decayed) in the 20th century, the Interstate Highway System was number one.

The possible and the impossible

What changes when we think of "culture" as being more like the Interstate Highway System than Beethoven's Fifth—more like architecture than like fine art? We begin to see that the most important thing culture does is *define the horizons of the possible and the impossible* for human beings. Culture determines what we can imagine doing and what we can actually do—and it determines what we cannot imagine doing and can never actually do.

Think of what the Interstate Highway System has made *possible*. In 50 hours (if you have a copilot or lots of caffeine), you can drive from Boston to Seattle on a single interstate highway: I-90, which stretches 3,100 miles from coast to coast. Before the vast, culture-making act that was the construction of Interstate 90, such a journey, in terms of speed and comfort, was impossible. Now it is possible. What made the difference was culture. Of course, most of us are too impatient to drive across the country, so if we can afford it, we avail ourselves of an even more audacious kind of culture—air travel—and cover the distance in a few hours. What was previously impossible, culture has made possible.

And even more remarkably, culture can make some things *impossible* that were previously possible. Reading David Mc-

Cullough's biography of John Adams a few years ago, I was reminded that not that long ago, a vast cultural infrastructure made it possible to travel by horse from Boston to Philadelphia. There were roads, wayside inns, stables, and turnpikes along which travelers could make a slow but steady journey from one city to the other. For more than a century, culture made interstate horse travel possible. But I dare say it would be impossible now. The inns and stables of the nineteenth century are long gone. Horses are forbidden from the shoulders of the highways that connect Boston and Philadelphia, even if horses could stand the roar of the traffic that would be rushing by them just a few feet away. To ride a horse any distance along what is now called "the Northeast Corridor" would be a feat of bravery, to say the least, and quite possibly also an act of cruelty to animals. Culture has made travel by horse, once eminently possible, impossible.

Moving the horizons

So this is what culture does: it defines the horizons of the possible and the impossible in very concrete, tangible ways. I don't just *believe in* fast and convenient travel by highway; I don't just *value* it; it isn't just something I can *imagine* that I couldn't imagine before. It is something I can actually *do*. And the only reason I can do it is because someone (President Eisen-

hower, the members of the United States Congress, and untold numbers of civil engineers and road builders and zoning commission members and accountants) created something that wasn't there before.

And, for that matter, I might *believe* that we'd be better off if we didn't spend 81 minutes a day in our cars (the American average, according to the *Wall Street Journal*), that the days of horse travel were actually better for people and animals, and that the rapid consumption of our planet's limited supply of fossil fuels is both greedy and foolish. But it's impossible for me to live as if the highways don't exist. And, again, those impossibilities are there, whether I like it or not, because someone created something that wasn't there before.

The horizon is the point we can't see beyond. Culture brings certain possibilities into view—into reality—even as it ushers other former possibilities over the horizon and beyond our reach. It's as though we human beings live in a valley ringed by imposing mountains on every side. We can climb part way up the side of the mountain, and a few explorers may even try to escape the valley, but most of us live our lives circumscribed by the horizons we can see. We live within the valley of culture, and most of what we believe,

imagine, value, and actually do happens within the constraints passed on to us by the culture others have created before us. But there's a twist. Culture is not static. The horizons do not stay exactly the same—as hard to move as they may seem to be. In fact, every time new culture is created, the horizons move a little bit—or, sometimes, a lot. After all, when Eisenhower signed the National Interstate and Defense Highways Act on 29 June 1956, the highways we now take for granted simply didn't exist. All that is possible for us now was impossible then; much that is impossible now was possible then. The only thing that changed was the creation of more culture. When culture is created, the horizons move.

Every act of culture making is an assault on the impossible. It doesn't have to be as grand as a national highway system or a headline-grabbing technological breakthrough. The horizons can move at small scales, too. Why does trash accumulate on a particular vacant lot next to a particular convenience store in my friend Paula's urban neighborhood, but the block around the small grocery store in my friend Adrianne's suburban town center is always perfectly clean? Because the horizons of possibility and impossibility are different in these two places. Cleaning up that vacant lot will require someone to breach the assumptions about what is possible (littering in that untended lot is convenient and consequence-free) and what is impossible (the city will never come to pick up the trash no matter how many times you call). And the way that will happen is to create something—perhaps a neighborhood committee, perhaps a sign saying, "Keep our corner clean," perhaps a monthly cleanup day. Without the introduction of some new piece of culture into the neighborhood—some concrete, tangible evidence of human beings making something of the world—the horizons will stay firmly in place. But if someone takes the risk of creating something new, the horizons may just budge a little bit. Or, in the long run, they may move so much that the new neighborhood is as different from the old as post-interstate America is from the days of horses and buggies.

The risk of failure

The key word in that last sentence is *may*. The horizons *may* move. Or they may not. They are, after all, the horizons of the possible and the impossible. Everything outside the horizons is, for the moment, impossible to imagine, let alone accomplish. Only if someone dares to push against the outer edges will we discover just how resistant the horizons are to change.

And much of the time, the horizons are very resistant indeed. Most attempts at cultural creativity—moving the horizons, offering something new that human beings haven't imagined before—fail. Consultants tell us that 80% of new product launches fail. (Pre-moistened toilet paper, anyone?) There are 12,000 members of the Writers Guild of America, the principal union of film and television screenwriters, most of them eager to move the horizons of TV and film, and make a living in the process—and in any given year, about 10,000 of them fail. The last ten years have been a golden age of church planting—but the North American Mission Board of the Southern Baptist Convention found that about a third of church plants fail within four years.

This shouldn't be surprising at all. There is simply nothing harder than creating new culture. Even people with tremendous cultural power fail at it regularly. Eisenhower's vision of an Interstate Highway System succeeded; Lyndon Baines Johnson's War on Poverty did not. Johnson's Civil Rights Act succeeded in many marvelous ways (though some of the horizons it attacked are stubbornly in place to this day); George W. Bush's attempt to move the horizons of the tragic impossibilities of the Middle East, so far, has not.

The ingredients of cultural change

Courage is the willingness to risk failure. And so courage is required for anyone who seeks to be part of changing culture, by creating something that will move the horizons of possibility and impossibility. Without courage, we won't be far out of the comfortable valley of currently realized possibilities before we turn around and head right back home. It is ever so much safer to simply live within the constraints of what is already possible. Little courage is required to pick your suburb, drive your 81 minutes, and go to a church that makes it seem like these horizons have always been there. It works the other way, too: it is much safer to live within the constraints of what is already *impossible*. We couldn't possibly see peace come to the land of Israel and Palestine, could we? Or see Americans reduce their outsized consumption of energy in a poor and thirsty world, or see the Gospel arrive in societies that know more about Coca-Cola than about Christ? If these things are impossible, after all, we're off the hook. Only courage will equip us to ask the question.

And I suspect we will only find that courage together, in community. The truth is that culture is simply never created in isolation. No one gets to move the horizons alone. Every cultural change worth making spreads through a network of people who know and trust one another. Indeed, the horizons are so powerful that only a relatively small, tight-knit group can sustain the belief that the horizons could one day move. That is why every technological innovation, every artistic movement, every academic breakthrough, every piece of legislation, every business, and every new church begins with a small group of believers who are willing to set out on a journey together to the edge of the current horizons—to create something together and then offer it to the wider world.

For the Church to become a source of cultural creativity, we're going to need to become more aware of the people already in our midst who are exploring those horizons. We need to make it safe for one another to fail at being culturally creative—because most of the time, we will indeed fail. But we also need to keep asking one another: Are the horizons misplaced? Are some things possible in our culture-shaped world that God never meant to be possible? Are some things impossible that God never meant to be impossible? If those horizons need to move, that will only happen when we quite literally encourage one another, take heart together, and dare to make something new in the midst of the world. **C**

Andy Crouch is editorial director of the Christian Vision Project and executive producer of the DVD *Where Faith and Culture Meet* (Zondervan, 2007). This article is adapted from his book *Culture Makers* (InterVarsity Press, 2008). Learn more at **www.culture-makers.com**.

1. How does the culture created by those who have come before you impact what you believe today?

2. Over the past decade, how have Christians expressed their values through the cultures they have created?

3. In what ways is your community of believers attempting to move horizons?

4. Why does changing culture require courage?

5. How have you lived safely within the constraints of what is already possible? How have you lived safely within the constraints of what is already impossible?

David Kinnaman

The Outside View
Why Outsiders View Us As unChristian

A Conversation with David Kinnaman and Gabe Lyons
By Tim Willard

Gabe Lyons

THREE YEARS AGO GABE LYONS (FOUNDER OF FERMI PROJECT) AND DAVID KINNAMAN (PRESIDENT OF THE BARNA GROUP) JOINED TOGETHER TO STUDY CERTAIN PERCEPTIONS OF 16-29 YEAR OLDS. THE TOPIC? WHAT THE NEW GENERATION OF "OUTSIDERS," OR THOSE OUTSIDE THE CHRISTIAN FAITH, REALLY THINKS ABOUT CHRISTIANITY. THE DATA THEY UNCOVERED AFFIRMED THEIR BELIEF THAT OUTSIDERS LARGELY VIEW THE ACTIONS OF CHRISTIANS AS CONTRARY TO WHAT JESUS STOOD FOR—THEY VIEW THEM AS UNCHRISTIAN.

It's no secret that over the years Christians have developed a somewhat ostentatious reputation, having been tagged as narrow minded, bigots, anti-intellectuals, right-wing nut jobs, and the list goes on. But could all of this negative press be the by-product of people who just have the proclivity to hate others, or is it self-inflicted? Unfortunately, Christians in this country are more known for what we hate rather than what we love. But every tide changes, and with their new book, *unChristian,* Kinnaman and Lyons are taking tangible steps to help Christians understand why the unchristian tide must turn sooner rather than later.

For Good Reason
The "why" behind the *unChristian* study isn't just the product of analytical minds wanting to solve a cultural problem. For Lyons, the passion to take on this project was fueled by several experiences with his peers. "These experiences led me to believe that this negative perception of Christians was a real problem and that it was a huge barrier that needed to be overcome, but nobody was addressing it." He continues, "We wanted to do a study that would stand the test of criticism and time to better benchmark where we sit as Christians—what our generation and the one behind us think of Christians."

But what does it matter what outsiders think of Christians? Aren't we to expect derision and hatred from the world? Didn't Christ say, "If they hated me, they will hate you"? On the surface that is a valid question, but if we dig deeper we discover that Christ never expected Christians to polarize the outside world by condemning it. If we are hated because we are living Christ-like lives, that's fine. But, as Lyons states, "To be despised for living a faith that's not authentic or true to who Jesus was or what He called His followers to be—that's a different story."

Reading through *unChristian* and seeing the research results is stunning. Lyons recalls his first look at the numbers: "I had an idea that some of the perceptions were probably going to be negative but the actual results left me in disbelief. Nine out of ten viewed Christians as anti-homosexual, eight and a half out of ten as judgmental—the numbers were off the charts."

"God pulled up the veil; He pulled up the blinds on my own barriers–the things I was doing and saying that were creating difficulty for people to see Jesus in my life."

It's numbers like these—startling numbers—that call out our actions as Christ followers. If we are perceived as haters and homophobes we aren't communicating Jesus' love—the Christ who died for all. But sometimes it's hard to see past numbers and make things personal. We must allow the *unChristian* findings to penetrate us on a deeper level.

That's exactly what happened for Kinnaman during this study. For him, the project revealed personal obstacles that might keep outsiders at bay. "This project is not just a glimpse into the process of how young people view Christianity," he said. "God pulled up the veil, he pulled up the blinds on my own barriers—the things I was doing and saying that were creating difficulty for people to see Jesus in my life."

Kinnaman started to realize that overcoming his barriers was more of a day-to-day proposition. "Apologetics in Bible college, for me, emphasized knowing all the answers, but the problems we are facing need more than pat answers—it's more of a spiritual battle and the answers come in a lifestyle apologetic."

All these confirmations lead to one thing … change. But how do you go about changing the face of Christianity?

Reclaiming The Name
Starbucks. Wal-Mart. Target. Apple. Nike. Each one of these brands carries with it a perception that's attached to a specific memory. Lyons points out, "When you hear the word 'Starbucks,' what im-

mediately comes to mind? A round green logo? The aroma of coffee? The taste of a vanilla latte? A warm place for conversation?" He continues, "The point is, when presented with a brand name, you immediately summon all your past experiences and interactions with a product and form an instant opinion."

The growing Christian subculture—Christian music, movies, action groups, schools, clothes—shifts public perception of Christianity. "To outsiders" Lyons says, "the word Christian has more in common with a brand than a faith." But this isn't a PR problem in the sense that a firm can come in and fix it. This isn't *Extreme Christian Makeover: The New Millennium Edition*. It's much deeper than that.

"What we're suggesting," Kinnaman says, "is that instead of just trying to do a face-lift, there's something fundamentally wrong with the way we've responded to people's skepticism." He continues, "For example: here are all these people who've had bad experiences with Christianity—they've been hurt deeply by churches or by Christians, or they don't understand what we're saying, or they believe that we're old fashioned—and they're hurt so badly that we can't address the problems of humanity.

"Those are not just things we should dismiss, 'Well those people just don't get it.' Christianity has the power to answer some of the age-old questions that humans are asking. And furthermore, it should be a place where skeptics find at least a spirit of humility and of reconciliation. What's so surprising to us is that a lot of con-

servative Christians are so busy defending the fort they forgot why they built the fort in the first place."

Some of us bristle at the thought that Christians are so misunderstood in the greater culture. This arises not from a desire to be liked or accepted, but from the standpoint of communicating the awesome experience that comes from a relationship with Jesus Christ. Kinnaman agrees and concludes, "The truth is, if we were to become more transparent with our own faults and more honest about our own doubts and more able to articulate the deep truths of Christianity, people would begin to have a different experience with Christians."

How Did We Get Here?
If you look across the Christian landscape, we've done a good job, like Kinnaman says, of building our own forts. Over the last few decades Christians have done a great deal of polarizing in the greater culture. And we've drawn hard lines on moral issues like abortion and homosexuality, often caring more about the issues at hand than the people dealing with the issues. But how did we get to this place—this great divide?

Lyons reflects, "When Christians in the early church put their faith into practice, the whole Roman Empire was changed. And throughout history we see that when Christians embody what it means to be Christ-like, instead of portraying Christianity as simply a list of rules to live by, influence is gained. People are attracted to those who care for them." So in the past the perception of Christianity wasn't always negative. Even though the early Christians suffered persecution, they were also known for caring for the poor and the sick, those infected by the plague, those whom no one else would touch. But more recently the divide has grown in large part to a separatist mindset.

Lyons goes on to say, "It's good for Christians to be counter-cultural but that doesn't mean detaching and creating our own culture. Disengagement leads to Christians becoming more pious, more focused on their own little community. And anyone who doesn't fit in that community typically gets shunned, as if they could defile us or keep us from being pure."

Though it's difficult to admit, the Christian community to a large degree has become pharisaical in its reaction to the sin of the greater culture. Kinnaman points to Matthew 23 when Jesus is talking to the crowds about the Pharisees—the hypocrites. Jesus calls them "blind guides" and says they, because of their lifestyles, will not enter the Kingdom of heaven. But the kicker is when Jesus holds them responsible for turning others away from God's Kingdom. Our actions carry great weight.

A Unified Front
But what is the right action? As Kinnaman points out, "This 'barriers' idea that *unChristian* talks about is nothing new—Jesus pointed it out centuries ago. However, though Jesus was bold in pointing out the barriers that kept people away from God, He also showed us how to bring people together. He showed us how to love one another, and that is to think of others first."

In this spirit, *unChristian* celebrates evangelical unity by pulling some of the most influential leaders in the Western Church together into one voice. Leaders such as John Stott, Andy Crouch, Gary Haugen, Margaret Feinberg, Chuck Colson, James Emery White, Jim Wallis, Rick Warren, Kevin Kelly, and Brian McLaren have set

aside theological differences and have offered commentary on why the message of *unChristian* needs to be heeded.

It is reminiscent of a time, not long ago, when church leaders came together to stand against theological heresy and behind the fundamentals of the faith. This new movement is less doctrinal but just as much fundamental. It is, as Andy Crouch would say, a posture shift.

In the afterword to *unChristian*, Lyons asks each of the leaders what they think Christians could be known for in the next thirty years. Brian McLaren projects the following:

Christians are the ones who love people, whoever they are—gay or straight, Jew or Muslim, religious or atheist, capitalist or not, conservative or liberal.

Christians are the ones who have done more than anyone in the world to stop the HIV/AIDS crisis.

Christians are the people who gravitate toward the poor and who show compassion through generous action and seek justice so that the systemic causes of poverty are overcome. They call the rich to generosity, and they call on rich nations to work for the common good.

Christians are people who believe that art and creativity are important, so they consistently produce the most striking, original, and enriching art.

Christians are willing to give their lives for the cause of peace. They oppose violence in all its forms. They will lay down their lives to protect the vulnerable from the violent.

Christians care for the environment. They don't just see it as raw materials for economic gain, but they see it as the precious handiwork of their Creator.

Christians have personal integrity. They keep their marriage vows and are aware of how destructive misused sexuality can be. Yet they are compassionate toward people who make sexual mistakes, and they never consider themselves superior.

Christians build harmony among races. You always know that you'll be respected when you're around a Christian. [1]

A tall order? A dream, perhaps? Maybe. But it has always been those who would spur us on to dream of a better time—a better way—to live and to be, that have been the catalysts for significant change. Imagine yourself as that Christian—the one Brian McLaren so vividly painted. Imagine the world impact we could make if we would live up to our name. Christian.

As C.S. Lewis believed, imagination precedes fact. Let's imagine together what *could* happen and then commit to *being* the change we want to create. [2] **C**

Tim Willard is a full-time freelance writer and graduate student (Gordon-Conwell) who serves as editor for the Catalyst GroupZine, and as Creative Content writer for the Prison Entrepreneurship Program. He and his wife, Chris, live somewhere north of Atlanta. Tim exclusively rides Kona mountain bikes and prefers French pressed to filter-drip coffee. To read more from Tim, visit **www.flickernail.com**.

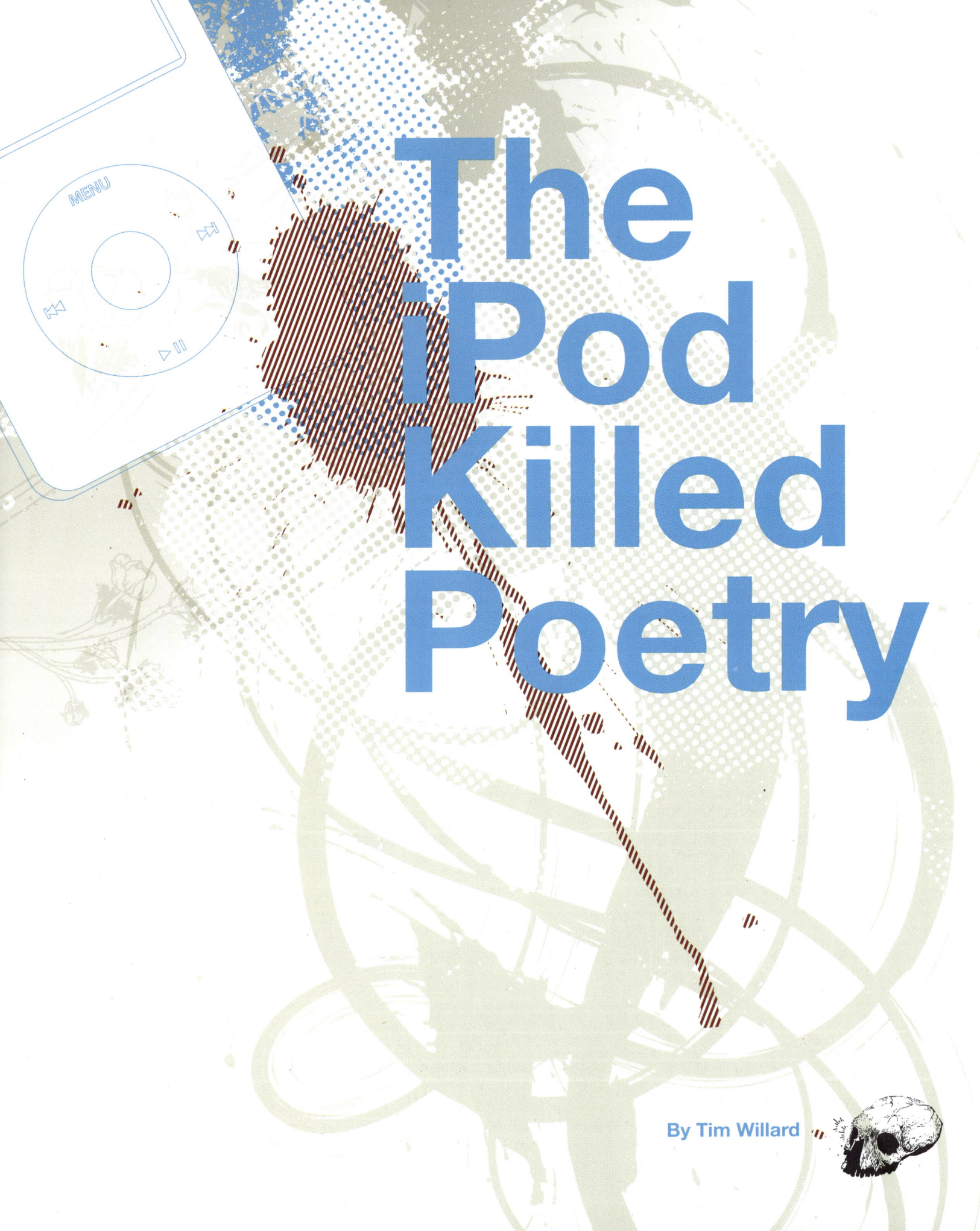

The iPod Killed Poetry

By Tim Willard

This is the dead land

This is the cactus land

Here the stone images

Are raised, here they receive

The supplication of a dead man's hand

Under the twinkle of a fading star.

—T.S. Eliot, The Hollow Men

IN A WORLD WHERE SPEED RULES AND FORMULAS EQUAL SUCCESS, WE HAVE RENDERED THE IDEA OF CULTIVATION OBSOLETE. BUSINESSES RE-CREATE THEMSELVES EVERY SIX MONTHS, CHURCHES ARE LAUNCHED INSTEAD OF GROWN, AND "AUTHENTIC COMMUNITY" IS NOTHING MORE THAN A TIME CARD WE PUNCH IN AN EFFORT TO FARM RELATIONSHIPS. AND CULTURE SHOWS NO SIGNS OF SLOWING.

Web 2.0, with its user-generated content and viral marketing potential, continues to bloat with digital giants Facebook, MySpace, and YouTube connecting people in social communities that exist only in the ether. Clearly these web tools serve useful purposes at some level—information sharing, entertainment, finding long lost friends—but the critique here gauges their impact on true community, which is life-on-life.

These cultural mediums represent the accelerating trend toward the speed and immediacy of our culture and the diminishing of things that take time to create and maintain, things like good food, love, symphonies, literature, poetry. This conversation centers on the loss of the ability to spend time building things that last—namely significant relationships. When we are honest about our everyday lives

we discover that beyond the cultural wow factor there is something decaying inside of us all, the ability to feel deeply and to relate beyond ourselves.

We feel that tug of eternity that the Teacher in Ecclesiastes describes (3:11) when we hear a story of someone overcoming significant odds to achieve an unthinkably high goal. Our goosebumps give way to tears when we watch movies and read books that tell of two lovers who endure life's worst and must bare their souls, clinging to one another, to survive the ordeal. What about these stories moves us? Is it perhaps the humanity of it all—the touch of the finite pushing through, reaching for the Divine?

Rob Bell says, "Our culture is thirsty for deep significant content." We are thirsty

because it is in such short supply—the beautiful and the deep have moved away from the shore and left us isolated and ignorant and blind. We find ourselves digging in the shallows for our food because we are too weak or too scared to chase after food that is sustaining, the food that may demand more from us than we are willing to give.

We all thirst for the physical and emotional touch of others, but often it is too costly; it asks for too much of a commitment to feel. The quickening we experience on the back end of a story or film dissipates into our decay and we walk away appreciating the depth of love and commitment but unwilling to put ourselves—our hearts—at risk in relationships. Honesty is too murky, and truth-telling, though romantic sounding, is better thought of

than acted out. So we cut our relationships short, absconding with time taken from others, and we retreat to our homes and our televisions and our computers and pray to God that He provide an outlet for authentic community. How quickly irony turns black.

Dead Poet Discussion

I have long found myself wondering about the validity of community within a culture that promotes isolation and narcissism. I can imagine myself as a superhero, rescuing others from a life of façade to a life of the real, only to see that black irony resurrected. I am just as isolated as everyone else, and I must forever be vigilant to pursue community.

My wonderings began to froth over into a conversation I had with my friend Ben. Ben is a talented writer and often surprises me with his commentary. I was lamenting over the fact that there are no poets today, not like there used to be. At the time I was considering a particular set of poems by T.S. Eliot, *The Four Quartets*.

I explained to Ben that after all these years of saying I was an Eliot fan, I found I was only fooling myself. I had never taken the time to delve deeper into his work, to allow them to seep in and, for a while, overtake my mind. I found that I wept while reading *East Coker*. So I asked Ben, "Where are the men who can pen immense verse, terse prose, and be masters in academia as well as the fantastical? Has culture stripped our hearts and minds? Have we become so thin, shadows of people who were once as deep as the ocean?"

I finished my rant, and Ben retorted in classic fashion, "The iPod has replaced poetry."

His comment startled me. He continued, "We don't need lines written on paper anymore. Convenience has won. It's easier to download music and books to our iPods and listen as we go. The speed of life has made poetry obsolete. It exists now in the songs that we listen to." We have morphed a once beautiful art form into a byte that we consume.

Ben was right. The iPod killed poetry.

Uncommon Commonality

If the iPod represents culture, then poetry represents more than a defunct literary form that takes long hours to write and understand. Poetry represents what has happened to you and me—our real-time interaction reduced to fleeting digital encounters. The Apostle Paul says that we are God's workmanship, or more accurately, God's poem, His opus, His masterpiece. We were crafted somewhere in the infinite deep, created to be in community with the Almighty and with each other.

And just as poetry takes time to write and understand, so too are we complex works of beauty, fashioned to unravel our wonders over time. Have you noticed that marriages become stronger over decades? Athletes blossom through the trial of injuries. We fall deeper in love with God as we spend more time in quiet communion with Him. Over time, the wonder of depth is revealed, a matchless glory which forces us to stop, reflect on what we have, and weep for our former blindness.

It is time to redefine community. Monthly meetings do not make the cut. Life-on-life happens in unglorious times during the week. We must be laid bare to one another, unraveled over time, sharing all things in common. Our uncommon commonality will draw others in who have been thirsting for something deep and significant. "And they'll know we are Christians by our love." And love, like poetry, takes time. **C**

We discover that beyond the cultural wow factor there is something decaying inside of us all.

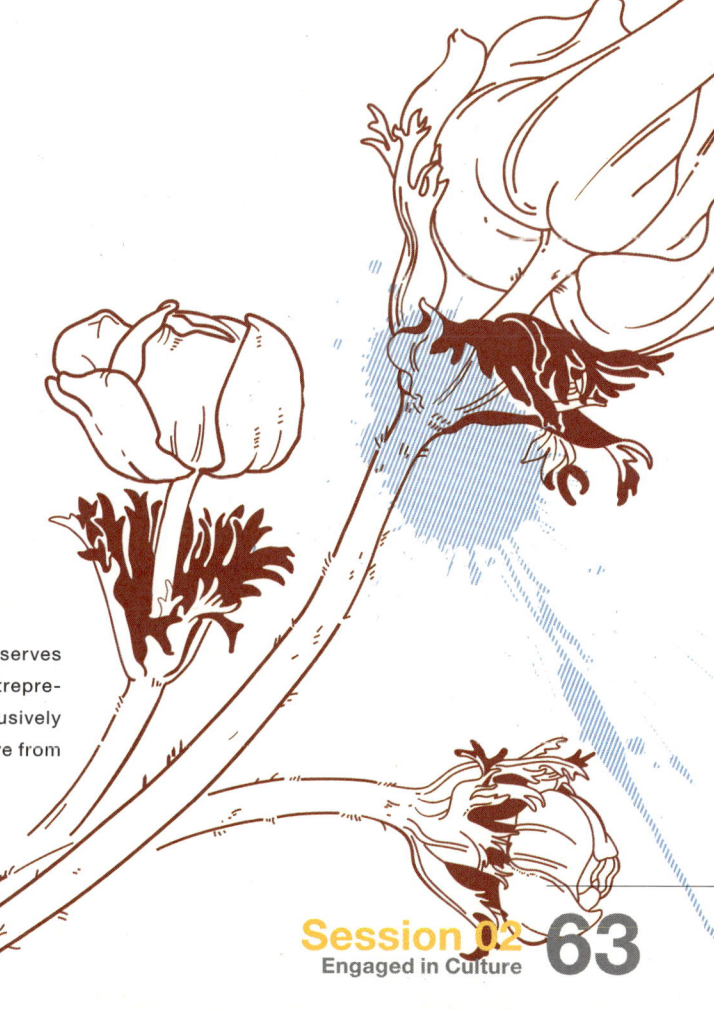

Tim Willard is a full-time freelance writer and graduate student (Gordon-Conwell) who serves as editor for the Catalyst GroupZine, and as Creative Content writer for the Prison Entrepreneurship Program. He and his wife, Chris, live somewhere north of Atlanta. Tim exclusively rides Kona mountain bikes and prefers French pressed to filter-drip coffee. To read more from Tim, visit **www.flickernail.com.**

Copyright 2007, Tim Willard.

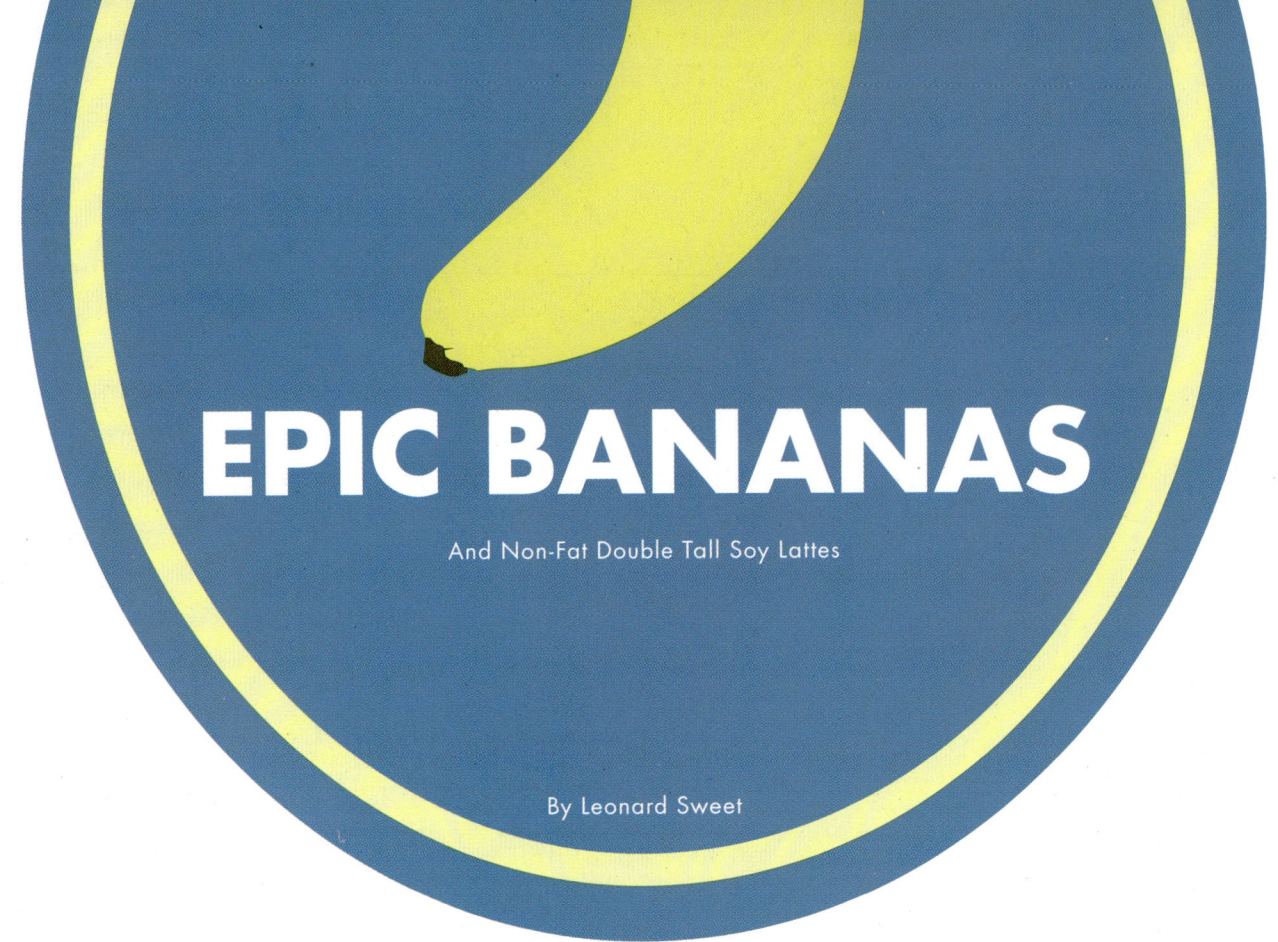

EPIC BANANAS

And Non-Fat Double Tall Soy Lattes

By Leonard Sweet

FOR A COUPLE OF MONTHS IN 2007, I LIVED IN FEAR OF TWO NAMES: 1) KATE AUDIE AND 2) DAN KIMBALL.

Since 2004 there is in England a Kate Audie Award for the most unoriginal book title. I lived in dread I'd win this award for the embarrassingly unoriginal title *The Gospel According To Starbucks*. Did the genre of "The Gospel According to ---------," really need another fill-in?

I breathed a sigh of relief when the Kate Audie Award (you know you've won when a copy of her book *The Kindness of Strangers* arrives in the mail) went to someone else. I can't remember whether the winner was *Never Had It So Good* or *In My Father's House*.

The other name I feared was Dan Kimball. Forget the fact that Dan is my doctoral student at George Fox University. Dan hated Starbucks. No polite way to put it. And before I knew how much Dan hates Starbucks, I asked the publisher to send a copy of the galley to Dan for his review and possible endorsement.

There is a comic artist who draws "Too Much Coffee Man" (**www.tmcm.com**). In one issue the lead character died and went to "hell" and hell turned out to be Starbucks. I tell Dan, "Hey, I can remember B.S.— Before Starbucks—when the US was coffee hell." But Dan only smiles and hands me a sticker he passes out like candy, "Friends Don't Let Friends Go To Starbucks."

It's not that Dan doesn't like the taste of Starbucks or that Dan doesn't credit Starbucks with starting a revolution. But in Dan's mind, Starbucks turned a movement into an empire just like Constantine turned a Christian movement into an empire, and the Star of Bethlehem has been dimmed and tilted out of its true and original shape ever since.

It didn't help my case when Howard Schultz, the chairman and founder of Starbucks Corp, shot a memo heard around the world on Valentine's Day (the day it was leaked) complaining to his ex-ecutives that in the interests of expansion and profits, the original "third-place" vision had been "watered down" and franchised, and that the stores were becoming too sterile, even corporate. I wondered if Dan had ghosted the memo.

"But Dan," I countered, "Starbucks isn't in the coffee business. They're in the people business." Dan nodded, but made that precisely the problem.

"I don't go to coffeehouses for the coffee really. I go to coffeehouses for being in a local cultural expression of the flavor of the community. What do the people dress like who work there? Starbucks uses all the same aprons, etc. What unique names of coffee and other drinks do local coffee houses come up with? Starbucks is uniform with names of coffees and drinks. What is the furniture, the decor? Starbucks uses the same everywhere. What is the art used on the walls from local artists? Starbucks uses generic art. What bands, poetry readings, events does the local coffee house hold? Starbucks doesn't have events or musicians, as it is mainly a get your coffee and go environment now, at least most of them."

By this time I was wishing I had chosen Cold Stone Creamery, or IKEA, or NASCAR, or American Idol, or any other company to make my case that digital culture wires the brain to be EPIC: E=Experiential, P=Participatory, I=Image-Rich, and C=Connective. In other words, Starbucks serves up Connective, Image-Rich, Interactive Experiences. Anything that is working is getting more EPIC, and our challenge is to turn whatever our activity into an EPICtivity.

In fact, maybe I should have used something as non-controversial as Dole Food: "The Gospel According to Dole ..." Well, maybe not. But even fruits and vegetables are becoming EPIC. In February 2007, Dole started labeling its bananas and some vegetables with "farm codes." The stickers send you to **doleorganic.com**, where you type in the three digit code that will identify the plantation that grew the banana, along with organic certification details, worker photos, and satellite map images via Google Earth. When you purchase a plum, you are now participating in a story that connects you to the people

who image that fruit. Organic Valley, the US's biggest organic farmer cooperative, has offered a similar feature on its soy milk cartons since 2004. Enter the expiration date at **organicvalley.coop/soy**, and it will bring up the bios and stories of the farmers who grew the soybeans.

Dan was relentless. "I'm not sure they can see all this in the Starbucks light, Len. Remember that favorite quote of yours from T. S. Eliot you keep citing to us: 'We had the experience but missed the meaning.'"

By this time I was beginning to feel like my book was a lost cause with Dan. Whatever tactic I took, he could find a negative comeback. I then thought of George Bernard Shaw's observations about preaching: "Some preaching is like

wine: it has colour and sparkle, but does no permanent good; some is like drinking coffee: it stimulates, but does not nourish; some is like carbonated water: a fizzle over nothing; some is like spring water: good but hard to get." Clearly Shaw wanted preaching that did all four, but I'm not sure I'd like a drink comprised of wine, black coffee, carbonated water, and spring water.

When my first copy of *The Gospel According To Starbucks* arrived in the mail, I squinted one eye and looked. There on the back cover was an endorsement from Dan Kimball. As much as he hates Starbucks, he still liked the book enough to risk his reputation and write some nice things about it.

That "C" in EPIC wins out every time. 🄲

Leonard Sweet, Ph.D., serves as the E. Stanley Jones Professor of Evangelism at Drew Theological School in Madison, New Jersey. He is also a Distinguished Visiting Professor at George Fox University in Newberg, Oregon, and founder and president of SpiritVenture Ministries. He is the author of *The Three Hardest Words* published by WaterBrook Press. He has also written *Out of the Question...Into the Mystery* and the trilogy *SoulTsunami*, *AquaChurch*, and *SoulSalsa*. Check out Len's newest project, **www.wikiletics.com**, the first wiki preaching resource on the web.

A MIND ABLAZE
The Vanguard of Christian Thinking

By James Emery White

CATHOLIC SCHOLAR GEORGE WEIGEL WRITES THAT IN JUNE 1959 THE COMMISSION PREPARING THE AGENDA FOR THE SECOND VATICAN COUNCIL WROTE TO ALL THE BISHOPS OF THE WORLD, ASKING THEM WHAT THEY'D LIKE TO TALK ABOUT. A FORTY-YEAR-OLD AUXILIARY BISHOP OF KRAKOW NAMED KAROL WOJTYLA—THE FUTURE POPE JOHN PAUL II—SENT A SINGLE, SHARP QUESTION: WHAT IN THE WORLD HAS HAPPENED? HOW DID A TWENTIETH CENTURY THAT HAD BEGUN WITH SUCH HIGH EXPECTATIONS FOR THE HUMAN FUTURE PRODUCE, WITHIN A HANDFUL OF DECADES, TWO WORLD WARS, THREE TOTALITARIAN SYSTEMS, AUSCHWITZ, THE GULAG, MOUNTAINS OF CORPSES, OCEANS OF BLOOD, THE GREATEST PERSECUTIONS IN CHRISTIAN HISTORY, AND A COLD WAR THAT THREATENED THE FUTURE OF THE PLANET?

What happened?

What happened, Karol Wojtyla suggested, was that the great project of Western humanism had gone off the rails. As John Paul's biographer, Weigel summarizes the thinking of the late pontiff: "Ideas have consequences, and bad ideas can have lethal consequences." [1]

Our purpose in developing our minds is our love for God; our mission, however, is to contend with the darkness for the sake of the Light. The exercise of our intellects does not exist merely to explore ideas and arguments. Those who study the history of Christianity as merely an intellectual history miss the point. As Robert Louis Wilken noted, "the study of Christian thought has been too preoccupied with ideas. Its mission is to win the hearts and minds of men and women and to change their lives." [2]

This is what *our* mind must be developed to understand in order to then offer something to the *world's* mind for consideration and challenge. If we cannot rise to this endeavor, we will have lost our place in the most critical of conversations—indeed, the only conversation that matters.

The mission of the church is paramount. And what propels the mission forward is an awakened mind, a mind ablaze with God and the things of God. This is the heart of the cultural commission within the Great Commission. The Great Commission calls us to reach out to every person with the Gospel of Jesus Christ; the cultural commission calls us to lay hold of every nook and cranny of our world for the Kingdom of God. They are not separate endeavors—they are the two edges of the single sword we are called to wield.

Though frighteningly few Christians embrace the true dynamic and practice of the Great Commission, even fewer take hold of the cultural commission. Too often we retreat into our Christian sub-culture, with its books, magazines, radio stations, and bumper stickers.

Henri Nouwen writes of a priest who told him that he cancelled his subscription to the *New York Times* because he felt that the endless stories about war, crime, power games, and political manipulation only disturbed his mind and heart and prevented him from meditation and prayer. "That is a sad story," writes Nouwen. "A real spiritual life does exactly the opposite: it makes us so alert and aware of the world around us, that all that is and happens becomes part of our contemplation and meditation and invites us to a free and fearless response." [3]

This is the difference between a Christian who is intelligent and a Christian who has an intellect. No one, argues Richard Hofstadter, questions the value of intelligence; that excellence of mind that is employed with narrow, immediate, predictable ranges that are undeniably practical. Intellect, on the other hand, is the critical, creative, and contemplative side of things. [4]

It is also the activist side of things.

For our minds to break free and loom large on the world's stage, we must recapture the lost art of thinking itself. Having a Christian mind means to think—and to think widely and broadly. This goes beyond the practice of reflection, important as this practice is, for reflection is more of a discipline or skill to be embraced. We are talking about application—prayerfully setting the mind to the task at hand. Nouwen's friend purposefully avoided the *New York Times*. Nouwen's reminder should not be lost: the point is to purposefully engage it.

This brings us to the heart of the mind applied. It is not simply *thinking* Christianly, for to know is to do. Our goal is to think in such a way as to know how to live. So what does it mean for Christ to lay claim to medicine? To law? To politics? To the economy? To a child in the womb? To sexuality? Consider the words of the prophet Micah: "And what does the Lord require of you? To act justly and to love mercy and to walk humbly with your God." [5] It is not enough to simply understand the nature of justice and love from within a Christian perspective. Then "we must go on," writes Dennis Hollinger, "to think about the strategies of justice and love in issues like poverty, race relations, abortion and political life." [6]

This is the vanguard of Christian thinking—knowing how to live, and then working to make the Kingdom of God a reality for others to be able to live as well. **C**

James Emery White is the president of Gordon-Conwell Theological Seminary. He holds M.Div. and Ph.D. degrees in theology, history and biblical studies. White is the author of twelve books, including *Embracing the Mysterious God, A Search for the Spiritual, Serious Times* and *The Prayer God Longs For*.

Excerpted from James Emery White's A Mind for God *(InterVarsity Press, 2006). Used by permission.*

A CONGREGATION OF PILGRIMS
AN INTERVIEW WITH EMMANUEL KATONGOLE

CHRISTIAN LEADERS FROM FIVE WAR-TORN COUNTRIES OF EAST AFRICA GATHERED IN KAMPALA, UGANDA, LAST NOVEMBER TO STRENGTHEN THE CHURCH'S WITNESS IN THE MIDST OF CONFLICT. THEY WERE CONVENED BY EMMANUEL KATONGOLE, A CATHOLIC PRIEST WHOSE BIOGRAPHY EMBODIES BOTH ETHNIC TENSION AND CHRISTIAN HOPE. KATONGOLE WAS BORN AND RAISED IN UGANDA, THE SON OF RWANDAN PARENTS. HIS FATHER EMBRACED CHRISTIAN FAITH AS AN ADULT, AND HIS JOYFUL SERIOUSNESS ABOUT CHRISTIANITY SHAPED KATONGOLE, WHO JOINED THE PRIESTHOOD AND TRAINED AS A PHILOSOPHICAL THEOLOGIAN IN BELGIUM. KATONGOLE NOW TEACHES AT DUKE DIVINITY SCHOOL, WHERE HE IS CO-DIRECTOR, WITH CHRIS RICE, OF THE CENTER FOR RECONCILIATION.

CVP: *You've lived on three continents and in four countries, and your parents were from yet another country, Rwanda. How does your story affect your understanding of God's mission in the world?*

KATONGOLE: Being an immigrant can be a blessing. God's mission, as I read it in 2 Corinthians 5:17, is new creation. God is reconciling the world to Himself. And there is a sense of journey that is connected with that. When, later on, Paul says that "We are ambassadors of God's reconciliation, God is appealing through us," He is inviting us into a journey toward a new kind of community. People looking at Christians should be confused. Who are these people? Are they black? Are they white? Are they Americans? Are they Ugandans? In Revelation, John sees people drawn from all languages and tribes and nations: an unprecedented congregation. Living on three continents has

deepened my understanding of the church as such a congregation; at the same time, it has heightened my sense of Christian life as a journey and of what it means to live as a pilgrim, a resident alien.

CVP: *Are specific places and local identities important in a life of pilgrimage?*

KATONGOLE: Absolutely. Pilgrimage actually makes us more aware of localness, because it brings us into contact with specific places and people. People sometimes ask me how "the church in America" should relate to "the church in Rwanda." But that level of abstraction grows out of a tower-building mentality. There are only specific Americans from specific places with specific gifts and stories; there are only specific Rwandans.

What would it mean for Christians to have a certain naiveté about all these things called *culture*? How do we inhabit what we might call tactics instead of strategies? Strategy is the posture of an army, of a nation state, of a business that is able to conduct surveillance of its territory and all others. Tactics, on the other hand, are weapons of the weak, of those who have no place to call their own, who live in a territory that is controlled by others.

CVP: *Isn't that a waste of our capacity to think strategically?*

KATONGOLE: There are two dominant models of mission in our time. There is the model of mission as aid, which arises out of the great need we see in the world—famine, AIDS, poverty—and also out of a recognition of how much American Christians have. So American Christians go to Africa to help. This can be criticized as giving a person a fish for a day, but if that person is starving, then this model of mission actually does some good. A lot of people are being helped by this kind of mission. But the problem is that from this mission, Christians return to a tower. Their world remains their world, and Africa's world remains Africa's world.

Then there is the model of mission as partnership. It arises out of a sense of mutuality and solidarity between churches in the North and the South. So churches develop sister-parish relationships and so forth. The hope is to teach people how to fish, to equip them to do the fishing.

This model also overlooks the difference in power between America and the rest of the world. One gets an impression that because of the numerical strength of Africa's church, African Christians can be equal partners with their Western counterparts. But we cannot pretend that the power of America does not exist. There is a new desire to learn from one another, but how deep does the learning go? I have

a hard time getting a serious answer when I ask American churches what they have learned from their African "partnerships." Perhaps instead of spending $2.5 million on a building, they scale it down to $2.3 million. But they're still constructing baptismal fonts that automatically adjust the temperature! In a world where millions of Christians have no clean water, how much has been learned here?

CVP: *Maybe they turn the temperature in the baptismal font down by two degrees.*

KATONGOLE: Right! I'm not saying that either of these models is heretical—they have biblical foundations. Mission as aid often draws from the story of the Good Samaritan, and mission as partnership invokes Paul's image of the Body, which has many parts. It is only that these models do not go far enough in bridging the neat divisions or tribalism between "us" and "them." That is why we need to learn another model—mission as pilgrimage, which is based on a vision of the Christian life as a journey. This

model grows out of the sense of being pilgrims together, pilgrims who feel the dust under their feet and come to know the places where they sojourn.

The problem with the world is not that we do not see others. We do. We know the needs of the world. But to *feel* the gifts and needs of the world—that means learning to journey with people in different parts of the world. This kind of journeying is slower than mission done as delivery of aid, slower even than partnership. But when we take time for that, it begins to transform the pilgrim. You have learned the names of people and places; you have inhaled the dust.

Mission as pilgrimage is about that transformation. It's not about fixing northern Uganda. You're not going to fix northern Uganda! It's not even about partnering with northern Uganda. Instead, the pilgrim begins to know, to feel, that northern Uganda, with all its tragedy and terror, is a Christian story. That it is not just *their* story, but that it is *our* story. **C**

For more from the Christian Vision Project and Emmanuel Katongole, visit **www.christianvisionproject.com**.

STEVE BEARD

EDITOR-IN-CHIEF, *RISEN MAGAZINE*
Age 42, Wilmore, Kentucky, www.thunderstruck.org

STEVE BEARD HAS BEEN WRITING AND EDITING SINCE 1988. SEVEN YEARS AGO, STEVE LAUNCHED **WWW.THUNDERSTRUCK.ORG** — A TRUCK STOP FOR THE SOUL THAT IS OBSESSED WITH ROCK 'N' ROLL, RELIGION, RED-HOT BARBEQUE, AND REDEMPTION. STEVE'S UNIQUE PERSPECTIVE AND WRITING TALENT CONTINUES TO AFFORD HIM OPPORTUNITIES FOR MAJOR CULTURAL INFLUENCE. HIS MOST RECENT VENTURE? EDITORIAL OVERSIGHT FOR *RISEN MAGAZINE*. SOME COMMENTS FROM STEVE ...

IT MAY NOT BE PRETTY

My writing tends to probe and investigate the mystical clash of faith in the creative arts. The people I like to profile—Bob Dylan, Johnny Cash, Albert Einstein—don't always provide neat and tidy conversion stories. They are the larger-than-life sagas that make believers nervous because of the lurid or open-ended nature of some of the journeys.

I believe that the lust for life has to be balanced with sweating it out to be in sync with the teaching and ministry of Jesus. I try to communicate the love and nature of God to a world that has been let down by flaccid and anemic religion.

LATENT CHRISTIANITY

This can be one of those endeavors that gets overused and cheapened. I simply think that Christians who can play music should play music, those who can surf should surf, those who can tango should dance, and those who can drive 180 mph should be involved in NASCAR. I believe in the sacramental nature of writing songs, taking photos, penning poetry, and producing films.

Our culture has a voracious appetite for spiritual engagement—even in our entertainment. There are tons of mainstream artists who are open about their faith struggles and journeys.

This new musical breed is not producing songs *about* faith, as much as songs *inspired by* faith. As C. S. Lewis wrote, "What we want is not more little books about Christianity, but more little books by Christians on other subjects—with their Christianity latent." [1] These musicians probe, lament, rejoice, and even banter with the Almighty—all the while giving flight to our discouragement and reminding us that there is hope.

It is rare that a book, film, or television broadcast actually converts someone to Christianity. Usually, people are drawn to God in tragedy, despair, or in rare, quiet moments of contemplation. They are often introduced to God through someone around them who loves them and loves God. We need to be vulnerable, available, and grace-filled to those inside and outside the four walls of the Church.

COURAGEOUS? COMPARED TO WHAT?

I am shamed when I read about how the early reformers found themselves ostracized, humiliated, or tortured for their faith. I consider that courageous. What I do should not be considered in the same category. I have always wanted to write a blog with complete anonymity so I could seriously vent about the way that I sometimes feel about God, my local church, or Christian leaders. I am not courageous like that.

I don't think it's courageous to want to write on things that matter. It is merely an impulse. I like telling stories. I love redemption. I have always tried to ask the rich to remember the poor, the hip to remember the lame, and the saved to remember those lost on their way. Sometimes that aggravates readers—but it's not terribly courageous. C

Church and Contemporary Culture

By Ed Stetzer

Like a giant tug of war, each side is pulling hard. The battle lines: Cultural relevance versus biblical faithfulness—a classic tyranny of the "or."

On one hand, the church can be so focused on cultural relevance that it loses its distinctive message. On the other hand, it can decide that culture is nothing more than the sinful world we live in and is to be ignored. Both scenarios lead to a church whose message is indiscernible and obscure to those who are outside of it. The Bible clearly gives us a mandate to make the message understandable. We do more than just translate it into a language: we must also translate it into culture.

Contextualizing may mean something very different in your church than it does in any other, and a culturally relevant church in your community may look very different from culturally relevant churches elsewhere. Simply put, you must passionately love the people God has given you—and the culture—in order to pastor those people well. John Knox said, "Give me Scotland or I die." We must have the same kind of passion and love for the people and the culture that exists outside our steepled structures.

Above all else, the church and its ministry must be biblically faithful. We must remember that the reason we engage culture is not to be cool, trendy, contemporary, or cutting edge, but so that those who live in our cultures can hear the message of Jesus. That message is more than just "come to Christ;" it involves how we structure our lives, and it matters deeply. Our churches should share the Gospel message wherever they are and whatever their cultural context. They should be known as people who love God's Word and seek to live differently because of it.

A church that is biblically faithful to God's mission must also work to relate to people in its own culture. If it doesn't, people will assume that being a Christian simply means dressing differently, listening to different music styles, and speaking a different language. They'll confuse becoming a Christian with a change of clothes, music, and vocabulary. Jesus said that we should be "in" the world but not "of" the world; many churches today do just the opposite. Christians should be living counter-culturally in their families, values, finances, and all other facets of life.

You may ask why, if we have the timeless truth of the Gospel, do we need to concern ourselves with culturally relevant ministry? Because if we don't, the message of the Gospel gets confused with the religion of old. The unchurched think that Christianity is a nostalgic culture rather than a living faith. Our job is to remove the extra stumbling blocks of culture without removing the essential stumbling block of the cross (1 Corinthians 1:23).

Consider emulating Paul's activities in Acts 17. Wander through your Athens. Look at the cultural idols. Let what you see break your heart and burden your mind. Let godly passion drive you to say, "Give me Athens or I die." Then confidently take the Gospel to those who'll see its uncluttered message, trust its validity, and receive its Savior—Jesus Christ. **C**

Ed Stetzer is Director and Missiologist in Residence at Lifeway Research. His most recent books are *Comeback Churches* and *11 Innovations in the Local Church*.

ENGAGED IN CULTURE

Are you living in the valley of culture? Dream a little—what lies just beyond the horizon of possibility? Is there something that you can create in culture that wasn't there before—like a park or clothing bank? How can you begin to shape your immediate culture? Write out your cultural manifesto—how will you engage culture through your giftedness and calling?

III. AUTHENTIC IN INFLUENCE

Leadership is influence. I am not a leader if others are not following.
Influence can't be forced or contrived. It can only be won over time. If I am living
out the six elements of a Catalyst Leader, influence will be natural, compelling, and attractive.
If not, it will be challenged by others and ineffective. My prayer is that God would
continue to expand and entrust me with greater influence.

CATALYST STUDY
AUTHENTIC IN INFLUENCE

MAVERICKS

THE PATH OF THE UNCOMMON

BY TIM WILLARD

AND AS HE WAS BROUGHT FORWARD, THE TUMULT BECAME GREAT WHEN THEY HEARD THAT POLYCARP WAS TAKEN. AND WHEN HE CAME NEAR, THE PROCONSUL ASKED HIM WHETHER HE WAS POLYCARP. ON HIS CONFESSING THAT HE WAS, THE PROCONSUL SOUGHT TO PERSUADE HIM TO DENY CHRIST, SAYING, "SWEAR, AND I WILL SET THEE AT LIBERTY, RE-PROACH CHRIST." POLYCARP DECLARED, "EIGHTY AND SIX YEARS HAVE I SERVED HIM, AND HE NEVER DID ME ANY INJURY: HOW THEN CAN I BLASPHEME MY KING AND MY SAVIOR." [1]

When I read the account of Polycarp something snaps inside of me. The thought of the bloody coliseum floor and the mangled bodies of Christians paints a much deeper picture of faith than I am used to. It's clear that the spilled blood of the martyrs was not just the life of Christians drying in the dust. It was like spring water falling on fertile soil—it would be the life-blood to strengthen the roots of the Christian faith for the next two millennia.

Church history is decorated with stories of men and women of ordinary station expressing their faith in extraordinary fashion. From its inception Christianity has faced opposition from governments from within its own walls, and from the greater culture. Yet each time the faith was pressed, Christians responded—winsome, vibrant, and fierce.

BLOOD ROOT

The martyr tradition of the early Church is one of the most beloved aspects of Christianity, and it stands as a testimony to the radical faith it took to claim the name of Christ in the first centuries. The martyrs reflected the deep love Christ had for humankind, and their influence shaped Christianity for ages to come.

At the time the Christian faith began to spread, Rome was highly tolerant of many religions and cults. In order to keep the peace and appease the enormous religious diversity, the government made it mandatory to worship foreign gods. The pluralism of the land was rampant; all was tolerated. Sound familiar?

You can imagine, then, the reaction of the Roman government when Christians began to claim that they worshipped the one true God and that to believe in the risen Lord was to believe in the sovereign God of the universe. This didn't sit well with the pluralism of the day. Because they did not believe in the "state gods" they were viewed as atheists, which was punishable by death.

Not only were they viewed as atheists, but their religious practices were seen as suspect. The "holy kiss" with which they greeted one another was blown out of proportion as the Christians were soon accused of incest. To make matters worse, their observance of the Eucharist was said to be a gross practice of cannibalism, as they would eat the flesh and drink the blood of Christ.

Polycarp's martyrdom is arguably the most recognized of all the early martyrs. Here was one of the last remaining connections with Jesus' disciples—a close friend of John the Beloved. He was old, he was dignified, and he was lovingly fierce until the end. His spirit of devotion encapsulated Christianity during the first four centuries, and he became the model for future Christians who would face similar governmental persecution.

FAITH. RISK. INFLUENCE.

So often we view leaders as men and women of great position, able to influence hundreds or thousands through various forms of media or the pulpit. But positions don't equal influence. I can hold a position in an organization and politic my way up the food chain—no problem. But in that case, the end goal is antithetical to that of an influencer—it is self-serving. "If anyone wants to be first, he must be the very last, and the servant of all." (Mark 9:35 NIV)

Influencers are doers, and they don't always hold positions within the church or the greater culture. Many times the great influencers throughout history were oppositional to traditional Christianity and its institutes. Polycarp was elevated to the status of a leader not because he did what it took to obtain a position, but because of the way he lived out his faith. We remember him not because of a successful church plant, but because he did not flinch when he was offered death as a reward to his faith.

John C. Maxwell says, "Leadership is influence—nothing more, nothing less." Too often though, people take this statement to mean that traditional (positional) leaders are the only influencers—especially in the Church. People in rock bands, producing movies, or writing excellent fiction influence in non-traditional ways but are often seen as mavericks or rebels. Maybe we should include headstrong monks with chips on their shoulders in that mix. No doubt in today's society Martin Luther would have more in common with religious activists than with MBAs or CEOs.

Strong leaders lead by what they do. It is *doing* something that inspires others to follow. Often the major influencers throughout history were misunderstood, highly imbalanced, and to, some extent, reckless. But the Christian faith isn't about the calculated and the safe; it's about radical transformation. And, as C.S. Lewis reminds us, it's about following the Christ who is good but not safe. [2] It is interesting that Martin Luther would conclude, in the face of his accusers, that to deny the authority of Scripture was neither right nor safe.

Perhaps something in our culture has made us too prudent—safe Christians. Perhaps influence is less about adhering to systems and programs and more about venturing out on the waters where Peter made his first steps toward understanding that attached to great faith is great risk.

The early martyrs laid a foundation of faith that would spread like wildfire all over the known world and would do so

WE CANNOT CHANGE OTHERS UNTIL WE FIRST CHANGE OURSELVES.

in the face of great risk. Their faith made them counter-cultural compared to Roman law, but their lifestyle was alluring and mysteriously beautiful. It seems the risk of faith doesn't always carry the promise of material success but the reward of trial and persecution.

A MONK AND A HAMMER

If the martyr tradition influenced the future of Christianity by standing for the faith against an intolerant government, then Martin Luther would be an example of an influencer who had to battle within the walls of Christendom to vie for true faith.

By the time Luther entered Wittenberg, the Catholic Church was already corrupted by power and money. When Luther hammered the Ninety-Five Theses on the church door he wasn't simply defying the Church in public—he was trying to engage dialogue with the hope of ensuing change.

But for Luther it wasn't just about the Ninety-Five Theses—he first struggled to come to terms with his faith. Was it actually his or something the Church manipulated? We see in Luther's life that massive reform wasn't something that interested him at first. Instead, we see him begin his spiritual journey in an attempt to understand a God that did not condemn, but loved. Luther sought personal reform, which translates into corporate reform. We cannot change others until we first change ourselves.

"The righteous shall live by faith." (Romans 1:17 ESV) Luther found that he could do nothing to merit God's grace. He would have to live this faith when it was not easy, when the whole world was barreling down on him. He would have to choose to stand upon faith and the Word of God, or to go the easy road and comply, compromise … cower. Another way to read this verse is, "By faith the righteous live." There is only one way to live, it is the only way that is redeemable to the Christian, that is a life of faith.

When we seek to glorify God with our lives, inevitably we will be called to make a stand that requires faith. These are the moments that define us as Christians. These are the moments that reform our hearts and minds. Luther didn't wake up one day with the notion to begin the Reformation. But he did wake up one day and consciously begin to pursue God, and in so doing he put into motion a pursuit that would lead to a personal reformation.

He wasn't the Monk of the Year, and he certainly wasn't in line for the next position in the Catholic Church. He was a maverick monk with a mission. His influence came not from position but from admission—admission that without God's grace, he was nothing. And as he faced death for his egregious beliefs, he left his fate in God's hands—"Here I stand … God help me. Amen." [3] His words defined his action—and both continue their influence to this day.

THE GANGLY FARM BOY

If there's one thing the Reformers taught it's that the Church always needs to be reforming. So fast-forward about five hundred years and you run right into the most prolific movement within Christianity—evangelicalism. Complete with its denominational divisions, the movement boasts a brilliant beginning and, as of late, a dim continuance.

Modern evangelicalism goes back a few hundred years. But the version we know emerged out of the fundamentalist movement at the turn of the twentieth century. Today fundamentalism carries a nasty stench, and rightly so. It started out as a positive expression of evangelicals everywhere who wanted to unite and stand for the fundamentals of the Christian faith, however, differences began to swirl and the hardcore fundamentalists withdrew from society. This resulted in many fundamentalists who sought a new way to express evangelicalism.

Enter the neo-evangelicals. These were evangelicals who still held tightly to the fundamentals of the Gospel message but sought to inject society with a winsome faith—redeeming the culture by creating it.

The poster-child for this movement was the Reverend Billy Graham. Graham, a gangly farm boy turned evangelist, used his famous "crusades" to spread the Gospel message. He cut his preaching chops on the stump for Youth For Christ, an eclectic group of evangelists and teachers with high passions to change the world for Christ. Billy Graham would move on to a world stage, preaching to as many as one million people in Seoul, Korea (1973).

His influence transcended church divisions, political arenas, and nations. He is arguably the most influential Christian of the age. He has preached to more people than any man in history and enjoyed unprecedented access to the President of the United States for decades. Unlike the staunch fundamentalists who retreated from culture, Billy Graham and the neo-evangelicals sought to engage it by establishing Christian colleges, charitable organizations, and various pursuits that infused the culture with excellence stemming from a biblical worldview.

Consequently, new Evangelicals became committed to re-engage the same institutions that many within the fundamentalist movement had abandoned. [4] This was perhaps the most notable movement since Continental Pietism to bring balance to the Christian faith in terms of encouraging a deep devotional life, intellectual pursuit, and cultural engagement.

But what sets Billy Graham apart from other evangelists or preachers? Many say that he's not the best speaker, nor is he the most brilliant theologian, but those same people describe him as the meekest and most humble man they've ever met. Because Billy Graham heeded the call on his life, the movement of evangelicalism has never been the same.

THERE IS NO SPOON

Billy Graham emerged from the pieces of fundamentalism with the intent to influence—not just his own ministry but he partnered with other evangelicals who didn't want to see Christianity curl up in a corner and wither in isolation. As he partnered with others he also continued to craft his own ministry, keeping it focused and simple. He operated in his giftedness and thrived.

We don't often discuss the fact that Billy Graham had to do business *with* God before he could be used *by* God. He faced serious doubts concerning the inerrancy of Scripture early in his preaching career and had to get to the point of total surrender to God.

The influencers we've looked at here all expressed their faith with their actions, and all of them did so after they were able to surrender all—many times this meant death. If your first notion in ministry is to wrestle with thoughts that ask, "How can I change the church?" or "How can I build a significant ministry or business?" without giving the proper time to cultivating your relationship with God, then your focus is askew.

Remember in *The Matrix* movie when Neo visits the Oracle to find out if he is "the One." In the waiting room he watches a child bend a spoon by looking at it. The child hands the spoon to Neo and advises him ...

"Don't try to bend the spoon, that's impossible. Only try and realize the truth."

"What truth?" asks Neo.

"There is no spoon. Then you'll see that it is not the spoon that bends; it is only yourself."

Stop trying to change things outside of yourself. Instead, operate within your giftedness, give up your control, and step out into the waters of your faith. This is the starting point of influence. If you want to be a shaper, you must journey through the process of being shaped—a process that begins with a lump of clay and ends with fire. C

Tim Willard is a full-time freelance writer and graduate student (Gordon-Conwell) who serves as editor for the Catalyst GroupZine and as Creative Content writer for the Prison Entrepreneurship Program. He and his wife, Chris, live somewhere north of Atlanta. Tim exclusively rides Kona mountain bikes and prefers French pressed to filter-drip coffee. To read more from Tim, visit **www.flickernail.com.**

GROUP STUDY QUESTIONS
FOR DISCUSSION

1. Why doesn't position equal influence?

2. What are you currently doing that inspires others to follow you as a leader?

3. As an influencer, what have you had to battle within the walls of the Christian culture today?

4. What do you need to change about yourself before you can think about influencing others?

5. How have you seen God shape you in order to become a shaper of others?

6. Why do you think the early martyrs had such a profound influence that shaped Christianity for the ages to come?

THE WHY, THE WHO, AND THE WHAT

CLEARLY DEFINE YOUR STRENGTHS

An Interview with Marcus Buckingham

GREAT LEADERS UNDERSTAND HOW TO UTILIZE STRENGTHS. MARCUS BUCKINGHAM UNDERSTANDS THIS CONCEPT BETTER THAN MOST. MARCUS HAS USED HIS 17 YEARS OF EXPERIENCE WITH GALLUP TO REDEFINE HOW LEADERS APPROACH THEIR STRENGTHS AND WEAKNESSES. HOWEVER, MARCUS REVEALS TO CATALYST THAT IT'S MORE THAN JUST GOING AFTER WHAT YOU'RE GOOD AT WITH PASSION—YOU MUST BE SPECIFIC.

TOO OFTEN LEADERS WHO WANT TO BE CHANGE AGENTS APPROACH A PROBLEM OR SITUATION WITH GREAT INTENTIONS WITHOUT HAVING THOUGHT THROUGH EXACTLY WHAT THEY BRING TO THE TABLE AND HOW THEY INTEND TO ACHIEVE THEIR LOFTY GOAL.

IN THIS INTERVIEW WITH MARCUS, WE FOLLOWED UP ON THE ISSUES RAISED IN VOLUME TWO OF THE *CATALYST GROUPZINE* BY ASKING HIM TO GIVE US INSIGHT INTO THE IMPORTANCE OF DEFINING OUR STRENGTHS AND HOW WE SHOULD GO ABOUT IT.

Catalyst: *Give us a snapshot of how people in America view their strengths versus weaknesses.*

Buckingham: In 2000 we (Gallup) took a poll and asked, "Which do you think will help you achieve the greatest success in life: building on your strengths or fixing your weaknesses?" forty-one percent of people said "strengths," and fifty-nine percent said "weaknesses."

In the intervening years, there's been a lot of movement toward the strengths side. Psychology has changed with things like positive psychology starting to dominate the curriculum of universities around the country. By far the most popular elective class at Harvard today in any discipline is an Introduction to Positive Psychology, which is a study of why people are happy, why people are joyful, why people are compassionate.

Over the last hundred years, psychology knew a lot about why people are depressed and sad and psychotic. But from all that knowledge we had inferred that to make people happy, you had to make them not depressed. Of course that's rubbish. People that aren't depressed are simply people that aren't depressed. If you want to actually get into what makes life meaningful, you better study people that have found meaning in life.

Catalyst: *So what about today? Are people more apt to work on their strengths than weaknesses?*

Buckingham: If you Google "strengths-based" today you get 42 million hits. Whether it's family therapy, growth of a church, or the legal system, we're starting to see approaches based on studying what works, studying the strengths of a person or a process.

But interestingly, people are still focused on weaknesses. Over the last 18 months when we asked people the same question we asked in 2000, 37 percent said "building on my strengths," and 63 percent said "fixing my weaknesses." When you ask, most people will bet their career and their success and their significance on finding out where they're weak and yet rarely spend time trying to improve those weaknesses.

Catalyst: *In your new book,* Go, Put Your Strengths to Work, *you say that strengths aren't necessarily what you're good at and weaknesses aren't what you're bad at. Explain that thought.*

Buckingham: Well, so often we say your strengths are what you're good at and your weaknesses are what you're bad at. But don't we all have some things that we're really good at but if we ever had to do them again, it would be too soon? Strangely, we find there are things that we're good at that drain us or bore us or deplete us; in that case you can't call them strengths because they do the opposite of what strengths do. They don't strengthen you; they weaken you.

It's as if you've been blessed with ability, but somehow God forgot to give you any appetite. The funny thing is you keep getting asked to do it because you're good at it. People don't know that you don't enjoy it, and you're kind of confused about it too because you're supposed to like what you're good at, right?

For example, there was a wonderful swimmer who, at the age of six, had such a beautiful swimming stroke that he was put into a swimming club and trained to become a truly fantastic swimmer. He won meets, set records, and was on the senior varsity team when he was only fourteen. He was a wonderful swimmer, but hated it so much that before every meet he would get a terrible migraine. His body was telling him something, but he didn't know how to express it.

Catalyst: *Is there perhaps a more accurate way to define strengths?*

Buckingham: If you think about strengths as in the swimmer illustration, then saying a strength is what you're good at is, at worst, inaccurate and, at best, incomplete. Perhaps a better definition of a strength is any activity that makes you feel strong. A strength is an activity that, before you do it, you look forward to it. While you're doing it, time doesn't stand still; it goes by quickly and you can concentrate. It's an activity that when you're done with it, you feel invigorated.

There are signs you can look for to determine a strength, like how you feel before, during, and after the activity. How you feel while you're doing it drives how good you get at it. You can discover your strengths in a regular week of life.

All of us have to realize that our appetites drive our abilities. There are some that would say, "Wait a minute. There are some things that I'm drawn to that I'm rubbish at, but I keep getting drawn to do them. No matter how much I feel like I want to do those things and no matter how much time zips by while I'm doing them, I'm still not very good." My response to that person is, "Those things are called hobbies."

They're hobbies, and they stay hobbies because no one pays us to do them. In the real world very few of us maintain a really strong appetite for activities we're clearly bad at.

Catalyst: *The last time we spoke you talked a lot about creating a strengths revolution.*

Thirty or forty years from now what does this strengths revolution look like?

Buckingham: Well, I think two things. If you ask people today in America "What percentage of a typical day do you spend playing to your strengths?" only 14 percent say, "Most of the time." I want that number to be 8 out of 10, not 1.4 out of 10. All of us were born with unique strengths and weaknesses. The purpose of life is not to transform ourselves into someone else. The purpose of life is to free up and focus the forces that are already there. Only 1.4 of us have figured out how to do that and that's a tragedy—a moral tragedy.

The second sign to me would be that we've changed the way we teach people in schools. I think our curriculum right now is designed to push children through a knowledge and skills acquisition system. We think of kids in a standardized way—thus the standardized tests. We believe that school is simply a knowledge transfer system used to push a certain precepts or knowledge through our kids. While some element of that must be there, schools should also be designed around helping a child to identify, name, and responsibly volunteer their strengths to the world.

Forty years from now I would like to see that we are teaching our children differently so that they become adults who contribute more of what they know they are good at. I don't want to see them volunteering in a blind way, "Hey I want to save the world." But saying, "I've got these three or four strengths that I'm bringing to do that."

Catalyst: *What's the correlation of our strengths to our heartbeats, what we're most passionate about?*

Buckingham: I think a proper definition of a strength is passion plus specificity.

IF YOU WANT TO ACTUALLY GET INTO WHAT MAKES LIFE MEANINGFUL, YOU BETTER STUDY PEOPLE THAT HAVE FOUND MEANING IN LIFE.

Passions by themselves are too far away; they're far too grandiose, and they can dissipate in the wind. But passion with specificity changes the world. Don't follow your heart. Follow your heart with specifics.

There are many practical examples of this. Some people join their church because they want to help it grow. But then they find out they're in charge of fundraising, and they hate fundraising. Their passion is to help their church grow, but there are no specifics to it. Suddenly, they find themselves calling people up every evening trying to raise money for some project, and it kills them. They feel guilty that it kills them because they think that they're following their heart. No they're not. If they don't get specific in their passion, then they're just chasing the wind; and wind chasers don't help anyone.

The bottom line is this: passions and strengths align very closely but only if you add passion to specifics. Ask yourself: What exactly am I going to be doing? Until you can take responsibility for knowing what activities invigorate you, you aren't going to be helpful to anyone by following your heart. In fact, you might end up getting

yourself in a situation where following your heart in a broad sense leads you into roles that burn you out or burn you up, without you even knowing why.

Catalyst: *That last statement is relevant to a lot of the pastors who may be reading this thinking, "I think I'm in the ministry to do the Lord's work or to serve people yet I'm miserable in the role I'm in." Can you give some practical advice to our readers who may be struggling in this area?*

Buckingham: I always say to people, "When you choose a career, there are three questions you have to ask yourself: The Why, The Who, and The What."

The Why: Am I invigorated by "the why" of this business or this enterprise? For pastors it's, "Am I invigorated by doing the Lord's work?"

The Who: Who am I doing it with? Do I enjoy the people that I am doing this around? People can be a life-blood for you or they can drain you—that's an important consideration.

The What: What activities am I going to be filling my week with? What are the actual things that I'm going to be doing at 9:00 a.m. on a Tuesday? What's important to remember is that "the what" trumps "the who" and "the why."

Pay incredibly close attention to how you feel before, during, and after an activity, because that is the clue to what your real strengths are. **C**

Marcus Buckingham is a graduate of Cambridge University, with a master's degree in social and political science. During his seventeen years at The Gallup Organization, he helped lead research into the world's best leaders, managers, and workplaces. He is the author of four books, including *The One Thing You Need To Know*; *Now, Discover Your Strengths*; and most recently *Go, Put Your Strengths to Work*. He lives with his wife and two children in Los Angeles. For more information, visit **www.marcusbuckingham.com**.

CHOOSE TO BE REAL

By Reggie McNeal

NO ONE WOULD ARGUE THAT INAUTHENTIC LEADERSHIP WAS EVER ACCEPTABLE. HOWEVER, THE STAKES HAVE NEVER BEEN HIGHER FOR LEADERS TO EVIDENCE AUTHENTICITY. THE NATURE AND PRACTICE OF LEADERSHIP HAS SHIFTED FROM POSITIONAL TO PERSONAL, FROM ROLE TO RESPONSIBILITY, FROM COMMANDING TO COVENANTING. LEADERS ARE ALSO INCREASINGLY EXPOSED RATHER THAN INSULATED. THE DISTANCE BETWEEN THE FRONT LINE AND THE BOTTOM LINE IS NARROWING. ALL OF THIS MEANS THAT SOME MAJOR THINGS HINGE ON THE PROMISE AND PRACTICE OF AUTHENTIC LEADERSHIP.

Spiritual vitality begins with authenticity

Spiritual formation is the number one issue for Christian leaders. This statement does not discount the need for leaders to be competent. In fact, personal, spiritual vitality should be seen as a competency issue for spiritual leaders. But too often this is overlooked.

Spiritual authenticity shows up in a number of key ways. The leaders' willingness to be open and vulnerable is just a start. The imprimatur of authenticity extends to the development of grace-based relationships with others that grows out of seeing others with Jesus' eyes. The authentic leader doesn't pretend with God or with others. They don't hide their weaknesses; neither do they ignore them. Authentic leaders struggle to grow and invite others to do the same. Authenticity promotes accountability, with the leaders going first.

The genuinely spiritual leader leaves others encouraged, refreshed, and hopeful. Their authenticity allows them to bless others, which reflects the heart of God to those in their leadership constellation.

Community-building rests on the foundation of authenticity

Jesus chose to do His work on earth as He had in heaven—in community. In heaven He enjoyed community with the Father and the Spirit. On earth Jesus chose to establish a faith-community to follow Him and to continue His work after He left. When the Spirit descended, it did so on a praying community.

Genuine community cannot thrive without authenticity, but dysfunctional community can. Non-community can. Bureaucracy can. Programs can. Clubs can. But communities of faith require covenant and accountability and a priority

on relationships. Life-transforming congregations and ministries provide healthy environments where people can be real with each other and real with God. Being broken is the entry requirement to the community, not having it all together.

Without leaders who traffic in honesty and grace, community breaks down. People then pretend and power up. They judge one another and exclude. When leaders practice candor, when they admit they don't have all the answers, when they acknowledge they have shortcomings, when they celebrate others' accomplishments, when they coach with grace—in short, when they act with authentic spiritual leadership, leaders foster community.

Team-based leadership requires authenticity

Teams use trust as currency. When it is in short supply, the level of teamwork is

poor. If trust abounds the team has large lines of credit between members, with each having access to others' gifts, talents, energy, creativity, love, and yes, even money. The development of trust, then, becomes a significant leadership strategy to increase missional effectiveness. Trust grows only to the extent that authenticity is present.

How does authenticity grease up the team's moving parts (read: people)? Team members need honest assessments of situations and skills. Knowledge workers expect to have the information they need to fulfill their own responsibilities as well as freedom to partner with others in alliances. This means that leaders cannot be isolated and insulated. Authentic leaders also take risks. They trust their teammates just as they want to be trusted by them. They give freedom for failure, but at the same time they ensure learning practices are in place to coach for life and ministry effectiveness. Authenticity also supports better team decision-making because options can be debated.

Practicing authenticity remains one of the best recruiting strategies for leaders who want to be a part of a championship lead-

ership team. Without authenticity, you get what you pay for … at best.

Pre-Christians search for authenticity

In an experience-based postmodern culture, the leader can no longer count on the authority of the Bible or the Church to challenge peoples' lives. What counts today is what counted in the first century before the New Testament was written or the institutional Church emerged—the power of an authentic life. Jesus is still held in high esteem today by those who are not a part of the Church, even while the institutionalized expression of the faith is suspect to many.

Pre-Christians aren't interested or impressed with the size of church buildings or membership rolls. They are not looking

for religious activity. They are looking for spiritual authenticity. They are desperate for God. Any Christian leader who takes seriously the Great Commission seeks for ways to reduce the barriers between people and God. This passion for people will drive the leader to authenticity.

The demands of authenticity

Practicing authentic leadership will demand two things from you. First, it will require a choice; actually, not just one choice, but thousands. Every encounter with God, with other people, with yourself, will create a choice for you of whether you will be authentic or something less. Second, authenticity will require courage—the courage to face your own self, to risk vulnerability with others, to place your life completely in God's hands. The courage to be a real person. **C**

Reggie McNeal enjoys helping people, leaders, and Christian organizations pursue more intentional lives. He currently serves as the Missional Leadership Specialist for Leadership Network of Dallas, TX. His books include *Revolution in Leadership*, *A Work of Heart: Understanding How God Shapes Spiritual Leaders*, *The Present Future*, *Practicing Greatness*, and *Get A Life!*

Management and Youth Soccer

By Patrick Lencioni

LAST SPRING WAS THE BIG DRAFT. YOU MAY HAVE HEARD ABOUT IT.

NO, I'M NOT REFERRING TO THE NFL DRAFT THAT TOOK PLACE IN APRIL OR THE NBA EDITION IN JUNE. I'M TALKING ABOUT THE MUSTANG BOYS' UNDER-NINE SOCCER DRAFT IN DANVILLE, CALIFORNIA. THAT'S RIGHT. AS RIDICULOUS AS IT SOUNDS, I'M TALKING ABOUT EIGHT-YEAR-OLD BOYS, THIRD GRADERS, ACTUALLY GETTING DRAFTED TO PLAY "COMPETITIVE SOCCER." AND THE PROCESS BY WHICH THEY'RE EVALUATED, RATED, AND SELECTED IS A SIGHT TO SEE.

Imagine a soccer field surrounded by clipboard-toting coaches (myself included) who are taking detailed notes as they watch little boys run and kick and dribble and scrimmage against one another. Afterward, those coaches sit down around a table and take turns selecting twelve players for their respective teams.

Luckily for me, I don't know a great deal about soccer. I played very little of the sport as a grade-schooler, though I've coached my sons' six- and seven-year-old teams. But to be fair, the nature of the game played by my boys' pee-wee teams more closely resembled a revolt within a prison than it did a sporting event.

I say that I'm lucky to be ignorant of soccer because it forced me to confront a brutal fact: I was going to be at a distinct competitive disadvantage when it came to assessing the technical skills of the munchkins on my list of draft-able players. You see, the other coaches in the league have all played soccer at collegiate, professional, or semi-professional levels, and they appreciate the nuances of the sport the way I do basketball or baseball. They are the type of people who not only understand the offside rule, but they actually like it!

Anyway, to mitigate my soccer naiveté, I made a decision that was motivated mostly out of desperation, with a little inspiration mixed in. In essence, I decided to completely change the criteria I would use to evaluate and select players for my team (which, by the way, is called The Swarm).

So, I took the official evaluation form that was given to me before the tryouts and crossed out the provided category descriptions like "speed," "field awareness," "touch," and "power," and replaced them with others like "attitude," "hustle," "skill," and "parents." Of course, that meant I would have to focus on observing different things than my peers would be looking for during the tryouts.

For instance, instead of spending most of my time looking at the players' feet, I

It's a lot easier to teach a humble, hard-working young man how to play goalie than it is to teach a spectacular athlete how to listen and put the team before himself.

tended to watch how they treated one another. I wanted to see how they responded when the instructor asked them to help move one of the portable goals or a bag of soccer balls to the other side of the field. I also watched the way they interacted with their parents during breaks. Were they respectful or inattentive? And I wanted to see how hard they played on the field. Did they only run when the ball came to them, or did they get involved and help out on defense?

During breaks I might slyly approach one of the kids and ask, "Hey there Billy, how do you like school?" or "What's your favorite subject?" And I was looking for someone who would say, "Yeah, I like school a lot," or "I like math, but not spelling so much." What I didn't want was a blank stare or an answer like "Nah, the only thing I like is recess."

Anyway, when the tryouts were over, my assistant coach (who never played or coached soccer before) and I ranked the players from top to bottom, according to our largely attitudinal criteria. When the draft began, we nervously waited our turn. By the time the draft had ended, we had picked more of our top "prospects" than we could have imagined and assembled a team that we felt had a very high likelihood of being positive and coachable.

Now, don't misunderstand this philosophy of mine for altruism or nobility. I have a competitive streak too, and I wanted our team to be successful. Certainly, I value character building and fitness more than winning, but I didn't want to field a team full of nice kids who couldn't score goals. And I would be lying if I said we didn't pay any attention to the basic athletic ability of the players we selected. But those skills took a distant back seat to attitude and demeanor.

As the season approached, my assistant coach and I wondered how much talent we had on the team. We hoped we'd have at least one good goalie and a few natural scorers. By the time our first practice was upon us, we didn't know what to expect. So we crossed our fingers, skimmed through *Soccer For Dummies,* and began the season.

That was six weeks ago. As of the writing of this article, we've played a little less than half of our games, and a few things have become crystal clear to us.

First, our team is a team. They treat each other well, encourage one another, and seek out collective attention more than individual praise. Second, they're having fun. They don't complain about practices, and they enjoy being together. Third, their parents are having fun. Many of them have approached me and my assistant coach to tell us how pleasantly surprised they are about the positive environment on the team and how much they enjoy being on the sidelines with the other parents.

What about the soccer? So far, so good. We've only lost three of thirteen games, and we've outscored our opponents 24-7.

Of course, that is not nearly as important as the other factors (I have to keep

reminding myself and the other parents about that), but it's a nice confirmation that our attitudinal approach is as viable on the field as it is off of it. It will be interesting to see how the team handles itself when we inevitably lose a few games in a row.

I'd like to say that this early success of the team is a result of great coaching and tactical training. But that just isn't the case. The fact is, as Jim Collins points out in *Good to Great,* getting the right people on the bus is the first critical step toward building a great organization of any kind.

Once the bus is full, then it's all about getting the right people in the right seats (or in our case, the right players in the right positions). But selecting the people who fit your culture, whether they are eight-year-old soccer players, senior executives, teachers, or church volunteers, is the first critical step.

Why? Because it's a lot easier to teach a humble, hard-working young man how to play goalie than it is to teach a spectacular athlete how to listen and put the team before himself. I'm guessing that applies to the organization where you work. Not the goalie part. Well, you know what I mean. ◼

Patrick Lencioni's six best-selling business books have sold over 2 million copies. After four years in print, *The Five Dysfunctions of a Team* continues to be a fixture on the *Wall Street Journal* and *New York Times* best-seller lists. The Dysfunctions model for teamwork has been embraced by a great variety of organizations, ranging from the NFL to the Blue Man Group to the 82nd Airborne to local schools and churches. Lencioni consults to organizations like Southwest Airlines and Cox Communications and speaks to tens of thousands of people each year. His latest book, *The Three Signs of a Miserable Job,* was released in August 2007. For more information visit **www.tablegroup.com**.

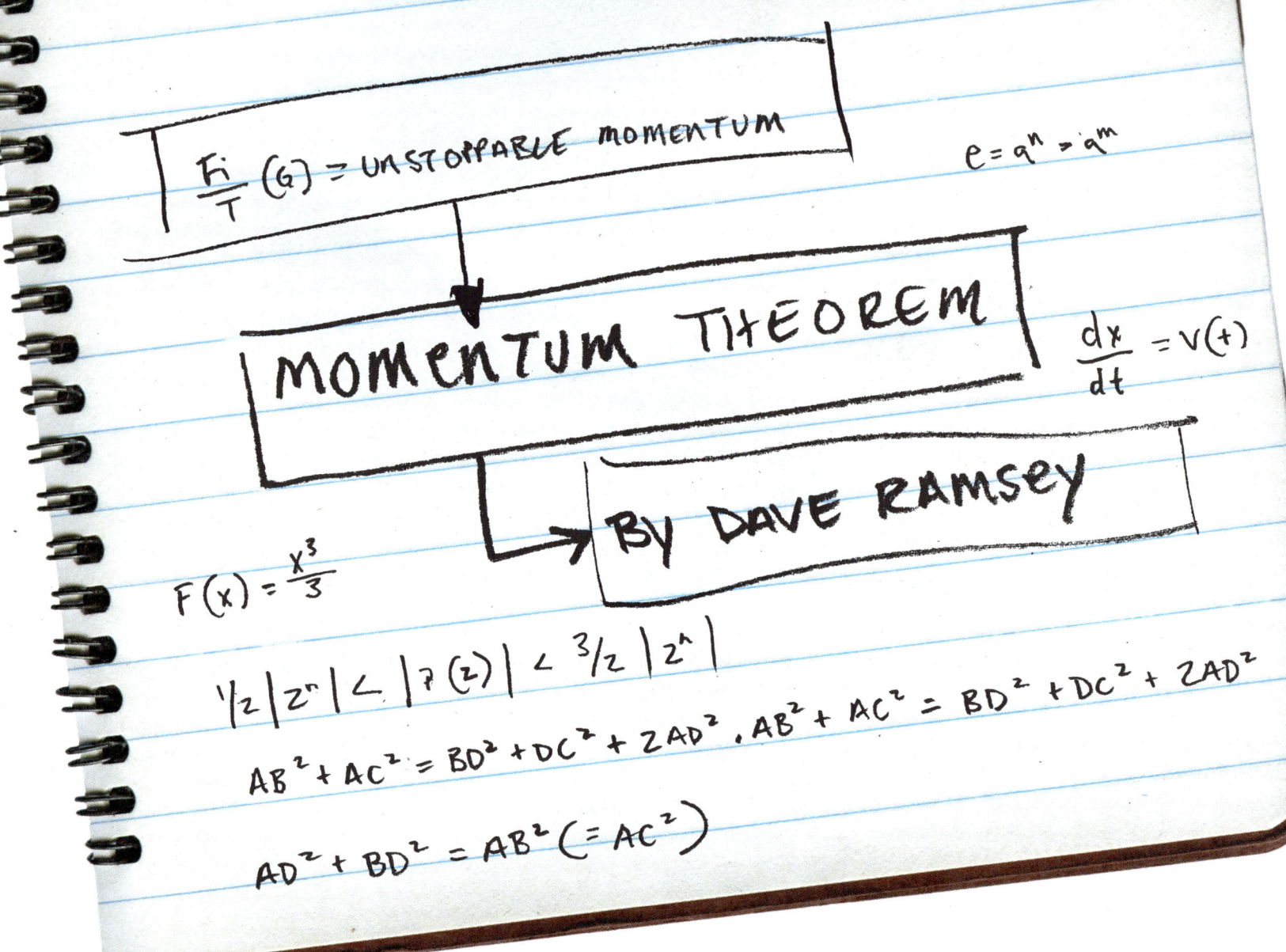

$\frac{Fi}{T}(G) = $ UNSTOPPABLE MOMENTUM

$e = q^n = q^m$

MOMENTUM THEOREM

$\frac{dx}{dt} = v(t)$

BY DAVE RAMSEY

$F(x) = \frac{x^3}{3}$

$\frac{1}{2}|z^n| < |f(z)| < \frac{3}{2}|z^n|$

$AB^2 + AC^2 = BD^2 + DC^2 + 2AD^2 \cdot AB^2 + AC^2 = BD^2 + DC^2 + 2AD^2$

$AD^2 + BD^2 = AB^2 (= AC^2)$

ISN'T IT FUNNY HOW MOST PEOPLE WORK THEIR TAIL ENDS OFF FOR YEARS ONLY TO BE LABELED AN "OVERNIGHT SUCCESS?" RIGHT NOW, OUR TEAM IS EXPERIENCING GROWTH LIKE NEVER BEFORE! BUT THIS ISN'T HOW IT'S ALWAYS BEEN. WE'VE PAID AN UNBELIEVABLE PRICE TO GET THIS MOMENTUM. WE'VE PUT IN THE TIME, THE MONEY, THE HEARTACHE, THE SWEAT, AND EVERYTHING ELSE WE HAD LEFT. AND THEN, EVERYTHING TOOK OFF. BUT IT SURE DIDN'T OCCUR OVERNIGHT.

One thing my team and I have learned over the years is that this type of unstoppable momentum doesn't just happen. Momentum has to be *created*. There is a process to go through before momentum can result. It takes focused intensity, over time, multiplied by God, to equal unstoppable momentum.

$$\frac{Fi}{T}(G) = \textit{UNSTOPPABLE MOMENTUM}$$

Begin: Focus
Focus? Really? In a society where everyone "should be" on Ritalin? Focus? In a time when my teenagers can have five IM screens open while checking their email, talking on the phone, keeping up with VH1, *and* doing the homework

that gets them on the Honor Roll? We live in a world of true multi-taskers, and I'm asking for focus!

But we have to learn—in our workplace, social lives, spiritual lives, and everything in between—how to *focus*. Whatever you focus on *will* happen. If you don't focus on anything, nothing will happen. Dispersed light lights up a room. Light that's focused can cut metal.

Let's use the analogy of a football player who's raking in millions. This guy's job—his only job for all that money—is to catch the ball! And yet, here comes the ball, heading straight for the numbers on his chest,

$$936 = 2^3 \times 3 \times 17^2,$$
$$200 = 2^4 \times 3 \times 5^2$$

> I'VE DONE THINGS IN MY OWN POWER, AND I KNOW WHAT THEY LOOK LIKE. THEY LOOK LIMITED.

$$F(x_i) - F(x_i - 1) = F'(c_i)(x_i - x_i - 1)$$

and he doesn't catch it! What happened? He lost focus. He either got greedy, taking his eye off the ball to look at the goal line before accomplishing the task, or he was overcome with fear (you would be too if some guy the size of a KIA was getting ready to mow you down). Being able to catch the ball in the midst of all that chaos is what marks the great ones. Concentration and focus make for success—which is just as true for you and me as it is for football players.

The Bible says the double-minded man is unstable in all his ways. [1] Get to one side of the road or the other. Be *somebody*. Focus!

Add: Intensity — Passion — Multiplied By Time

And remember, momentum doesn't come easily. You must possess intensity and passion for what you're doing. Be fired up and wired up. If you don't love what you're doing, you won't be intense, so get to doing something else. You might not be able to quit and start totally fresh today, but start making plans. Start taking classes that have something to do with what you're passionate about. It's time to get with it! Get the mentality that what you're doing matters because whatever you're doing *can* matter. And you can do it with excellence and intensity at a level of attack that awes everyone around you.

A lot of us think we *can* do that, but few of us actually do. Most people are just plain lazy. If you go to work and *work while you're at work*, you're ahead. Most people won't even do that. Sure, maybe they'll do it for a few days, maybe even a month. Maybe somebody will make it a whole year. But

how many people actually make it a decade or two with that focused intensity?

Another huge factor in reaching the goal of unstoppable momentum is time. Most of our culture isn't willing to put in the *time* it takes to be a success! Sure, you'll have problems and "down days" along the way, but it takes an overall, determined willingness to get up in the morning, leave the cave, go kill something, and drag it home.

Think back to one of the foundational tales of childhood – The Tortoise and The Hare. Every time you read that story, the tortoise always wins. He *always* wins! The slow and steady win the race. The slow and steady—those willing to put in the time as they're intensely focused—succeed and gain momentum.

You — To The Power of One

If you think you can do all this stuff by yourself, you're naïve. I've been fortunate to experience success as a leader and speaker. It's what I do; it's my craft. And we have a fabulous organization. But there's no way I could've created all this on my own—I don't have enough juice for that! I've done things in my own power, and I know what they look like. They look limited. But we don't have to be bound by limitations. We have access to the multiplying factor who is the ultimate

deal-changer, who shifts *everything* over time. With God, all things are possible. [2]

Without God in the equation, our efforts would look like just a bunch of "good ideas." But God has a way of taking our ordinary attempts and ideas and desires and making them extraordinary. It's because of God that the information we market is influencing our culture on such a massive scale.

Also, without God, none of the work we do would really matter. Maybe it could still get pretty big and somewhat successful. But the power to change people's lives and see new truth, hope, and peace infiltrate their entire families would be extremely limited. God brings meaning and reason to all things, and without Him our efforts would be just a drop in the bucket. Our work would be about changing people's minds instead of their *lives*. I don't know about you, but I want to change some lives!

Momentum is not something that just occurs. Momentum is something that is *created*. Have some focus, some intensity, some patience to let things unfold over time, and to allow God to permeate, penetrate, and multiply everything you do. If you stay focused and intense over time, if you let God do things His way, you'll experience unstoppable momentum! **C**

Dave Ramsey is a nationally-syndicated talk radio host. He has written 14 books, 3 of which have been on the *New York Times* Best Seller list. He is also the creator of a 13-week video training series known as Financial Peace University, and a school program known as Financial Peace for the Next Generation that is offered in more than 1300 schools in 46 states.

RELEVANCE IS A TOOL, NOT A GOAL

BY ED STETZER

I'VE GOT A DEWALT 12-INCH DUAL BEVEL COMPOUND MITER SAW WITH A SLIDE. (GRUNT.) OH YES, IT'S A SERIOUS TOOL AND, NO, YOU CAN'T BORROW IT.

I TELL MY WIFE THAT I HAVE TO HAVE THE RIGHT TOOL FOR THE RIGHT JOB. SHE SMIRKS AND POINTS OUT THAT I HAVEN'T USED IT IN 4 YEARS— BUT I KNOW WHAT REALLY MATTERS: I MIGHT. AND WHEN I DO, I NEED THE RIGHT TOOL.

TOOLS MATTER. THEY MAKE IT POSSIBLE TO ACCOMPLISH THE GOAL. RELEVANCE IS LIKE THAT—IT IS A TOOL TO ACCOMPLISH A MORE IMPOR-TANT PURPOSE, COMMUNICATING CHRIST IN CULTURE.

Relevance is a word seen more and more these days on church marquees, yellow page ads, and websites. It seems that every church wants to make sure everyone else knows how relevant it is. This strikes me a bit like the advertising agency named "Creative Ads." If you are so creative, could you not share that with me in a more creative way?

No one advertises a lack of relevance. Who wants an irrelevant church? (Well, it must be a lot of people, but that is another story.) For most of us, we are tired of people criti-cizing culturally relevant churches. I have heard dozens of sermons against contem-porary worship, music, and casual dress. Been there, done that, got the T-shirt (or the tie, depending on your perspective).

But, we also need to be careful. Relevance can be (and sometimes is) over-empha-sized. The problem isn't found in the desire to be relevant. After all, the word relevant means, "to be pertinent." The problem is that sometimes we have too lit-tle confidence in the Gospel and its abil-ity to prove relevant on its own merit.

The Gospel is relevant, in this and ev-ery culture; it is often our churches and ministries that are not. We can find ourselves putting too much emphasis on relevance itself and not enough on what we're trying to make understand-able—the Gospel.

While relevance can bridge some gaps to the Gospel, it is only a tool, not a goal.

Recently I shared some thoughts with a group at the National New Church Con-ference to illustrate this point. We cannot lose the Gospel in order to find relevance; relevance must be a tool that spotlights the Gospel within culture.

Are you focusing too much on relevance? Here are some ways you can know that relevance has become more important than the Gospel to you:

1. If we focus on personal transformation and not Gospel transformation.
Too often our messages are driven by the steps method (i.e. five steps toward fi-nancial freedom), when oftentimes these steps have little to do with biblical advice on the subject. If this is the case, you'll

find more secular advice than biblical advice on certain subjects. It's not that we can't learn from others in the world; however, the goal of our churches isn't to simply reflect the culture but to impact it. The danger of relevance in this area is to enforce an already narcissistic mentality that permeates our culture. The consumeristic, me-istic mindset is thorny ground that threatens to choke out the Word in people's lives.

2. If your sermons are so practical they lack any Gospel.

Do not preach any message that would not be true if Jesus had not died on the cross. It is great to be practical in what we teach; but, if we hesitate to share about the work of Christ, what is the eternal value? Using practical messages can help us share biblical truth, but ultimately our goal is that they leave with the Truth, not just true stuff. The Truth is the person of Jesus. Think through the inner logic of Jesus and His very character. How does His viewpoint—what He really treasured—shine through your message? The very essence of Jesus should waft through the room during your sermons.

3. If you talk about practical more than you talk about biblical.

This is more than simply how we preach, it is how we carry out our duties in the ministry. When sharing the vision of your church, what is prominent? What do peo-

ple walk away with? What strikes them as being at the very heart of what your ministry is all about? There are many pastors who have visions of a new building, higher giving, and so forth. While these fit practical needs, many focus on them more than focusing on a biblical aspect of our faith. You want the people you are leading to be built on the solid foundation of God's Word—not the wood, hay, and stubble that will eventually fade away.

4. If your outreach demeans others that preach the Gospel.

This shows that your confidence is in your relevance and not His Gospel. Do not communicate anything that feeds people's tendency to devalue other churches that preach the Gospel. There are plenty of churches today promoting their church by diminishing the ministry of another. While some of these churches may be irrelevant to much of the community, we shouldn't make an extra effort to prove this to the community. Those churches are probably able to reach some people you couldn't. We are all on the same team, even if our methods and styles are very different—so let's begin to act like it—even when others do not.

5. If your approach makes you the hero and not Jesus.

It seems that many ministries are driven by personalities. It is not a good thing that the number one reason someone stays

at a church is because they like the pastor. It is inevitable that personalities will drive some ministries, because people will obviously come to listen to this person. Seek for ways to promote others and their unique gifts. When you do so, you emphasize the astounding body of Christ and the phenomenal power that comes when that body is truly connected and functioning. This brings glory to Jesus and not you.

6. If "personal evangelism" is an oxymoron at your church.

Simply put, disciples share their faith. If our goal is to make disciples, we don't just hope to have plenty of seats filled on a given weekend at our church. Instead, we hope to see people respond and be moved by the Gospel. This is evident in their personal devotion toward sharing the Good News with others. Train your people to share their own stories of encountering Jesus.

7. If "invest and invite" never leads to evangelism.

Many church structures emphasize to their members to simply "invest and invite." This is a great strategy toward getting their friends, families, and neighbors in the door. But if this is the means to an end, you might be placing too much emphasis on relevance and not enough on the Gospel. Once we have invested and invited, we need to share the Good News

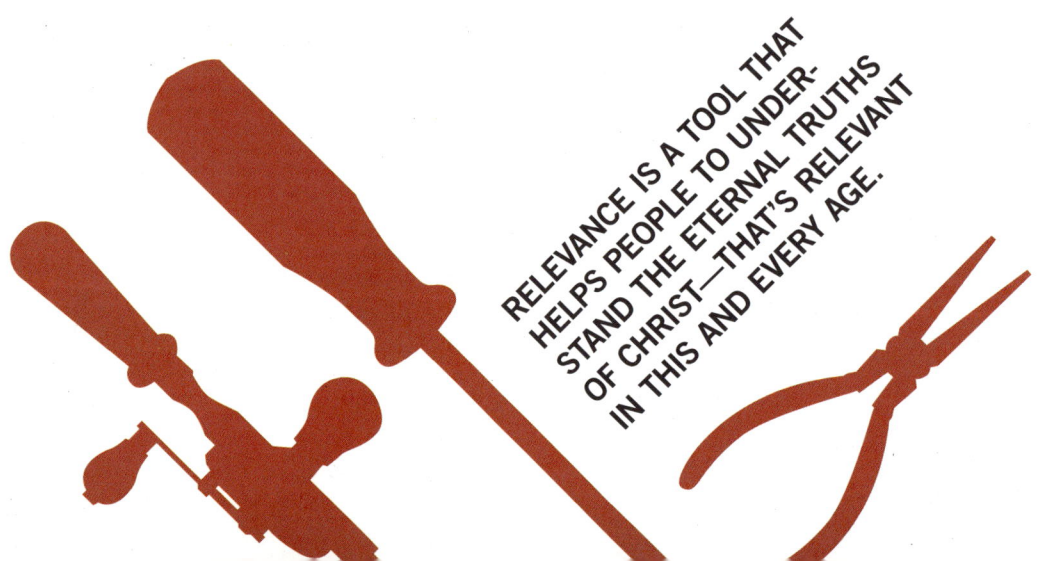

RELEVANCE IS A TOOL THAT HELPS PEOPLE TO UNDERSTAND THE ETERNAL TRUTHS OF CHRIST—THAT'S RELEVANT IN THIS AND EVERY AGE.

with them. If you are really developing disciples, you are training your people in the full set of discipling skills.

8. If attendance is a greater value than conversion.

Everyone wants to know numbers. Deep down, many pastors equate attendance with success. It definitely does make sense in some ways, but the fastest growing religion in the world is a works-based falsehood. Face it, Donald Trump or Madonna can draw a crowd. Don't be fooled into believing your ability to fill seats is effecting redemption in others. Numbers can help us only if we have already defined our win on the response to the Gospel.

9. If the cross gets less focus than the church.

Typically, we don't talk about the cross enough. The cross should be central to the vision and direction of our churches. Without the cross, none of us would even be where we are today—and without the cross, our churches will never be where they need to be. We must lead people to depend on the cross and not our programs and systems. Help your church learn that the path to redemption in their individual lives and circumstances can lead straight to the cross. It does not have to go through a relevant church first.

10. If not offending seekers is more important than telling the Gospel.

The Gospel is offensive. When it comes down to it, eventually we're going to have to pull the trigger, and we may end up being the stench of death to someone. But, if we take the risk so they can hear the truth, we must move forward regardless of the relational cost. Don't try to sand down the cross and make it smooth and lightweight. Be "seeker comprehensible" and quit trying to be driven by seekers.

The sad truth is that some churches sacrifice their God-given message on the altar of relevance, and the Gospel is what is seen as irrelevant. We need to recapture a genuine faith in and love for the Gospel. We need to re-kindle a desire to let it do its thing in our congregations. We can use relevance as a tool to connect with people, but even the best tool can't do its work if there is not a clear goal. As my wife reminds me, there is no point in having that beautiful yellow miter saw if it is not building something (like that new swing set she wants me to build).

Let's be relevant—but let's make sure that relevance is a tool and not the goal. Relevance is a tool that helps people to understand the eternal truths of Christ—that's relevant in this and every age. ▣

Ed Stetzer is Director and Missiologist in Residence at Lifeway Research. His most recent books are *Comeback Churches* and *11 Innovations in the Local Church*.

LIVING IN PAKISTAN

JOSHUA WHITE

EVANGELICAL CHRISTIANS HAVE BEEN LEARNERS IN THE ARENA OF MISSIONS FOR SEVERAL HUNDRED YEARS. ENTER JOSHUA T. WHITE. A 27-YEAR-OLD GRADUATE FELLOW AT THE INSTITUTE FOR GLOBAL ENGAGEMENT AND A STUDENT AT THE JOHNS HOPKINS SCHOOL OF ADVANCED INTERNATIONAL STUDIES, JOSH EMBODIES A NEW GENERATION OF MISSION-MINDED CHRISTIANS. AS JOSH'S STORY SHOWS, THEY BRING WITH THEM A COMMITMENT TO INCARNATIONAL WITNESS THAT TRANSCENDS POLITICS AS USUAL.

It was a rather large funeral. When I arrived on the third day, the colonel at the gate informed me that "about 125,000" people had already filed through the Durrani home to pay their respects. It was a staggering number for such a remote corner of northwest Pakistan, but I believed him. No one goes to Bannu just to visit. Yet, when news spread that the uncle of the province's chief minister had been killed, people came.

By strange providence, I was the chief minister's guest in northwest Pakistan. It was an unusual relationship, begun in 2005 when the Institute for Global Engagement (IGE) invited Durrani to Washington, D.C. for a week of face-to-face conversations about the troubling new *Shari'ah* law his party had proposed. In 2002, for the first time in Pakistan's history, Islamists had been elected outright in the North-West Frontier Province.

In spite of our political and religious differences, we found the chief minister to be something of a moderate in his con-

text. Before departing, Durrani invited us to see the frontier for ourselves. A few months later we did.

I was so taken with the history and hospitality of the frontier that I decided to stay for a year in the provincial capital of Peshawar. That a 27-year-old American Christian was in Peshawar as the guest of an Islamist political party caused no end of wonder to the local diplomats and church community. For me, it was an extraordinary opportunity to glimpse Islamist political leadership from the inside; to get to know these people as people; and to find myself as the only Westerner making a trip down to Bannu.

THE ART OF DOING PRAYER
Arriving in Bannu, I was ushered into the family courtyard. When the chief minister saw me, he stood and smiled. I greeted him as best I could, with a hand over my heart and the phrase, "I am an equal partner in your sorrow." I added, simply, "We're doing prayer for your family."

Muslims in Pakistan speak of two forms of prayer. The obligatory prayer practiced five times a day is *namaz*. The other form of prayer is *du'a*. To do *du'a* is to offer a prayer on someone's behalf.

When honoring the dead, a silent *du'a* is said. It is said communally, such that when I sat down and softly said *du'a kare*, "let us do prayer," the whole tent instantly responded by raising their hands with me, praying in absolute silence for the soul of the departed.

In so many ways, my worldview differed from that of the people in the tent. Yet a communal prayer for a lost family member is a profoundly human moment. The image of that moment has stuck with me, because it is a picture of two things I found to be true of northwest Pakistan.

First, the majority of people I met were gracious to a fault and quick to condemn violence in the name of religion. They were, at the same time, uninterested in trying to delineate the boundaries of religion in public life. Coming from an American culture where religion is often unwelcome in the public square, this was a real change. Religion in Pakistan is more than the language of private devotion; it is still the most potent language of public life as well.

Second, in spite of feeling far from home, I felt surprisingly comfortable in Pakistan, precisely because it was a deeply religious society. I believe differently than the Muslims I lived with and prayed among. But I still came away appreciating a society in which religious conversation and values are honored.

EASTER AS A SECURITY EVENT
Of the 20 million people in the North-West Frontier Province, Christians number only 100,000. They have learned to

live with the constant anxiety of being a minority. One of my most memorable experiences in Peshawar reflected this deep and unending tension.

I was invited to participate in the annual Easter march in Peshawar's Old City. At three o'clock in the morning I joined what was an extraordinary scene—hundreds of Christians marching through dark, narrow streets, with candles lit, in a line that stretched for an entire block. And all around this scene were policemen.

It was my first Easter celebrated within a police cordon.

What dissonance to be saying, "Jesus is risen!" in the streets of an ancient Muslim city while surrounded by men with batons. Part of me felt awe that an Islamic republic would go to such lengths to protect a declaration that has no standing in its received revelation. Another part of me felt sadness that Easter needed to be managed as a security event.

In light of my experience with the suffering Church in Pakistan, I feel deeply that the Church in the West needs to "suffer with those who suffer"—with Christian brothers and sisters, but also with the whole

range of religious communities worldwide who feel beleaguered and forgotten.

We also need to find ways to broaden the way we practice Christian witness in this post-9/11 world. As my experience in Pakistan unfolded, it stung to find I had been sold a bleak picture of the Muslim world so at odds with my experience of the Pakistani people.

Never once in Pakistan did I bring up the subject of religion, yet somehow I was always talking about it. My Muslim Pakistani friends were gracious enough to interpret for me their world and their faith. We Christians ought to be more eager to do the same.

This kind of interpretive witness is one calling of a true global citizen and certainly of a Christian who takes seriously the way of Jesus. It is a witness that doesn't ignore the realities of politics and the brutalities of modern terrorism, but responds with something more than power and pragmatism. Above all, it is a witness that stitches together humility and conviction in the messiness of the real world—and does so in a way that points quietly, but inevitably, to the faith we profess. **C**

For more from the Christian Vision Project and Joshua White, visit **www.christianvisionproject.com**.

© *2007 Christianity Today International. All rights reserved. Used by permission.*

ZACH HUNTER

ABOLITIONIST, AUTHOR, *BE THE CHANGE*
Age 15, Atlanta, Georgia, www.lc2lc.com

ZACH FIRST HEARD ABOUT THE PLIGHT OF MODERN-DAY SLAVES THREE YEARS AGO. HE REALIZED SLAVERY IS NOT JUST SOME OUTDATED THING FOUND IN HISTORY BOOKS, AND HE FELT MOTIVATED TO DO SOMETHING. AT AGE 12, ZACH LAUNCHED A CAMPAIGN CALLED LOOSE CHANGE TO LOOSEN CHAINS TO RAISE AWARENESS AND FUNDS TO HELP END SLAVERY. HUNDREDS OF GROUPS ARE NOW FURTHERING THE CAMPAIGN, AND STUDENTS AROUND THE WORLD CONSIDER THEMSELVES ABOLITIONISTS.

I HAVE A DREAM

My dream is that my generation would develop a love for the poor and the oppressed; that we'd serve them and in doing so would grow closer to God. God tells us who He's "for" and who He's "against." He's always on the side of the poor, the orphan, the widow, the oppressed. When we get closer to the hurting people in the world, we get closer to the heart of God. Specifically, I hope that in my lifetime we will see the end of slavery. A big dream, but one I believe we can see happen.

GATHERING UP COURAGE

In May 2006, I was given an opportunity to speak about modern-day slavery to nearly 15,000 people—one of the biggest crowds I'd ever seen, let alone spoken to! I previously struggled with an anxiety disorder in elementary school, and when I looked out on the crowd, some of those old fears came rushing back. But I knew I had the chance to let people know of the millions who are suffering around the world as slaves. I decided to take the stage, trusting God would give me courage. I explained the truth of slavery to thousands of people that night.

The courage I need to show is nothing compared to the courage of many others who face death and danger every day. Soldiers who put their lives on the line to defend their countries. Firefighters who enter burning buildings. And certainly, the courage required of every man, woman, and child in slavery who must wake up today and face their oppressors. Each of us faces situations in which we need to gather up our courage. When we do, it's as though the courage multiplies like yeast in dough, allowing us to be even more courageous the next time we're called upon.

PASSION AWAKENED

My generation has been numbed to passion in many ways. We have been anesthetized by all of the stimulation in our culture. But I also hear in students a desire to wake up and feel something deeply—to be moved. It seems as though God is doing this as my generation comes face to face with some of the awful suffering occurring around the world. When I speak, I often meet students afterwards who are experiencing something new—passion. It's like a troubling in their spirits that I believe is the call of God to join Him in bringing relief to others. I'm confident that if they answer, they will experience the closeness to God that they dream of. **C**

Conflict is Everything

By Nancy Ortberg

One comment said it all. "We never run into any tension; it's just that we aren't moving forward."

Exactly.

In our first phone conversation, a client diagnosed his company's problem—unintentionally. He meant the first part of his sentence as a compliment. But in reality, it was the symptom that described their outcome. On a regular basis, healthy, high performing teams must engage in what Patrick Lencioni refers to in *Five Dysfunctions of a Team* as "passionate, unfiltered debate." Conflict is a necessary and important part of great teamwork.

Your organization depends on great decisions, stellar implementation and complete "buy-in." Without those three things, you aren't positioned to get the results you're working so hard to accomplish. Nor are you building a cohesive leadership team. Healthy conflict is the precursor to those three things.

One of your primary jobs as a leader is to create a culture that fosters this kind of interactive discussion. Intel has coined a great phrase that they practice and teach in each new employee orientation class—"Disagree and commit."

Without a culture that encourages conflict, here's what happens. In our rush to make decisions, we short-circuit the process, leaving many great ideas and opinions unspoken. Not only have we failed to unearth contrary strategies, the very people responsible for implementation are only partially committed. Harley-Davidson calls this "malicious compliance." This is a great way to describe what siphons off great forward thinking energy that ought to be spent on implementing the decisions we come to as a team.

So what's a leader to do?

First, understand that in order for you to create this kind of a culture, *you* have to be very comfortable with conflict. Take a look at your family of origin. Was it a place of passivity, avoiding conflict? Or was your family more aggressive, taking the offensive in conflict? I can guarantee that you bring a certain style of conflict resolution to work with you, and your style is rooted in the home where you grew up. In order for your team to be comfortable with conflict, you need to be well on your way.

Secondly, know that your role as the leader is to demand spirited debate. Tell your team you want it; and empower them to engage in this kind of debate. Great leadership desires great leaders at every level in an organization, and leaders have opinions and passion. Encourage your team meetings to be places of passionate debate in order to get the kind of commitment that drives decisions into great implementation.

Remember, moving a team from "artificial harmony" takes time ... give your people permission to do it poorly in order to do it well.

Finally, celebrate when passionate debate renders terrific results and reward teams that have the courage to disagree and commit. In addition to great results, you will experience healthier teams. That is a dynamic combination! **C**

Nancy Ortberg is a founding partner of Teamworx2, a leadership consulting and coaching firm in Westlake Village and Menlo Park. Teamworx2 is an affiliate of Patrick Lencioni's Table Group.

AUTHENTIC IN INFLUENCE

Influence begins when you answer God's call. What are some tangible ways to broaden your influence in your cultural context? Is God calling you to influence a different channel of culture? What is that big idea that is brewing in your heart—the one that scares you a little bit? Map it out right now.

IV. UNCOMPROMISING IN INTEGRITY

Character, conviction, discipline, and decision-making—these all make up the inner qualities and integrity of a Catalyst leader. I understand that my integrity is the guard to my soul and ultimately my life. This can't be let go or delegated. It's the foundation of who I am as a person and as a leader. It's the basis from which my moral authority is grounded. It must be nurtured, guarded, and found true under testing.

SILENCING
THE NATIVE TONGUE

SESSION 04

He who conceals his sins does not prosper, but whoever confesses and renounces them finds mercy.
Proverbs 28:13

ENCING THE NATIVE TONGUE

By Craig Groeschel

HAVE YOU EVER TOLD A LIE? NO? LIAR!

SERIOUSLY, WE LEARNED EFFORTLESSLY TO LIE AS CHILDREN. PARENTS DON'T HAVE TO GIVE THEIR KIDS LYING LESSONS. IT'S ALMOST NATURAL. ONCE I WALKED INTO MY KITCHEN, AND ONE OF MY KIDS WAS STANDING THERE, COVERED IN CHOCOLATE—IN HIS HAIR, ALL AROUND HIS MOUTH, ALL OVER HIS HANDS. I ASKED, "DID YOU EAT THAT CANDY BAR?" HE INSISTED, "NOOOO!"

I've never done anything like that. Okay ... that was a lie.

As hard as it is to admit, I've been known to exaggerate the truth. Occasionally, I've avoided revealing the whole truth. More than once, I've simply blatantly lied to avoid some undesirable consequence.

As a pastor, I can't count how many times someone would say with extreme caution, "What I'm about to tell you, I've never told anyone before." Then they would carefully reveal some deep, dark secret generally rooted in some form of deception.

Over the years, my burden for personal truth and truth in our church family has grown exponentially. Finally, after agonizing in prayer, I embarked on a personal crusade to combat lies and pursue truth.

MySecret.tv

As part of a series at our church called My Secret, we launched a website, **www.mysecret.tv**, where people could anonymously post their secrets. Our hope was that this first step toward full-blown confession would free the logjam in their minds. It was an opportunity to move toward real forgiveness, real healing. After opening in the summer of 2006, MySecret.tv took on a life of its own. Within the first two months, we saw more than 5000 confessions and over 2.5 million page views. (Should you decide to visit www.mysecret.tv, be forewarned: the content is inappropriate for children. People are honest about their hurts and mistakes ... and life can be messy.)

Most telling were the confessions from pastors. Examples include:

"I've always struggled with lying. My problem is that I want everyone to like me. I lie to impress people, to cover for mistakes, or to make a boring life seem better. I even lie regularly when I'm preaching. God help me."

"I act like everything in my life and marriage is perfect. But the truth is that it's all a lie. I don't even think my wife likes me. I know I don't like myself. My church doesn't have any idea."

"For several years I lived two different lives: One as a husband, father, and pastor, and the other as a homosexual."

"I am a pastor who is addicted to pornography and masturbation. My wife would die if she knew. And if my church knew, I'd lose everything. I hate myself. The only way I stay alive is by lying. The truth is just too painful to face."

I find it useful to consider lies in categories—like the ones below.

1. Occasional liars. A friend asks, "Do these jeans make me look fat?" The person thinks, "*Yes!*" But instead answers, "No. You look great." Occasional liars often exaggerate the truth a little to get a job, or they "stretch" the truth here or there, or they don't want to hurt people's feelings, or they want to impress people.

2. Frequent liars. These are people who create a false persona for one reason or another. Perhaps they lie about finances.

, "I act like everything in my life and marriage is perfect. But the truth is that it's all a lie. I don't even think my wife likes me. I know I don't like myself. My church doesn't have any idea."

truth, and therefore I don't really trust God. When I lie, I don't really trust the

They *look* like things are going well, but maybe they're living beyond their means. Maybe they lie about other people to make themselves look better, or to "get ahead" at work. Some people lie for no reason.

3. Habitual liars. As a teen, and into my early years of college, I was this person. My life was a complicated tapestry of lies. I was a different person to each group in my life: my parents, my sports friends, my party friends, my teachers, and to girls. I would tell one lie to one group, a different lie to another group. I lied so much that eventually I believed my own lies. I forgot what the truth was.

I believe that many people—even some pastors—fall into this last category. They're ministers, but their lives look just like unbelievers: their marriages, the way they handle money, the "pastoral gossip," bitterness, addictions, etc. Burying their secrets, they hope and pray nothing comes to light because everybody thinks they're something they're not. They live a lie.

Why Does It Matter?
What's the difference between these categories? Honestly? Nothing. God hates *all* lying, period. Proverbs 12:22 says, "The LORD detests lying lips, but he delights

in men who are truthful." (NIV) Proverbs 6 lists seven things the Lord finds detestable. Two of them are lies. How much does God hate lying? Well, the Hebrew word for "detests" is *tow' ebah*—literally, something disgusting, an abhorrence, something nauseating. Lying lips make God want to vomit.

Why does God hate lying *so much*? John 8:44 gives us some insight:

"... *(Satan) was a murderer from the beginning, not holding to the truth, for there is no truth in him. When he lies, he speaks his native language, for he is a liar and the father of lies.*" (NIV)

Lying is sin. Sin separates us from God. But lying is even more diabolical than that. When we lie, we actually partner with Satan, speaking "his native language."

Contrast Satan with Jesus. Satan is a liar, the father of lies. Jesus said He is the way, the truth, and the life (John 14:6 NIV). Jesus is *The Truth*.

Why Do We Lie?
Are you ready to get free from the web of lies? Are you sick of playing the games? Performing? Acting? Pretending? Posing?

First (and this may be challenging), I'll encourage you to identify *why* you lie. People lie for different reasons. If my wife lies, it might be for what she considers a noble reason. She doesn't want to hurt someone's feelings. (Like when I come home knowing my sermon bombed and I ask her, "What did you think about the message?" And she smiles politely and says, "You did great.")

Other people lie for different reasons. In the past, I've lied to make myself look better or to get ahead. We're all motivated by different things. Why do you lie?

For me, as hard as it is to admit, I generally lie because I don't fully trust God. (I hate to even see that in print. But it's true.) When I lie, I'm basically saying, "I believe my lie will work better at this moment than the truth."

Consider the phrase, "the moment of truth." In stories, the moment of truth is when we find out what a character is made of. But what is truth? Jesus said He is *The* Truth. God is truth. When I lie, I don't really trust the truth, and therefore I don't really trust God.

Lies Lie

Lying itself tempts us with a lie: "Avoid the truth right now, and I'll get you off the hook." Maybe the truth is uncomfortable, and lying helps us avoid the pain of confronting that truth. Or maybe lying will get us more of something. Either of these things makes us *feel* more secure ... at least for the moment. But the truth is: there's no security in lying. At its core, lying is based in selfishness. I'm lying to you either to protect myself or to get something. The truth always tries to creep in, and our only alternative is ... to tell more lies. The idea of a lie promises us an immediate payoff. And then later, the lie breaks its promise. A lie ... lies.

Lies are a perversion of genuine relationships. A relationship based on lies is not *really* a relationship. It's not real. Ironically, the thing that I think I want—to "protect" or maintain the relationship by hiding the truth—keeps me from what I *really* want—a real relationship with genuine intimacy.

Translate that to ministry. A ministry based on lies is not really a ministry. It's a lie. And a lie won't set anyone free.

Maybe you have a secret. Maybe you did something years ago and lied to your spouse to cover it up. Secrets breed lies. Somebody said, "The only thing that grows in the dark is mushrooms." You know, mushrooms break down dead (or dying) things. Maybe you have this other "thing" going on—just you and your computer when you're alone, doing something you shouldn't do. Maybe you have some kind of addiction. Maybe you're having an emotional affair. Whatever it is ... *you know,* and *God knows.* You have a choice: deal with the truth, or continue living the lie—and die a slow, painful death.

Truth Frees

"If you hold to my teaching, you are really my disciples. Then you will know the truth, and the truth will set you free." (John 8:31-32 NIV) Jesus is the truth who sets us free. But how? In two simple steps:

1. Confess to God. "If we confess our sins, (God) is faithful and just and will forgive us our sins and purify us from all unrighteousness." (1 John 1:9 NIV) Confess to God and receive His forgiveness. It really is that easy, but this is where many leaders stop. Maybe you've done this. You've prayed to God. You know He has forgiven you, and you believe it, but ... you're still drawn to the sin. You still feel vulnerable. You still feel dirty. Something is just not right. The problem is that you've only done part of what God called you to do. You've confessed to God, but you continue to struggle. Why? There's still one thing left to complete the process ...

2. Confess to the appropriate people. "Therefore confess your sins to each other and pray for each other so that you may be healed." (James 5:16 NIV) Confessing to God gets you forgiveness. Confessing to others gets you healed. And exactly who are these "appropriate people?" Definitely, without any reservation, the answer is: *it depends.*

True Honesty

Honesty means that everything you say must be true, not that everything true must be said.

Not everyone needs to know everything. Let me give you an example. As a pastor of a large church, I hear rumors about myself all the time. They're rarely true, and often, they're very strange. Occasionally, they're even appalling. A few years ago, a man walked up to me and introduced himself. I had never met him before. He doesn't attend our church. He began, and I'm paraphrasing, "I'm so sorry." *Uh-oh.* He continued, "I know we've never met, but I used to really despise you. In fact, I hated you so much that I decided it was my responsibility to destroy your reputation. I feel really bad about this, but for years ..." and this part is a direct quote, "... I told *hundreds and hundreds* of people lies about you." He went on to confess that he had told lies about me to Christians, to non-Christians, to pastors. He even admitted that many people he lied to about me tried to defend me. They told him he was wrong. He finished his confession with, "God has convicted me. I know what I did was wrong. Will you forgive me?"

I weakly managed to squeak out, "Yes, I will forgive you."

Relieved, he smiled and said, "Oh, I feel so much better! Now I can go on with my life."

He cheerfully bounced away, a new spring in his step. I just kind of stood there, emotionally bleeding. Hearing his confession did not "restore" our relationship, even though I genuinely forgave him. We didn't *have* a relationship! To whom should he have confessed? Well, the "hundreds and hundreds of people" he had lied to about me would be a good start—his spouse, his pastor, his accountability partner ... but not me.

So, Now What?

So, to whom should you confess? I wish I could tell you. *It depends.* You'll need to ask God's Spirit to direct you. As you do, perhaps you should consider the following question:

Could the short-term pain caused by my confession lead to deeper intimacy?

No? Then maybe you shouldn't confess to that person. On the other hand, if you have a secret that involves your spouse ... it's going to hurt, both your spouse and you. But the alternative is that you continue living the lie. That lie is a wall between you and your spouse—a wall that your spouse doesn't even know is there. If you confess, it'll hurt. But it could lead to healing, and thus to deeper intimacy. That's a confession you probably should make.

Bottom line? Stop believing lies. Stop telling lies. Stop living a lie. Live in the truth. And the truth will set you free. **C**

Craig Groeschel is the founder and senior pastor of LifeChurch.tv, an evangelical Christian multi-site church with multiple locations in Arizona, Oklahoma, and Texas that feature live satellite video services. Craig is married with six children and lives in Oklahoma. Learn more at **www.lifechurch.tv**.

GROUP STUDY QUESTIONS
FOR DISCUSSION

1. Which category of lies do you most easily slip into?

2. Identify why you most often lie.

3. How do lies evidence "the moment of truth" in relation to our integrity?

4. How do lies affect our community as believers?

5. Are there any "appropriate people" in your life that you need to confess to?

6. What is meant by the statement, "Honesty means that everything you say must be true, not that everything true must be said"?

Nun Chucks, Warriors, and Master Po

By Mike Foster and Jud Wilhite

"HE WHO CONQUERS HIMSELF IS THE GREATEST WARRIOR."
—Master Po, *Kung Fu*

Kung fu and hard knocks drove us to this place.

Maybe you're here with us. Not physically, of course. Just at this place in life.

We write this from Jud's Man Cave. Rest assured, this is no bunker filled with raw meat and rifles. It's just a converted part of Jud's garage with a couple of leather chairs, a TV, and some good action movies.

Not long ago, we were in the Man Cave watching the *Kung Fu* episode where Master Po says—gently, wisely—"He who conquers himself is the greatest warrior."

For some reason, we paused and just had this "moment." We put down our four-cheese pepperoni and sausage pizza slices simultaneously. Was it guilt? Was it a strange sense of our own mortality? Was it simply that we forgot the mushrooms?

The episode droned on though we weren't listening to it anymore.

Mike took the opportunity to ask, "Hey Jud, how's it going? Really, how's it going?"

We talked over the stresses of our work, our marriages, our friendships, and life in general. We kicked around our options for the future. We talked about our dreams for our kids and our roles as leaders. We hashed over the possible pitfalls of life. (Mike heads up a design firm; Jud's a pastor.) That night we got honest with each other and ourselves and asked each other some pretty straight up questions:

- How come we never talk about the really important stuff?
- What are those big and nasty issues lurking out there ready to take us down?
- What are those stupid choices we are on the verge of making that would deliver a knockout blow and wreck our lives?

- How could we help each other be healthier leaders and find true meaning for our lives?

LADIES AND GENTLEMEN, WE INTRODUCE YOUR ENEMIES
That conversation in the garage led us to consider the different things that could destroy our families, our ministries, and the things we hold most important. We refer to these things as "The Deadly Viper Character Assassins." Who are these kung fu killers? They are bloodthirsty hit-men lurking in the shadows, plotting to undermine your leadership, integrity, and success. And because of their stealth MO, we often don't see them 'til it's too late. By then, they're chopping us up into sushi rolls and folding us into puny cream cheese wontons.

The Deadly Vipers are some bad dudes who take great pleasure in what they do. They eat your kind for lunch and are skilled in the arts of annihilation, pain, and destruction. These ninja experts are working 25 hours a day, 8 days a week to undo you. They don't rest. These forces of darkness are fully funded and well resourced. They possess the weapons, they've plotted the strategies, and they kick more tail before 7 a.m. than most of us will in our entire lives.

They include *the Assassin of Character Creep*, who would love to see you erase some lines and violate the values you hold most dearly—one expense report, or flirtatious meeting, at a time.

Then there's *the Assassin of Zi Qi Qi Ren*, which is a funky Chinese word that means, "self deception while deceiving others." He'd love to get you lying to yourself and others about who you are and what you do. His goal is to lead you into concealment and hiding so he can undermine your integrity.

The Assassin of Amped Emotions wants you going nuts on petty and insignificant things. He wants you to act out and go postal so you embarrass yourself in front of your friends, co-workers, family, and associates. This Assassin wants you to feel threatened, insecure, and to be overly focused on your shortcomings. When this happens, he controls you and the timing of your ultimate downfall.

The Assassin of the Headless Sprinting Chicken wants to keep your schedule so overwhelmed that you cave under the pressure and do something really foolish. He'll beat you to a pulp, lop your head off, and take nun chucks to your loved ones all while you buzz around from one manic appointment to another. You'll be found in a corner curled up in a fetal position, a headless twitch. He won't even break a sweat.

The Assassin of Boom Chicka Wah Wah wants you walking a little too close to the sexual edge. The hormones get raging. An innocent lunch meeting turns into dessert in the back seat of the Chrysler. A night of celebration with a colleague on a business trip can lead to a night of pleasure. A few drinks, a few thousands miles from home, and Boom Chicka Wah Wah.

The High and Mighty Assassin is also coming for you. He bases his attack on you having a false estimation of yourself. When you're struck by the High and Mighty Assassin, you can overestimate your giftedness and your chops and your all-that, and find yourself in real trouble.

The Bling Bling Assassin wants you never satisfied. He's always challenging you to desire more, irrespective of the personal cost. He's out there constantly seeking to bury you under debt, or get you to falsify the expense report, or fudge on your word.

And then there's little old us looking like schoolgirls with plaid skirts on because we are unskilled and undisciplined in the area of character. We're weaklings with rail-skinny arms and toothpick legs. Too many of us think we can skate by on our business savvy, stellar successes, and our impressive ability to jive talk ourselves out of anything. But here's the deal: the Deadly Vipers aren't in the mood for small talk. They're in the mood for spilling blood. They're like our favorite karate legend Chuck Norris; the Deadly Vipers don't go hunting, they go a-killing.

The Deadly Viper Character Assassins are brutal slayers. Are you ready to face them? We want to help turn you into warriors who are trained and ready for wherever and whenever the attacks may come. And let's make this one truth crystal clear: the Character Assassins are on their way. For some of you they are pressing a steely blade to your throat even now.

UGLY DANCE PARTNERS
Here is a fundamental problem as we see it. Character and integrity are like those girls or guys at the high school dance you would only cut the rug with as a last resort. It's as if they are sitting across the dance hall wearing headgear, braces, and Coke-bottle glasses. Want to dance? No thanks!

For too long the discussions on character have been marginalized by politically correct business jargon, legalistic strategies

from do-gooders, and concepts that only fire up sixty-something IBM execs. Deep down we know we need to keep the issues of character and integrity, and the ongoing options to screw them up, before us.

NO PERFECT PEOPLE
Many think being a person of integrity is about perfectionism, legalism, and the glow of a halo illuminating your face. Please don't make us hurl. Unfortunately, the issue of character has often been hijacked by behavior Nazis who wield their nattering lists of dos and don'ts. We will have none of that here.

We would rather bring the decades-old wisdom of the great Eagles musician, Glenn Frey, to the table: "Rock and roll isn't about perfection. It's about excellence."

So is integrity. No one passes through life's rich pageant without character flaws. No one bats a thousand in integrity, either.

See, whether it's big or little stuff, we all got stuff. Maybe we:

- under-report our taxes
- exaggerate successes
- say things we don't mean
- carry on an illicit affair
- take advantage of people

Maybe we:

- steal pens and paper from the office
- surf porn during work hours
- enjoy gossiping and undermining people
- rip our kids off with the lack of quality time
- bail on friends in their time of need

Bottom line: We're all a mess, and we all have character issues.

THE DESTINATION WILL COME. THE JOURNEY IS NOW.
Emerson wrote, "The force of character is cumulative." We need leaders to slip into a rhythm of making right choices. Imagine character just naturally flowing from you because you have trained and disci-

plined your mind, body, and soul. Choosing honor, nobility, and the good can become extensions of who we are. We reject the small-minded, ineffective approach of those who focus simply on specific bad behaviors and miss the lifestyle approach. All of us want to get to the point where living with integrity is as simple as clubbing baby seals over the melon (BTW, we love baby seals so don't miss our point).

You can get good at this if you want to, but ultimately it's your choice. It will come with a cost, and there will be sacrifice. You can treat this like all those other "nice thoughts" or "leadership concepts" you've heard from well-meaning folks, or you can train your mind, body, and soul to flow with integrity.

NO LONE RANGERS

It's also important to understand that character is both a personal AND a community concept. If you are a person of great character, all those around you benefit. The organization, the relationships, the families—they all win. If you lack character, everyone pays.

The building of character is a community thing. There are no Lone Rangers. We need to train together, fight together, and watch each other's backs. True leaders make tough decisions to battle for integrity together, no matter how inconvenient or how it may stretch us.

Most of us are simply not inclined to talk about our struggles, our inadequacies, and our vulnerabilities with each other. This is counter-culture. But we must. We must defend each other in this battle and carry each others' burdens. If Jud was ever to be peering at the tip of a saber belonging to a character assassin, without question Mike would fiercely battle for his friend. If Mike was in a potentially deadly place, Jud would do the same. We are linked together, each and every one of us.

If you are not willing to defend and come to the aid of a wounded, struggling, even fallen leader, then your character is vacant and empty. If you lack the guts to risk your personal reputation for someone else, then Master Po rejects you. And yes, we are dead serious. In fact, we're not sure there is anything more cowardly, more anti-warrior, less noble than attacking an obviously bruised leader—or standing on the sidelines, silently and smugly taking in the spectacle of it all.

THE GRAND MASTER CHALLENGE

Our basic conclusion: we need to make character and integrity THE priority. We need to train, get ripped, and be ready for the fight. You want to rock the world, Grasshopper? Then make these issues the foundation for life.

Let's go back to those questions we began with in Jud's garage:

- Do you talk about the really important stuff?
- What are the big and nasty issues lurking out there ready to take you down?
- What are those stupid choices you are on the verge of making that would deliver a knockout blow and wreck your life?
- Who could you reach out to in order to be a healthier leader and find true meaning for your life?

We are asking you to make a choice and a decision right now. We are asking you to let it all hang out with us and become warriors, fighters, and black belts in the art of integrity. For some, this might be painful. For others, this will simply validate your leadership choices and good decisions.

This is the grand master challenge to conquer yourself. We want to party with Master Po!

We are warriors in the making. [C]

Mike Foster and **Jud Wilhite** are the authors of *Deadly Viper Character Assassins*, a kung fu survival guide for leadership integrity. Driven by the core themes of radical integrity and radical grace, Mike and Jud are reinventing the conversation on character for next generation leaders.

Mike currently serves as the President of Ethur and Jud is the Senior Pastor of Central Christian Church in Las Vegas. For more information visit **www.DeadlyViper.org**.

FAILURE

WHAT IS TRUE SUCCESS?

BY JIM COLLINS

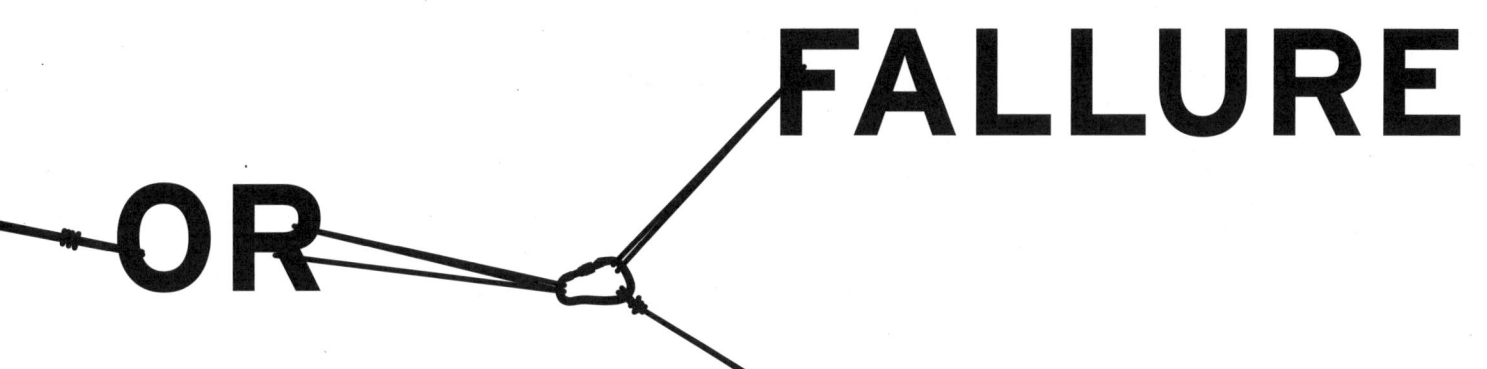

OR FALLURE

SOME OF MY MOST VALUABLE LESSONS ABOUT LEADERSHIP AND LIFE HAVE COME FROM A SPECIAL CLASSROOM: THE SHEER ROCK WALLS OF COLORADO AND TOWERING CLIFFS OF YOSEMITE VALLEY. IN THIS LABORATORY OF PERSONAL CHALLENGE—HANGING BY FINGERTIPS FROM LITTLE EDGES, TETHERED TO A GREAT PARTNER, CONFRONTING FEAR AND DISCOVERING PERSONAL WEAKNESSES (AND AN OCCASIONAL STRENGTH)—I'VE COME TO SEE THE PURSUIT OF EXCELLENCE AS A QUITE DIFFERENT CONCEPT THAN PURSUIT OF THE SUMMIT. IN FACT, SOME OF THE PROUDEST DAYS COME IN NOT REACHING THE TOP, AND SOME OF THE MOST DISAPPOINTING DAYS COME WITH SUMMIT SUCCESS.

Matt and I stood below an absolutely beautiful sheet of rock—smooth and overhanging, with a finger-tip sized seam splitting the middle of the grey and silver granite wall. "You can see why I named the route Crystal Ball," Matt said, pointing to a baseball-sized quartzite handhold fifty feet up the climb.

We roped up and I set off up the route, shooting for an on-sight ascent. An "on-sight" means that on your first try you lead the climb without any prior informa-

tion about the moves. For you, the route is an entirely blank page, no matter how many other climbers have ascended the route. Once you start to climb, if you blow it (and thereby fall onto the rope), you've forever lost the on-sight.

Ten feet below the crystal, my feet began to skitter, slipping off slick pebbles, and I curled my thumb around a little edge, thinking to myself, "If I can just get a little weight off my fingers ..." The adrenaline made me over-grip ev-

ery hold, sapping strength I would need higher on the climb. A hard sport climb is a race to the top before you run out of power; moves that would be easy if they came at the bottom are much harder when found higher on the route when you hit those moves already fatigued. As climbers like to say, "the clock is ticking" from the moment you leave the ground. You only have so many minutes and seconds before your fingers uncurl off the holds, and you plummet down until (hopefully) the rope catches.

"Breathe, Jim. Relax." Matt's voice soothed me for a moment.

I gathered a bit of composure, while hooking my thumb and resting my fingers, trying to get my breathing to settle down. But to little avail. My mind chattered away: "Not sure whether to go right hand or left hand to the sideways edge above ... If I get it wrong, no way I can reverse ... and even if I get it right, I'm not sure I'll have enough power to pull up to the crystal ball ... and if I can't get to the crystal ball, there's no way I'll be able to get the rope clipped into the next point of protection ... how far would I fall? ... But I don't like to take big falls ..."

Tick, tick, tick—the clock ran on while I hesitated.

"Okay, Matt, here I go."

Right hand to the side pull. Left foot to the edge.

Uh oh, wrong call. I should have gone to the edge with my left hand! I rolled my body to the left, groping for an edge, a pebble, a wrinkle—something, anything—that would allow me to pop my right hand up and move my left onto the side edge. I smooshed my right fingers into a little edge that pointed down and sideways—the wrong direction for a good pull. I now had a less than twenty percent chance of success. If I tried to make the move up, I'd almost certainly fall. Even if I did manage to surge upward, the higher I went without making the next bolt clip, the bigger the eventual fall. (To "clip" means to get the rope into the carabiner hanging off a protection bolt. If you fall when leading, you descend about 2.5 times as far as the distance to your last successful clip.)

"Off!" I called down to Matt.

"No," he yelled back. "You're only three moves from the crystal."

"OFF!" I repeated, with angry emphasis. And I let go, dropping onto the rope in a nicely controlled fall.

I hung on the rope for about ten minutes, recovering, and then swung toward the rock on the end of the rope, pulled myself back on to the holds and climbed to the top. But of course it didn't count. I hadn't done a clean on-sight. And even though later in the day, I managed to ascend the route from bottom to top in one shot—a success by most measures—I had nonetheless failed. When confronted with the moment of commitment, the moment of decision, the moment of go-for-it on the on-sight ... well, I let go. I went to failure, not fallure.

Failure and fallure. The difference is subtle, but it is all the difference in the world. In fallure, you still fail to get up the route but you never let go. Going to fallure means full one hundred percent commitment to go up, despite the odds against you. You'll only find your true limit when you go to fallure, not failure. Sure, I had less than a twenty percent chance of pulling through to the crystal ball, but because I let go, I'll never know for sure. Perhaps I would have had an extra reserve, perhaps I would have surprised myself and had an extra bit of power to hang on for one more move. Or perhaps—and this turned out to be true—the very next hold is better than it looks. And that's the rub. It's the ambiguity—about the holds, the moves, the ability to clip the rope—that makes one hundred percent commitment on the on-sight so difficult.

LIKE AN ON-SIGHT ATTEMPT, THE NEXT HOLDS IN LIFE REMAIN UNCLEAR, AMBIGUOUS. AND THAT VERY AMBIGUITY HOLDS US BACK FROM MAKING A FULLY COMMITTED ATTEMPT.

One of my mentors, the design guru Sara Little Turnbull, built a distinguished career as a design consultant to major corporations. (The Corporate Design Foundation once described her as "the CEOs' secret weapon in product design.") Turnbull once told me that some of her best designs came when she was on the brink of a failed concept but didn't let go. Of course, many—indeed, most—of her brink-of-failure designs ended up being failures. But every once in a while, by not letting go, she would push herself to a completely different level and something extraordinary would come about. "And of course, that's when breakthroughs happen," she told me. "If you don't stretch, you don't know where the edge is." Fallure, not failure.

Some of the best business leaders in history intuitively understood this idea. Darwin Smith made a fallure versus failure decision in vaulting his company to greatness. For one hundred years, Kimberly-Clark languished in mediocrity, with most of its business in traditional coated paper mills. Smith realized that the company's best shot at greatness lay in the paper-based consumer goods arena, where it had a side business called Kleenex. But how to get the company to fully commit to making the consumer business great, when the bulk of the company's history and revenues lay in the traditional industrial paper mills?

Like the general who burned the boats upon landing, leaving no retreat for his soldiers, Smith decided to sell the mills. He would sell even the mill in Kimberly, Wisconsin, and throw all the proceeds into the consumer business, going head to head with consumer rivals Scott Paper and Procter and Gamble. Wall Street derided him, the

business media called the move stupid, and the analysts wrote merciless commentary. But in the end, Smith's decision paid off. Kimberly-Clark became the number one paper-based consumer products company in the world, eventually beating Procter & Gamble in six of eight product categories. Of course, there was no guarantee that Kimberly-Clark would succeed in the consumer business—it could have taken a huge leader fall—but Smith understood the only path to success lay in a full commitment to climb to fallure.

I now see life as a series of choices between going to failure or fallure. Like an on-sight attempt, the next holds in life remain unclear, ambiguous. And that very ambiguity holds us back from making a fully committed attempt. We fail mentally. We let go. We take a nice controlled fall, rather than risking a bigger fall. But as with most hard sport climbs, going to fallure in life is scary, but not dangerous. Whether it be starting a business or publishing a book or trying an exciting new design, fallure rarely means doom. And most important, the only way to find your true limit is to go to fallure, not failure.

Facing 50, my body does not allow me to pull as hard on holds as when I was 20. But I've since learned that what you lose in physical strength you can gain

by increasing your mental strength. I've even redefined "success" less in terms of getting to the top and more in terms of the quality of my mental effort. I keep a record on my Palm Pilot of my hard on-sight attempts. A recent listing reads:

HARD ON-SIGHT ATTEMPT LOG

REACH THE TOP:	24
CLIMB TO FALLURE:	18
FAILURE (LET GO/QUIT):	16
TOTAL ATTEMPTS:	58
% SUCCESS RATE: (TOP + FALLURE)	72%

Note that I calculate the "success rate" not just as the percentage of times to the top, but the percentage of times to the top PLUS percentage of times to fallure. During a recent climbing session, I did not make it to the top of a single route. Not one. Still, it was one of my most successful days of climbing ever, because I went to fallure on every single attempt. I felt good on the way home because my mind felt strong that day, compared to the weak feeling on most days. For in the end, climbing is not about conquering the rock; it is about conquering yourself. And this is what fallure is all about. **C**

Jim Collins is the author of *Good to Great: Why Some Companies Make the Leap ... And Others Don't* and co-author of *Built to Last: Successful Habits of Visionary Companies*. A recipient of the Distinguished Teaching Award while a faculty member at the Stanford University Graduate School of Business, Jim now works from his management-research laboratory in Boulder, Colorado. More of Jim Collins' work can be found at **www.jimcollins.com**.

Article has been adapted from Author's chapter "Hitting the Wall" from the book UPWARD BOUND: 9 Original Accounts of How Business Leaders Reached Their Summits, *Edited by Michael Useem, Jerry Useem, and Paul Asel, published by Crown Press (2003).*

TO TELL THE TRUTH

HONESTLY, CAN YOU TRUST ANYONE AT WORK?

BY JOHN BRANDON

WHEN I GRADUATED FROM COLLEGE IN 1977, I WAS HIRED AS A SALES REP FOR TEXAS INSTRUMENTS. THE FUNNY THING IS, I WAS A HISTORY MAJOR AND I'D NEVER SOLD ANYTHING BEFORE, LET ALONE ANYTHING IN THE TECHNOLOGY REALM. I WAS A BIT OVERWHELMED, SO I WENT TO SOMEBODY I CONSIDERED A BUSINESS MENTOR, AND I SAID, "I'M GOING TO BE A SALES PERSON. WHAT ADVICE DO YOU HAVE FOR ME?"

We were sitting at lunch and he looked at me and he said, "Well, I only have one piece of advice." I'm thinking, "Oh boy, this is going to be the key to my business success." He said, "Learn to tell the truth. If you learn to tell the truth, you will absolutely stand out from all of your peers."

We finished that lunch, and I started my career. But the interesting thing is, those words kept ringing around in my head. I decided that I was going to make that one of my lifetime goals—I was going to be a truth teller. Along the way, I've learned three lessons about telling the truth:

No.1: Consider the cost, because the price tag might be high.
No.2: People are attracted to the truth.
No.3: It's a lot easier to tell the truth if you know the Author of the truth.

And I've come to the conclusion that telling the truth should be a lot like the golden rule: we should tell to others what we personally would want to be told.

LESSON NO. 1: CONSIDER THE COST, BECAUSE THE PRICE TAG MIGHT BE HIGH.
During the first part of my career, I was with Texas Instruments, a highly ethical company. During the years I was there, every employee worldwide went through ethics training annually.

I decided to leave there in the mid-'80s to join a startup that was founded by a brilliant professor from UC Berkley. I was lucky enough to be the first sales person they hired, employee number 17. We had great technology, which we turned into a fantastic product. After two years, we were able to take the company public. We had some of the best venture money in the world behind it, and we were on a rocket. I really felt like I had won the lottery. I tasted the upside of the Silicon Valley, and I really liked it.

There was, however, a problem in how the CEO dealt with people. It was pretty unpleasant. He had a nasty habit of pitting the management team against each other. And he would normally pit the team against a person who wasn't in the room. He decided to start one particular meeting by making an accusation about the one senior manager that wasn't in the room. He said this guy had done something the previous week to intentionally damage the company.

Well, it was one of those things that not only wasn't true, it was so outrageous, that people didn't even want to acknowledge it. The CEO decided he was going to call on each one of us to see if we agreed with him. I was sitting to his immediate right, but he started on his left. He literally went around to each of the people at the table, looked them in

the eye, and said, "This is what I believe. Do you agree with me?" I sat there and watched every senior exec crumble under the pressure of the CEO.

I was thinking, "What am I going to say?" The words that came to my mind were, "Be a truth teller. Tell the truth." So I decided to do that. When it was finally my turn, he looked at me and said, "Do you agree with me and everyone else?"

Being the sales guy that I am, I attempted a little humor. Nobody was laughing. So I swallowed hard, and I looked him in the eye and I said, "Well, actually if you really think he did that intentionally to damage the company, I disagree. And by the way, I'm personally really uncomfortable that we're talking about one of the senior managers that is not here to defend himself."

I wish I could say that at that moment the CEO jumped up and said, "Finally, an honest man. I'm looking for my successor, and he'll be the next CEO of this company." That's what I was hoping. It's not what happened. He kind of glared at me, changed the subject, and finished the managers' meeting.

The next morning, the CEO's administrative assistant called me. She said, "John, you need to know, he started a search this morning to replace you."

Ninety days later, I'm out of the company. I had my tail between my legs; I was all chewed up. I was trying to figure it all out, "Lord what in the world are You doing in my life? Haven't You noticed we're wearing the same color jersey? I thought I was on Your team." There I was, on the street looking for a job, wondering what had happened to me.

LESSON NO. 2: PEOPLE ARE ATTRACTED TO THE TRUTH.
People are desperate for the truth. I've learned over the years that telling the truth is an amazing thing. Even if they don't do it themselves, people want the truth to be told to them. And they almost expect it.

When I left that company with my tail between my legs, I took the only job that I could find with a little software company that was trying to decide if they were going to go get into the application software business. That company was Adobe Systems. Adobe was a highly ethical company, just the opposite of the experience I had come out of with that start-up company.

All my friends thought I was brilliant. I was just desperate for a job because I was married with two little kids, trying to make a mortgage. At Adobe, we were committed to annual reviews for every employee. But even though we would train our managers, they didn't do a very good job with it. There's a dirty little secret that's part of corporate America. While many companies are committed to annual reviews, most managers won't tell the truth in the reviews. They won't tell the employee what's going on.

I was developing a reputation that I'd tell employees the truth, so I would find that around review time, employees in completely different parts of the organization would want to meet with me. They would walk in and say, "I'm desperate to know the truth. I got my review. I don't believe it. What's going on?"

Some of them I had to look in the eyes and say, "I'll tell you why. We view you as a brilliant engineer, but you're so difficult to do business with nobody wants to be on your team, let alone let give you the responsibility to lead a team. Go back and ask your boss, 'How are my people skills?' Get some honest feedback."

After a great 10-year run at Adobe, I got a phone call from one of the most powerful and influential venture capitalists in the world. He offered me the opportunity to be-

TRUTH IN NUMBERS

Years ago, I decided that my best chance of success at being a truth teller and living a life of integrity was to share my life with a handful of guys. I have a very strong support system. I actually have two accountability groups: one with guys that are in the marketplace; the other with the elder board of our church.

There is no major decision or anything that happens in my life that I don't share with those guys. I've just made that part of a decision grid that with every major decision, I run it through those guys.

Those groups have told me the most difficult things I've ever heard about myself. But we made a covenant with each other that we love each other enough to tell each other the truth.

Do not walk this path alone.

PEOPLE ARE ATTRACTED TO THE TRUTH BECAUSE THEY'RE FINDING IT TOO RARE THESE DAYS.

come the CEO of a company he was involved with. So I became a CEO for the first time. I showed up on my first day of work and met my new team. The second day, we worked through all of the presentations for the board meeting, which was to be held the very next day. The third day, we went to the board meeting. My new team walked through the presentations and they had all of the answers to every question. It could not have gone any better.

At the end of the day, I called all of the execs back into my office and said, "I thought you guys did a really good job today. I'm really proud of you. Let's go over a few of the numbers. I just want to go over the risk one more time." The room got quiet. One of them handed me an email from the controller that basically said the numbers that we had used to raise our money were bogus.

I said, "Guys, I have a big problem with this." One of the company's cofounders looked at me and said, "You really don't get it, do you? If you let them know these numbers are wrong, we won't get this next round of funding. We're living on a bridge loan. It's going to run out in less than 30 days, and you will have to lay off every employee in the company."

I looked at him and said, "Actually, I do get it, and you need to know that we are not going to take people's money based on things we know are not true."

I didn't sleep very well that night. The next morning at 7:30, I called the lead venture capitalist. I said, "I just went over the numbers. Contrary to what you heard at the board meeting, they're not right. There's enormous risk in them. We need to be upfront." Needless to say, he was angry.

He said, "I need you to call all of the rest of the investors, especially the new lead investor in this round." He was a CEO in New York. I called him. If the first guy was angry, this guy was really angry.

When I finally got to the last investor, she said, "You're calling about the numbers, aren't you?" I said, "How did you know?" She said, "We did our due diligence, and we knew the numbers were squishy. We just wanted to find out how long it was going to take you to find out how squishy they were and when you were going to tell us."

Amazingly, we closed the round at the valuation and took the company forward. But the really amazing thing is that through a rough set of circumstances, I discovered a team of investors that was attracted to the truth. People are attracted to the truth because they're finding it too rare these days.

LESSON NO. 3: IT'S A LOT EASIER TO TELL THE TRUTH IF YOU KNOW THE AUTHOR OF THE TRUTH.
Even though I've got some interesting war stories, I still struggle all the time with telling the truth. I'm just not that good. I still struggle with wanting to make up excuses when I'm late for dinner. Or why I've not called somebody back. Or why I haven't done something that I've committed to.

I've found that my only hope comes out of my relationship with Jesus. It's the only hope. Jesus said, "I am the way, the truth, and the life. No man comes to the Father but by Me." I decided that I am going to take Him at His word … and I've found that it's true. I have found that no matter what the circumstances, out of my relationship with Him, I somehow am able to step up to this issue of being a truth teller.

If you're going to live in the marketplace, if that's where the Lord has placed you, you're going to get challenged about issues of telling the truth every day of your existence. If you think you can do it on your own, if you think people are going to step up because they're basically good and they have good intentions, you're going to be disappointed.

But if you realize that there is hope in a relationship with Jesus, there is true hope. And there is truth. **C**

John Brandon has served as Vice President of the Americas and Asia Pacific for Apple Computer since 2001. Before joining Apple, he spent 24 years with other high-technology companies. He also leads a team of Silicon Valley executives who speak at the nation's top business schools on the subjects of integrity and business ethics. John lives in Atherton, California with his wife and three children.

RELATIONAL CURRENCY

By Andy Stanley

TRUST IS THE CURRENCY OF RELATIONSHIPS. GREAT LEADERS CULTIVATE A CULTURE OF TRUST, AND THUS A CULTURE WHERE RELATIONSHIPS THRIVE. BUT HOW DO YOU FOSTER TRUST BETWEEN MEMBERS OF YOUR TEAM?

For some, trust is not the intuitive choice. However, I believe it is just that. A choice. In 1 Corinthians 13, Paul says that along with forgiving, enduring, and bearing all things, love *believes* all things. We must reconcile the scriptural charge to believe all things with the fact that it is not always easy to do. If we believe it is possible for us to *choose* to love, or be kind, or be patient, then we must also believe we can *choose* to trust.

But the gap between what we expect of people and what they actually deliver makes it hard to trust. We can either fill that gap with *trust* or with *suspicion*. How we handle these opportunities is the greatest determining factor in the success or failure of the relationships in our organizations.

I started by saying that trust is the currency of relationships. Currency implies an exchange of one thing for another. Relationally, we give trust, and we expect trustworthiness in return. But trustworthiness is not a synonym for perfection. Trust is not built on flawless character but on authenticity. I will extend trust to people who will admit their imperfec-

tions. It is people who defend their infallibility who make me suspicious.

There are situations that merit suspicion. What's important is how we handle them. When over time a person's actions erode our trust, and we believe those actions leave the organization vulnerable to harm, we have a responsibility to talk to that person about it (*not the rest of the team*), to address the gap, and to give that person the opportunity to re-establish their trustworthiness. Trustworthy people will address the suspicion they've created.

I wish this principle were easy to implement. It's not. But it is crucial for building a strong team. Here are three things to keep in mind when a trust versus suspicion issue surfaces:

1. When there is a gap, choose to trust.
2. When you see others filling the gap

with suspicion, come to the defense of the *suspect*.
3. If what you see continues to erode your trust, go to the person directly.

Great leaders create a culture in which people have learned how to trust. Modeling biblical trust as outlined in 1 Corinthians 13 is one of the greatest leadership strategies you can employ. Biblical trust is not denial—pretending that you don't see behavior that erodes your trust. It's not withdrawal—refusing to confront. The key is to choose to trust. When it becomes impossible to fill the gap between expectation and behavior with trust, ask for clarification.

Trust is the currency of relationships. Trust is a dynamic your team cannot afford to be without. Model it. Extend it. Choose to trust. **C**

Andy Stanley is the lead pastor of North Point Community Church in Atlanta, Georgia. (**www.northpoint.org**) He is the bestselling author of *Visioneering*, *The Next Generation Leader*, *The Best Question Ever*, and the recent *It Came from Within*. Andy and his wife, Sandra, live in Atlanta with their two sons and daughter.

GLOBALSHIFT

TIM WILLARD

THE LANDSCAPE OF CHRISTIANITY IS SHIFTING INTO A VIBRANT GLOBAL COMMUNITY. HOWEVER, THE HEART OF THIS FAITH AWAKENING IS NOT THE UNITED STATES—IT IS THE GLOBAL SOUTH. IT SEEMS THAT FOR THE FIRST TIME IN A LONG TIME, CHRISTIANS ARE BEGINNING TO TALK ABOUT THEIR FAITH, NOT IN DENOMINATIONAL TERMS BUT IN TERMS OF UNITY. IT IS THE ADVENT OF A NEW CHRISTIAN PERSPECTIVE AND PERHAPS A NEW CHURCH UNIVERSAL. SO WHAT EXACTLY IS THE GLOBAL SOUTH, AND HOW DOES IT AFFECT US?

The Global South refers to what used to be called the "Third World," mostly the under-developed countries in Asia, Latin America, and Africa, among others. It is here that Christianity is exploding. This unprecedented growth marks the epicenter of what Philip Jenkins calls *The Next Christendom.* [1]

From a historical standpoint, Africa is accustomed to being at the center of the Christian world. Some of the greatest minds in Christian history hale from Carthage, Alexandria, and Hippo. If these cities do not sound familiar perhaps names like Tertullian, Origen, and Augustine ring a bell. It could be said that Christianity is moving back to its origins.

Former Bush (W) speechwriter Michael Gerson reports, "The center of gravity of the Christian world is now arguably in central Africa, with more than a third of a billion Christians on that continent." [2] Recently the Passion conference testified to this shift by canceling its 2008 con-

ferences in the U.S. in favor of its first world tour. Don't look now, but the world doesn't revolve around North America.

LEADERSHIFT

Some believe that even though the growth of the Global South is intense and deep, the leadership center of Christianity remains in America. Really? Jenkins reports,

Under the leadership of the Nigerian Church (over 20 million strong), an alliance of conservative Global South churches flatly accused the Americans and British of departing far from biblical principles: 'The unscriptural innovations of North America and some western provinces on issues of human sexuality undermine the basic message of redemption and the power of the Cross to transform lives.' [3]

So who is leading whom? These comments come from the Nigerian Anglican leaders who recently split from and reprimanded their Western (New Hampshire) counterparts. Their lack of industrialized development notwithstanding, the Global South churches are pressing forward towards biblical fidelity, and a type of Christianity that we in the West would be wise to learn from.

The interesting aspect of the Global South is its ecumenical makeup. For some pure fundamental evangelicals the term ecumenical might cause bristling. However, this ecumenism is defined by a strong adherence to the Scriptures. Jenkins notes, "These newer churches preach deep personal faith and communal orthodoxy." [4]

Visionary evangelist Billy Graham took major heat decades ago from fundamental Christians for his ecumenical stance in regards to convert follow-up after his crusades. Graham and his band of neo-evangelicals sought to bridge the gap between the broader culture and the fundamentalist withdrawal that threatened to create a polarizing evangelical subculture. Now in the 21st century we are trying to pick up where Graham left off—breaking down denominational barriers to unite Christendom in order to bring the Good News of Jesus Christ to the world.

Douglas Sweeney intimates that a kinder, gentler Protestantism is on the horizon, one with less opposition between "mainline" and evangelical churches. He suggests that, "Fresh leadership is required, as well as a new, global vision, a humbler spirit of partnership, and a stronger support for the common good (especially the welfare of the poor)." [5] This means that the Western church must begin looking outward, beyond its borders, and be willing to shift focus off itself, with its divisions, and embrace global Christianity.

SHAPESHIFT
While the Church of the Global South grows because of a thirst for spiritual depth, a winsome social awareness, and

persecution, the modern North American church finds itself struggling to overcome issues of purpose, mission, and methodology: "Should we be missional? How do we get more people to come to our church?" "Should we subdue the messages in order to be less offensive to unbelievers?"

Brennan Manning observes, "The North American Church is at a critical juncture. The gospel of grace is being confused and compromised by silence, seduction, and outright subversion." [6] There grows a great disparity between the Global Church and the Western Church—a divide that alienates the West as it strives for relevance in a world that is desperate for relationship.

Have we in the West become so spiritually latent that we no longer pine for

the rich blessings that come from deep communion with God? We must look to our global family and join with them in strengthening a faith that historically has led the way in assisting the widows and orphans, giving to the poor, and seeking social justice.

Let us not sit idly by as spectators as Christianity blossoms—as lives and nations are changed. Instead, let us pick up the plowshare and begin the work Christ set before us—to make disciples of all nations. God did not make Christianity for the West; He offered redemption for whosoever will. We must remember that "There is not a square inch in the whole domain of our human existence over which Christ, who is Sovereign over all, does not cry: 'Mine!'" [7] ■

For more from Tim Willard, visit **www.flickernail.com**.

PERRY NOBLE

SENIOR PASTOR, NEWSPRING CHURCH
Age 36, Anderson, South Carolina, www.newspring.cc

I REMEMBER THE FALL OF 1999 SO CLEARLY. I WAS MEETING WITH A GROUP OF 15 PEOPLE IN A LIVING ROOM DREAMING ABOUT WHAT WOULD SOON BE KNOWN AS NEWSPRING CHURCH. WE HAD OUR FIRST SERVICE ON A LOCAL COLLEGE CAMPUS ON JANUARY 16, 2000 WITH 115 PEOPLE IN ATTENDANCE.

We grew so rapidly, we moved to the largest auditorium on the campus, adding multiple services to accommodate the growth. We quickly reached maximum capacity with a weekly average attendance of 4,500. We began building a facility of our own and moved into it in February, 2006. God has continued to bless us and blow our minds. In a recent weekend, we saw 9,260 people here at NewSpring, with 250 making first-time decisions to receive Christ.

I had no idea this was going to happen, *but* I have managed to learn a few things through this experience:

1. I AM IN WAY OVER MY HEAD!

I feel that if God is in something, then the person leading it will never truly feel like it is manageable ... because it isn't. I have discovered that God's desire for me as a pastor is to never be comfortable. When God is moving within your ministry, you will always feel like you are in way over your head.

2. I HAVE TO CONTINUALLY LISTEN TO GOD.

Some of the biggest mistakes I have made as a leader have happened when I tried to substitute my vision for God's. As I've studied the Old Testament I've discovered that Moses was *always* successful when he did exactly what God told him to do. This principal has challenged me to seek God in every decision we make as a church. Listening to God reduces our "screw-up" factor and allows us to function with confidence.

3. I MUST CONTINUE TO SURROUND MYSELF WITH QUALITY LEADERS.

When you start a church, you can either surround yourself with "yes men" or reformers. So in the beginning of New-Spring, I chose to go the reformer route, and I have *never* regretted that decision.

Developing a strong leadership team takes time. One of the biggest mistakes that church planters often make is to form a senior management team right out of the gate. I encourage pastors to wait because the best leaders might not even be at the church yet.

4. THIS TAKES WORK.

If a church wants to reach people who are disconnected from Christ as well as assist others in making their connection stronger, it's inevitable that there will be hard decisions to make. There can't be a half-hearted effort by the leaders to see how fast they can get through a meeting. It takes time, effort and a willingness to work through really hard decisions. If a church is growing, it isn't by accident.

We are not the perfect church. But we know that as long as we continue to seek God's direction with a willingness to do what He tells us to do, there is *no limit* to where He can take this thing! C

The Way of Wrigley

By Sarah Cunningham

My dog, Wrigley, has a "one-track" mind. As he tears after the squirrels in our backyard, I imagine his mental sequence goes something like this: "Squirrel, squirrel, squirrel." Then a bird flies by and his mind switches gear. "Bird, bird, bird."

I am not a pet psychiatrist, but I would wager that Wrigley does not have the ability to separate his thoughts from his actions. Even if he wanted to, I doubt Wrigley could auto-pilot after a squirrel while thinking, "I hope there's pizza crust in my food bowl today."

Wrigley's maniacal focus is the source of constant humor. However, I am a little jealous of my dog's one-track consciousness—his ability to fiercely focus on the exact moment he is currently living.

Humans have a unique and confusing ability to separate thoughts from actions. We can be doing one thing but thinking something completely unrelated.

On the plus side, our split-track minds allow us to multi-task, to iron while talking on the phone. But on the minus end, this also allows us to slip into hypnosis where we iron over our hand without thinking.

Even scarier is that entire chunks of my existence are directed by ritual familiarity—I wake up, I go to work, I eat, I sleep. I am startled when ordinary things like the descent into my pillow or a new grey hair remind me that real-life days, weeks, and years have passed while I operated in zombie mode.

This separation of thoughts from actions is not what God intended because when I check out of the moment I am living, I cannot keep even my simplest physical or spiritual goals in mind. I go through the motions of my day while my mind is absorbed in tangent topics.

I don't even realize my own obliviousness until regret surfaces just before I fall asleep. Here, I must admit that I have made it to another day's end without applying myself toward my spiritual goals.

This is the darkness of daily disillusionment, when I must give up my illusion of a well-managed life and see the gaps between who I want to be and who I was today.

In the mornings of life, when I seek renewal, I desperately want to rejoin my thoughts and actions. I want to gradually reform my daily rituals, so that all the hypnotic, repetitive moments are laced with reminders of my spiritual intentions. Perhaps this is why God told the Israelites to discuss His commandments while they did everyday things like walking along the road. (Deuteronomy 6)

I am on this chosen-people quest to rejoin my thoughts with my actions and fully live the moments God gives me. If I can wake up and think of rising to a new life, or eat Rice Krispies while remembering I am first and foremost a spiritual bread eater, then I can begin to pray continuously, and to borrow from the way of Wrigley. To inhale and remember the good things of God I breathe in each new day, to exhale and remember God is purging my life of flaws and dysfunction. In consciously letting my moments become reminders of my aims, I bring my life back into alignment with my goals. I begin to tour my world in pursuit of God, thinking "God, God, God." **C**

Sarah Raymond Cunningham is a high school teacher from Jackson, Michigan and the author of *Dear Church: Letters From A Disillusioned Generation*. She travels and speaks to groups of all ages about fighting disillusionment, keeping the faith, and harnessing the energy of twentysomethings. Sign up for Sarah's free newsletter at **www.dearchurch.com**.

UNCOMPROMISING IN INTEGRITY

Who are you when no one is around? How do you bend the truth to make yourself look and sound better than you are? Truth can be frightening, but it is the language God expects us to speak. Spend some time confessing façades you are sustaining with lies. Ask God to strengthen you to speak the truth in love. Find a friend you trust to hold you accountable to living in truth.

V. PASSIONATE ABOUT GOD

I must be aware of my small role in God's big, developing story. This is critical to my
humility, faith, and trust in Him as the definer of how He will use me and my calling. To
increase my awareness, I must connect with God without ceasing through all of life, whether in
study, music, art, film, vocation, or relationships. My passion for God to receive
Glory must be bigger than my desire for Glory.

What I Want To Be When I Grow Up

Add to Your Faith ... Godliness

By Mark Buchanan

SIMON PETER, A SERVANT AND APOSTLE OF JESUS CHRIST, TO THOSE WHO HAVE OBTAINED A FAITH OF EQUAL STANDING WITH OURS BY THE RIGHTEOUSNESS OF OUR GOD AND SAVIOR JESUS CHRIST: MAY GRACE AND PEACE BE MULTIPLIED TO YOU IN THE KNOWLEDGE OF GOD AND OF JESUS OUR LORD. HIS DIVINE POWER HAS GRANTED TO US ALL THINGS THAT PERTAIN TO LIFE AND GODLINESS, THROUGH THE KNOWLEDGE OF HIM WHO CALLED US TO HIS OWN GLORY AND EXCELLENCE, BY WHICH HE HAS GRANTED TO US HIS PRECIOUS AND VERY GREAT PROMISES, SO THAT THROUGH THEM YOU MAY BECOME PARTAKERS OF THE DIVINE NATURE, HAVING ESCAPED FROM THE CORRUPTION THAT IS IN THE WORLD BECAUSE OF SINFUL DESIRE. FOR THIS VERY REASON, MAKE EVERY EFFORT TO SUPPLEMENT YOUR FAITH WITH VIRTUE, AND VIRTUE WITH KNOWLEDGE, AND KNOWLEDGE WITH SELF-CONTROL, AND SELF-CONTROL WITH STEADFASTNESS, AND STEADFASTNESS WITH GODLINESS, AND GODLINESS WITH BROTHERLY AFFECTION, AND BROTHERLY AFFECTION WITH LOVE. FOR IF THESE QUALITIES ARE YOURS AND ARE INCREASING, THEY KEEP YOU FROM BEING INEFFECTIVE OR UNFRUITFUL IN THE KNOWLEDGE OF OUR LORD JESUS CHRIST. FOR WHOEVER LACKS THESE QUALITIES IS SO NEARSIGHTED THAT HE IS BLIND, HAVING FORGOTTEN THAT HE WAS CLEANSED FROM HIS FORMER SINS. (2 PETER 1:1-9 ESV)

"If You Love Me, You'll Love Me as I Am."

That's a refrain I use with my wife. She points out some minor flaw in me—I mean *minor*, minor as in petty, miniscule, incidental—and I retort, "If you love me, you'll love me as I am!" Love me with all my smells and noises, my quirks and whims and warts.

Well, it's true. The nature of deep love is its capacity to love what is unlovely, even unlovable. Deep love—what the Bible calls *agape* love—transcends our inborn tendencies of attraction or revulsion. It subverts ingrained prejudice. It trumps our niggling irritations. It annuls our sticky and picky conditions.

Deep love loves simply because its nature is to love.

At just the right time, Paul says, *Christ died for us, while we were still sinners.* (Romans 5:6) When I was utterly unlovely and unlovable, God's love found me.

He loves me just as I am. That's real love. But that's only half of it.

Real love loves us, not just *as we are*, but *so that we can become what we are to be.*

That, too, is its nature. It's a love that won't let us go. It is hardy and feisty and relentless. It loves at great cost. *For God so loved the world, He gave His only son that whoever believes in Him might not perish but have eternal life.* (John 3:16)

Such love. It takes hold of us as we are, in our prodigal stench and squalor, but loves us until it cleanses us head to toe, inside out, and dresses us in royal robes. I mention love because godliness—*being Christ-like in character*—is what God wants to love us into. It's the endpoint of divine love. When you have arrived at the fullness of godliness, the measure of that is that you are fully Christ-like, and the work of divine love is complete. It has accomplished what it set out to do.

Take a moment and reread the opening passage from Peter. Read it slowly and carefully—its message is the core of our discussion. It's a message Peter sums up with his pithy imperative (one he stole from Leviticus)—*Be holy as God is holy.*

This is the virtue that defines God's purpose for everyone: to be godly.

But there are mountainous, treacherous obstacles to godliness. The work of be-

coming godly—holy and pure and Christlike—makes His work of conversion seem a simple matter. Conversion—where you were dead in sin and now are alive in Christ—is an astounding miracle, no question. But the miracle of godliness is, I think, greater yet—because with that, God not only makes me alive *in* Christ, He makes me to live *as* Christ.

Conversion—pulls that off in a blink. Sanctification—God typically needs a lifetime to accomplish.

Take A Step Back

Let's nail down a precise definition of *godliness*. In some ways, I've already given it: godliness is Christ-likeness. But let's tighten that up.

The Greek is *eusebeia*. It's the same word Peter uses in 2 Peter 2:3, where he says we already have everything we need for life and *godliness. Eusebeia*—sometimes translated "holiness"—means "good devotion" or "genuine devoutness." It describes the inward quality of a heart set completely on God, His Kingdom, and His purposes. In short, *eusebeia* is God-centeredness.

The New Testament passage from Peter's first letter lends special aid in getting us to grasp the substance of the word:

In your hearts, set apart Christ as Lord. Always be prepared to give a reason for the hope that you have. But do this with gentleness and respect, always keeping a clear conscience, so that those who speak maliciously against your good behavior in Christ may be ashamed of their slander. (1 Peter 3:15-16 NIV)

Godliness begins with a resolve of heart: *In your hearts, set apart Christ as Lord.* Before godliness shows up in how you talk or act or think or dress, it has to do with what you do with Jesus. Is Jesus at the table or still outside the door, knocking? Is Jesus telling you how it is, or are you telling Jesus what's what? *In your heart, set apart Jesus as Lord.* Everything follows from that.

But what does that mean? Simply, who Jesus is and what Jesus desires always—always—takes precedence. It takes precedence over your politics, your prejudices, your emotions, your upbringing, your opinion. All must step aside if in any way it stands in the way of Jesus and what He wants.

And then, right on the heels of that heart resolve, godliness requires a change of behavior. *Always be prepared to give a reason to everyone who asks.* Two things are clear here, one implicit, one explicit. The implicit thing is that godly people live in such a way that they arouse curiosity. They provoke questions. People start to wonder about you. You're different. You're peculiar. You can't be accounted for by the usual theories, assumptions, and explanations.

That peculiarity can be summed up in a word: hope. Godly people live in hope and offer hope. They bring hope into situations of fear and worry and despair and darkness and disappointment. Where others turn to complaining or panic or resignation or protest, the godly embrace hope. And Peter makes it clear where such hope springs from: "Through Him you believe in God," he says in 1 Peter 1:21, "who raised Him from the dead and glorified Him, and so your faith and *hope* are in God." (NIV) The hope of the godly is rooted in God, who can take the bleakest situations—crucifixion, death, the shattering of a dream—and turn it into the best thing imaginable. If we have a God like that, why wouldn't we be hopeful?

That's the implicit thing: godly people live lives so filled with hope they arouse wonder and provoke inquiry.

The explicit thing is this: the godly are prepared to tell anyone who asks them about the reason they have hope. Godly people live in a readiness to seize opportunities that their peculiar living creates. When someone asks, "What is it about you, anyhow?" godly people don't get all shy and evasive. They don't say, "Well, I eat well, I exercise regularly, I try to get eight hours of sleep a night." No, they're ready to tell the reason that they are hope-filled.

Another fact about the godly is that they seize those opportunities with grace. They show gentleness and respect to people. Godly people are not mouth-frothing, placard-waving, curse-spewing crusaders. But they also don't conceal or compromise who they are or what they believe, either. They do what they do with boldness and a clear conscience. The godly are not arrogant or bullying, but neither are they cowardly or apologetic. They don't shout at people or mock them for what they believe or how they live, but they don't join in with their debauchery, either. Rather, the godly live in such a way that the godless, some anyhow, start to ask questions. And if they don't—if they abuse the godly—the godly live in such a way that the godless one day will be ashamed of what they've done.

The godly set apart Christ as Lord in their heart. They live with such hope that people become curious. They answer anyone who asks them about their hope. And they speak with gentleness, respect, and a clear conscience.

A Note of Mystery

From the pen of the Apostle Paul, we can further grasp the meaning of godliness.

Great indeed, we confess, is the mystery of godliness: He was manifested in the flesh, vindicated by the Spirit, seen by angels, proclaimed among the nations, believed on in the world, taken up in glory. (1 Tim 3:16 ESV)

Godliness is not an option for any Christian, but for church leaders it is foundational. Before we look for anything else in a leader, we're to look for godliness. If that's absent, it matters little how otherwise gifted, virtuous, or capable they are. Godliness is the one ingredient that empowers and redeems all the others. Christian leaders especially need to exhibit godly character.

Paul says godliness is a mystery. After all is said and done, there is no earthly explanation for it. The power for this kind of living is only available from above. It is a Spirit work. So there will always be an element of the inexplicable among those who are godly. Once again, as Peter says, the godly are wonders, arousing curiosity. They are peculiar people.

But Paul, in his definition of godliness, takes a step beyond Peter. Peter says godliness begins by *setting apart in your heart* Christ as Lord. Paul adds this: godliness involves *setting your eyes* upon Christ as Lord. "You want the supreme example of godliness?" Paul, in effect, says, "Look to Jesus. He is the perfect embodiment of *eusebeia*."

He tells us six things about Jesus' godliness. He implies that these six qualities are worthy of our imitation:

1. Jesus appeared in a body. Godliness makes God personal. Godliness brings God close. Godliness is the presence of God among us. When you stand among the godly, you have a sense of God Himself hovering near.

2. Jesus was vindicated by the Spirit. The godly entrust justice to God. They do not exhaust themselves trying to manage what others think about them.

3. Jesus was seen by angels. He lived His life with an awareness that the real drama took place in a realm beyond the visible world. The godly believe that we are engaged in something much bigger than ourselves, bigger than even earth can contain, bigger than mere humans can comprehend or even notice.

4. Jesus was preached among the nations. His life had global influence. His identity and work cast a net far beyond the narrow geography in which He moved. And so do the godly: they have potential for influence far beyond the confines of their time and place.

5. Jesus was believed in the world. His life had impact beyond the Church. He changed things on the inside but also on the outside. Quite simply, the godly change the world they live in. They change the way people see, the things they believe, the values by which they live. Their influence translates into transformation.

6. Jesus was taken up in glory. His life had ultimate purpose and reward. The godly live in the here and now but live with their eyes fixed on forever. They live in light of eternity. What motivates the godly is not earthly reward. It is the glory that will be revealed. Their treasure is in heaven.

That's godliness. But there is one enormous hurdle …

Worldliness
The opposite of godliness is not deviltry or demonism. That is the extreme opposite but not the common garden variety. Its opposite is worldliness. John describes worldliness this way: *For everything in the world—the cravings of sinful man, the lust of his eyes, and the boasting of what he has and does—comes not from the Father but from the world.* (1 John 2:16 NIV)

Worldliness is, in a word, selfishness. If godliness is God-centeredness, worldliness is self-centeredness. It's craving, lusting, boasting. It's me, me, me. It's getting what I want when I want it and then ballyhooing about it.

Here's my own homespun definition of worldliness: *Whatever makes sin look more attractive than God.* Whatever makes you think that defying God will bring you more reward than obeying God. That is worldly.

Worldliness is not the same thing as earthiness. Earthiness is an admission of our limitations, our frailties, our needs, and our possibilities as humans made in the image of God. In fact, worldliness and earthiness are so different as almost to be opposites. At some level worldliness involves a denial of our humanness.

I mention this because the cure for worldliness and the path to godliness is in fact to become more human. It is to live in an awareness of your creatureliness, so much so that you are utterly dependent on God. The worst thing you can do if you seek to be godly is to deny your creatureliness. You'll only end up faking it. Godliness is beautiful when it's the real deal and revolting when it's pretense.

So Two Things Are Needed
One, look and look and look again to Jesus. Come to Him you who are weary and heavy laden—He will give you rest for your soul and more besides. He will remake your soul. As you abide in Him, He promises, you will become like Him. For those who seek godliness, there is no substitute to being with Jesus, God in the flesh.

And two, practice and practice and practice the daily discipline of dying to yourself. This is worked out in the mundane more than the heroic. It is faithfulness in the small things before it can be carried off on the grand scale. It is the barb of sarcasm or the morsel of gossip or the retort of self-vindication that you *don't* speak. It is the flare up of anger that you take to prayer rather than take out on your wife. It is the burning lust or haunting loneliness that you refuse to treat in the habitual way. It is the quiet prompting to give to another that you obey rather than make excuses for why you cannot give this time.

As a boy, I wanted to grow up to be a cowboy, or a fireman, or a cop—something adventuresome, valorous, dangerous. Plus, with two of those vocations, you got to pack a gun and with one wield an axe. It amazed me that people got paid to do that.

I never got to be any of those. But it's okay. More and more, I'm setting my sights on something else, something higher, something that cowboys and firemen and cops and dentists and pastors and homemakers and students all can aspire to be.

I want to be a saint.

I want to be godly.

And you? **C**

Mark Buchanan lives on Vancouver Island, Canada, with his wife and three children. He is a pastor and the author of *Your God Is Too Safe*, *The Rest of God*, *The Holy Wild*, and his new release *Hidden In Plain Sight*. Some days he is restful or playful without shame. Check out his blog at **www.markbuchanan.net**.

Adapted with permission from Hidden In Plain Sight: The Secret of More *by Mark Buchanan, ©2007, Thomas Nelson, Inc., Nashville, Tennessee. All Rights Reserved.*

GROUP STUDY QUESTIONS
FOR DISCUSSION

1. As you examine your life implicitly, how can you live in such a way that others are aroused by the peculiarity of your hope?

2. As you examine your life explicitly, what response would you give when questioned about the reason for your hope?

3. What current opportunities surround you in your particular living environment, affording you the prospect to explain why you are hope-filled?

4. How can you best start to live so that the godless start asking questions?

5. How do you think worldliness stunts the development of godliness in your life?

6. How can you practice the daily discipline of dying to yourself in the mundane of your personal life?

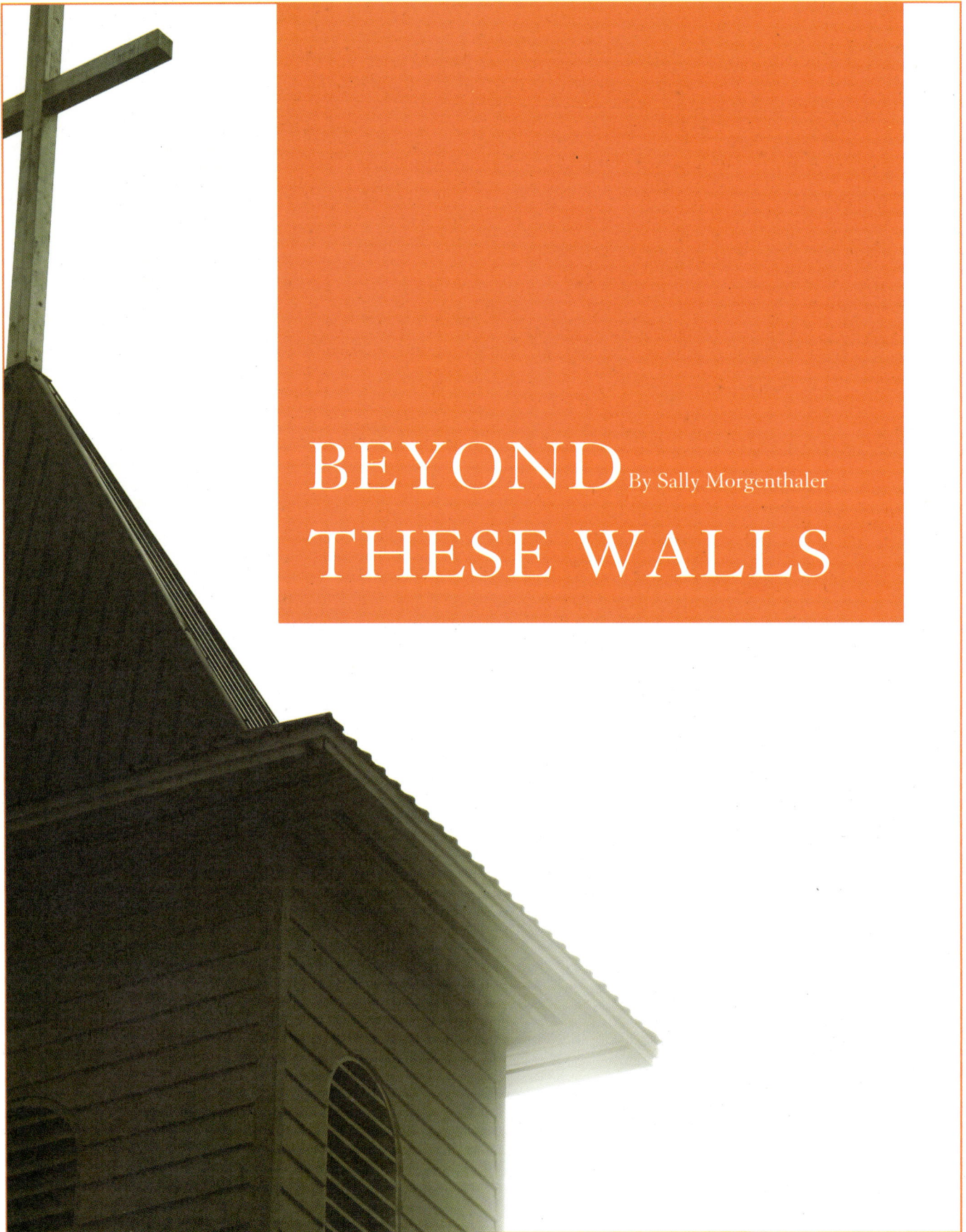

BEYOND By Sally Morgenthaler
THESE WALLS

A YEAR AND A HALF AGO, I TAUGHT MY LAST SEMINAR ON WORSHIP. A YEAR AGO, I DISBANDED MY WORSHIP RESOURCE SITE, *SACRAMENTIS*. MY COLLEAGUES WERE CONCERNED. HOW COULD I LEAVE THE WORK I'D BEGUN? DID IT MEAN I NO LONGER BELIEVED WORSHIP WAS IMPORTANT? WHO WAS GOING TO TAKE UP THE TORCH OF WORSHIP EVANGELISM? WAS I JUST GOING TO WASTE MY LEGACY? WAS I CRAZY?

Maybe I was, but a storm had been brewing in my soul for five long years. I remember meeting with the worship leader of a well-known church in the fall of 2000. He had followed my work and respected many of my viewpoints. When we met over coffee, he shared a concern he'd had for awhile. In his view, *Worship Evangelism* had helped to create a "worship-driven subculture." As he explained it, this subculture was a sizeable part of the contemporary church that had just been waiting for an excuse not to do the hard work of real outreach. An excuse not to get their hands dirty.

To be honest, I wasn't surprised. The attitude he described certainly didn't fit every congregation out there in contemporary worship-land, but it matched too much of what I'd seen. The realization hit me in the gut. Between 1995 and 2000, I'd traveled to a host of "worship-driven" churches, some who openly advertised that they were "a church for the unchurched." On the good occasions, the worship experience was transporting. Too many times, I came away with an unnamed, uneasy feeling. Something was not quite right. The worship felt disconnected from real life. Then there were the services when the pathology my friend talked about came right over the platform and hit me in the face. It was unabashed self-absorption, a worship culture that screamed, "it's all about us" so loudly, I wondered how any visitor could endure the rest of the hour.

Were worship-driven churches really attracting the unchurched? Most of their pastors truly believed they were. In a few cases, they were right. The worship in their congregations was inclusive, and their people were working hard to meet the needs of the neighborhood. Yet those churches where the emphasis was dual – celebrated worship inside, lived worship outside – were the minority. In 2001, a worship-driven congregation in my area finally conducted a survey to discover who they were really reaching, and they were shocked. They thought their congregation was at least fifty percent unchurched. The real number was three percent.

By 2002, a few pastors of praise and worship churches began admitting to me that they weren't making much of a dent in the surrounding non-Christian population, even though their services were packed and they were known for the best worship production in town. Several asked me to help them crack the unchurched code. One wanted to invest in an expensive VJ machine and target twenty-somethings. Another thought a multi-sensory, ancient-future, or emergent twist might help. However, when I visited their congregations, it was not hard to see that the biggest barrier to reaching the unchurched had little to do with worship technique or style—it had to do with isolation and the faux-worship that isolation inevitably creates.

BUT NUMBERS DON'T LIE. RIGHT?

As negative attitudes toward conservative Christianity among the unchurched increased in the late 1990s and early 2000s, most large congregations' growth efforts became more focused on the churched consumer, even as their written and spoken visions remained focused on the unchurched. These star-performers became masters at what the churched wanted.

They raised the bar several times over as to what could be expected out of a Sunday morning experience, and they worked tirelessly to develop the quality, practical programs that churched people now viewed as norm. Having excelled at making theirs the best-churched experience on the market, they were perfectly positioned to absorb the windfall of disgruntled attendees from both dwindling mainline congregations and failed, contemporary start-ups.

As influential as they are, mega-churches aren't the whole story of American religion. To get a complete picture of church growth in the 1990s and new millennium, we need to look at overall church attendance patterns. Traditional pollsters conduct telephone interviews and expect people to be honest about their religious practices. According to the numbers gathered this way, we're still at a forty percent attendance rate.

But pollsters who actually do seat counts and take exit polls tell a different story. The average weekly church attendance when measured by actual bodies present was at 17.4 percent in 2005, down from 20.4 percent in 1990. [1] David Olson of **TheAmericanChurch.org** remarks, "You'd have to find 80 million more people that churches forgot to count to get to 40 percent." [2]

The upshot? For all the money, time, and effort we've spent on cultural relevance, it seems we came through the last fifteen years with a significant net loss in church-goers, even with the proliferation of mega-churches.

THE TIDE CHANGES

In 2003, the film *Saved* debuted at the box office. Many evangelicals were horrified and panned the movie. The fact that the film was produced in the first place should have tipped us off that something was a-foot. The fact that it opened in theaters nationwide should have provoked a sizeable dialogue among contemporary church leaders about attitudes among the unchurched. It didn't.

Was the film exaggerated? Yes. It's satire. Was it "slanted?" Yes. But then, wasn't that the point? It was the chance for non-Christians to reflect back to us how some

of them perceive us. Truth hurts. Here was a film that depicted the smug, self-absorption of an evangelical school culture—complete with narcissistic praise and worship. I wondered if the dozen or so who walked out on it were Christians who didn't want to face themselves on the screen. If it hadn't been for my colleague drawing me aside in 2000, I could have been one those.

The question is, should cultural and missional realities have anything to do with worship? Perhaps not. It would appear that we're more than capable of creating our own view of the world, and we tend to promote and perpetuate that view in our sanctuaries and worship centers. Somehow, the show goes on … even if most of the unbelievers we thought we were reaching either weren't there in the first place, or they left the building some time ago.

NO MAGIC BULLET

Early in 2005, an unchurched journalist attended one of the largest, worship-driven churches in the country. Here is his description of one particular service:

"The (worship team) was young and pretty, dressed in the kind of quality-cotton-punk clothing one buys at the Gap … Male singers at (this) and other mega-churches are almost always tenors, their voices clean and indistinguishable …"

"They sound like they're singing in beer commercials, and perhaps this is not coincidental. The worship style is a kind of musical correlate to (their pas-

tor's) free-market theology: designed for total accessibility, with the illusion of choice between strikingly similar brands. The drummers all stick to soft cymbals and beats anyone can handle; the guitarists deploy effects like artillery but condense them, so the highs and lows never stretch too wide. Lyrics tend to be rhythmic and pronunciation perfect, the better to sing along with when the words are projected onto movie screens. Breathy or wailing, vocalists drench their lines with emotion, but only within strict confines. There are no sad songs in a mega-church, and there are no angry songs. There are songs about desperation, but none about despair; songs convey longing only if it has already been fulfilled." [3]

No sad songs. No angry songs. Songs about desperation, but none about despair. Worship for the perfect. The already arrived. The good-looking, inoffensive, and nice. No wonder the unchurched aren't interested.

The contemporary church—including the praise and worship church—was in a holy huddle, and I began to talk about it. It was excruciating. It was career suicide. But from pastors' conferences to worship seminars to seminaries, I began challenging leaders to give up their mythologies about how they were reaching the unchurched on Sunday morning. Yes, worship openly, unapologetically, and deeply. But let our deepened, honest worship be the overflow of what God does through us beyond our walls.

Let our deepened, honest worship be the overflow of what God does through us beyond our walls.

Conference organizers were confused. They wondered what had happened to me. Where was the worship evangelism warrior? Where was the formula? Where was the pep talk for all those people who were convinced that trading in their traditional service for a contemporary upgrade would be the answer?

I understood their dilemma, and secretly, I wished I had a magic bullet. But I didn't. And I wasn't going to give them false hope. Some new-fangled worship service wasn't going to save their church, and it wasn't going to build God's Kingdom. It wasn't going to attract the strange neighbors who had moved into their communities, or the generations they had managed to ignore for the last thirty years. As I pulled the *Sacramentis* site off of the web, I posted this statement:

"*Sacramentis* has been a pioneer site on worship and culture for seven years. From the beginning, it has been a gathering spot for the most helpful worship ideas and resources we could find. *Sacramentis* has also been a place where church leaders could go deeper into what classic Christian worship is and does and where they could re-imagine worship for communities where church-going is no longer the norm. But as culture has become incessantly more spiritual and adamantly less religious, we at *Sacramentis* have become convinced that the primary meeting place with our unchurched friends is now outside the church building. Worship must finally become, as Paul reminds us, more life than event. (Romans 12:1-2) To this

end, we will be focusing on the radically different kind of leadership practices necessary to transform our congregations from destinations to conversations, from services to service, and from organizations to organisms."

A NEW DESTINATION

Recently, *USA Today* featured an article entitled, "Can the E-Word (Evangelical) Be Saved?" [4] I think we need to ask a parallel question. "Can the W-Word (Worship) be saved?" Can it be saved from the definition that it's just what goes on inside the tent? Or from the lie that worship is a place you go, not what you do or who you are?

Ah, but aren't buildings important? Yes, they are. Jesus Himself spent crucial time in synagogues and the temple. He affirmed that the worship of God is central to what it means to be a disciple. But here's the catch. He did not make the building—or corporate worship—the destination. His destination was the people God wanted

to touch, and those were, with few exceptions, people who wouldn't have spent much time in holy places. Jesus' direction was always outward. Centrifugal. Even in death, He was broken and poured out for the sake of a needy world. God's work may not be all outside, but if we look at where Jesus spent his time, I think we can safely say that most of it is.

I am currently headed further outside my comfort zones than I ever thought I could go. As I exit the world of corporate worship, I want to offer this hope and prayer. May you, as leader of your congregation, have the courage to leave the "if we build it, they will come" world of the last two decades behind. May you and the Christ followers you serve become worshipers who can raise the bar of authenticity, as well as your hands. And may you be reminiscent of Isaiah, who, having glimpsed the hem of God's garment and felt the cleansing fire of grace on his lips, cried, "Here am I, send me." [5] **C**

Sally Morgenthaler has been a major influence in the worship world for fifteen years. Known best for her book, *Worship Evangelism*, Morgenthaler helps missional congregations craft worship that moves beyond the Christian subculture. Morgenthaler can be reached at **www.trueconversations.com**.

Reprinted by permission, Rev! *Magazine, Copyright 2007, Group Publishing, Inc., Box 481, Loveland, CO 80539.*

An Organic Appetite

By Margaret Feinberg

IT WAS ONE THING FOR MY JEWISH FATHER TO MARRY MY NON-JEWISH MOTHER. IT WAS ANOTHER THING COMPLETELY FOR BOTH OF THEM TO BECOME CHRISTIANS WITHIN A MONTH OF EACH OTHER EIGHT YEARS INTO THEIR MARRIAGE. LET'S JUST SAY THAT THE DECISION DID NOT GO DOWN TOO WELL WITH THE JEWISH SIDE OF THE FAMILY. (IMAGINE *MY BIG FAT GREEK WEDDING* WITHOUT THE HAPPY ENDING.) A MONTH AFTER THEIR CONVERSION, I WAS CONCEIVED, AND LESS THAN A YEAR AFTER MY PARENTS BECAME CHRISTIANS, I WAS WELCOMED INTO A WORLD OF RELIGIOUS TENSION. I DIDN'T KNOW IT AT THE TIME, BUT I BECAME THE BUNDLE OF GLUE THAT HELD THE FAMILY TOGETHER, BECAUSE AS UPSET AS MY JEWISH GRANDMOTHER WAS AT MY FATHER, SHE WASN'T GOING TO GIVE UP ACCESS TO HER ONLY GRANDCHILD.

As a result of my parents' backgrounds, I was raised in a Christian home with hues of Judaism. Think matzo ball soup at Christmastime. I never knew how many gifts my Jewish grandmother was going to give—whether I would hit the jackpot with the stack-o-gifts that accompany Hanukkah, or receive the one big present that inadvertently acknowledged Christmas even though it was still wrapped in Hanukkah paper. The confusion ended when Grandma began giving the gift that embraced the fullness of my Jewish heritage: a check.

Throughout the years, I managed to learn a few random words in Yiddish, develop a quirky Jewish sense of humor, and inherit an undeniable sense of chutzpah. I developed a desire to know how these worlds that seemed so opposed in my childhood could ever get along. I also developed a hunger to know God. This hunger wasn't anything I conjured up but rather seemed to be part of the "me-package," like a strand of DNA, though it took years to fully manifest itself. My initial interaction with Scripture wasn't so much out of longing as it was out of desperation. I was having terrible nightmares—the kind you can't forget even when you're an adult.

These night terrors continued for months. My parents held me. Prayed for me. Comforted me when they heard my screams. But the dreams didn't stop until I made a personal discovery. Somehow as an eight-year-old, I figured out that if I read the Bible before I went to bed, I would sleep soundly.

Two plus decades later, I'm sometimes tempted to shrug off my miracle cure as an oddity or merely chance, except for the fact that those evening readings made God all the more real and personal. I'm humbled that God would so tenderly and intimately embrace a child with simple faith. And I am staggered to realize how God was preparing me, even then, to know Him better.

Failure To Focus

Now there were a few years when I forgot about my experience as a young girl. I tried to run away from God and engaged in an extracurricular activity better known as partying like a rock star. But after a while, I returned to the routine I had learned at eight and began reading my Bible again.

All too often I find myself tempted to live a distracted life. You know the kind—the one where within the busyness of life you still manage to perform the stand-up, sit-down, clap, clap, clap of regular church attendance, hope for a new nugget of knowledge or insight from the weekly sermon and check off a random, albeit short, list of acts of kindness.

That's when the hunger appears in my belly and overtakes my soul, grumbling that there must be more. More of God not only to understand but to discover.

Deep down inside, I still hunger for a true, pure relationship with the Organic God—the One True God.

Real.Deep.Hunger.

While organic is usually associated with food grown without chemical-based fertilizers or pesticides, organic is also used to describe a lifestyle: simple, healthful, and close to nature. Those are all things I desire in my relationship with God. I hunger for simplicity. I want to approach God in childlike faith, wonder, and awe. I long for more than just spiritual life but spiritual health—whereby my soul is not just renewed and restored, but it becomes a source of refreshment for others.

I want to discover God again, anew, in a fresh way. I want my love for Him to come alive so that my heart dances at the very thought of Him. I want a real relationship with Him—a relationship that isn't altered by perfumes, additives, chemicals, or artificial flavors that promise to make it sweeter, sourer, or tastier than it really is. I want to know a God who in all His fullness would allow me to know Him. I want a relationship that is real, authentic, and life-giving even when it hurts. I want to know God stripped of as many false perceptions as possible. Such a journey risks exposure, honesty, and even pain, but I'm hungry and desperate enough to go there.

In some regards, the journey to know God isn't too different from a first encounter with someone you've never met. I want to know what God looks like and what His interests are. I want to know His likes and dislikes. I want to know what makes Him tick and also what ticks Him off. I want to fall in love all over again. I want to know God.

I want to know the Organic God. C

Margaret Feinberg (www.margaretfeinberg.com) is a speaker, blogger and author of more than a dozen books.

Taken from The Organic God *Copyright © 2007 by Margaret Feinberg. Used by permission of Zondervan.*

HALF-HEARTED KAMIKAZES

By Tim Elmore

Moving Generation Y from Involvement to Commitment

I HAVE A FRIEND WHOSE SON MADE THE VARSITY BASKETBALL TEAM HIS FRESHMAN YEAR. HE WORKED HARD TO MAKE THE TEAM, SO WE WERE ALL PROUD OF HIM. BECAUSE HE WAS A FIRST YEAR STUDENT, HOWEVER, HE DIDN'T GET A LOT OF PLAYING TIME. HE APPROACHED HIS DAD WITH AN IDEA. "DAD, I'M SITTING ON THE BENCH MOST OF THE TIME. I THINK I'M GOING TO QUIT THE TEAM AND DO SOMETHING ELSE. THE VARSITY TEAM ISN'T AS FUN AS I THOUGHT IT WOULD BE."

My friend's response was amazing. He sat down with his son and replied, "I know you had hoped to get more playing time this year, and I am sorry you're watching most games from the bench. It's tough when you'd rather be having fun on the court. But, son, I can't let you quit the team. Several other boys wanted the spot you won, and I am not going to let you flake now just because it isn't fun. You made a commitment to be on this team, and I want you to keep that commitment until the end of the season. Next year, if you don't want to risk sitting on the bench, it's OK. Don't try out."

These words, spoken with grace, are exactly what students need to hear today—especially if they are going to be leaders. Commitment comes with the territory. One psychologist said it this way, "The ability to keep a long-term commitment is one true sign of maturity."

If you're like me, you've moaned under your breath: where is the long-term commitment in this generation of kids? Why do so many seem like they have ADHD? Their attention spans last two minutes! The sad truth was summed up by a friend of mine who works at a college. "This generation of kids talks about changing the world, but they won't stay committed long enough to even change their campus." One Associate Dean told me, "Students want to change the world, but before they're ready to take any action, they change their minds instead."

This is the paradox of being part of the millennial generation. Students have a strong belief that they can transform society, but find it difficult to stick to an idea once the novelty of that idea wears off. It is easier to return to the comfort of their iPods and cell phones. According to *Weekly Reader's* Insider's Survey, half of students (ages 6-18 years old) believe one kid can change the world. Unfortunately, only 31 percent are actually doing any volunteer work that aligns with that belief. In other words, their optimism doesn't always equal action.

Let's face it. We should have predicted this. Many of these kids grew up being affirmed for every step they took, winning trophies, ribbons, prizes and pats on the back for anything—even finishing in 9th place. Parents clapped for everything. Few learned anything about perseverance. If a child failed, parents often swept them away before it could hurt their self-esteem. Unfortunately, life doesn't work that way. As an adult, work isn't always that rewarding. Projects can be hard and slow. And when colleagues don't continue to affirm a commitment, it's difficult to sustain that commitment.

WHEN CONVENIENCE ECLIPSES COMMITMENT

Let me summarize what I believe has happened, then suggest how commitment works with students. We live in a world of convenience. Kids today have been called the "disposable" generation because everything can be thrown away when they're finished with it. Likewise, they've been conditioned to believe that no commitment has to last too long. This can create problems morally and spiritually. For instance, during the summer following 9/11, France lost thousands of people in a heat wave. It was awful. But the worst part of the story came after the deaths. When the heat wave struck, 15,000 elderly people died in nursing homes and hospitals. Unfortunately, it was August and many families were on vacation. The children of those elders didn't even leave the beaches to come back and take care of their bodies. Institutions had to scramble to find enough refrigeration units to hold the corpses until family members finally came to claim them.

The loss of life was five times bigger than the terrorist attack of 9/11, yet it didn't trigger any change in French society. Why? Because keeping Mom and Dad alive is costly and inconvenient.

Convenience has eclipsed commitment. Sticking to what we believe to be right is hard because change is normal today—and because few are able to endure what is inconvenient. We complain about traffic lights being too long. We fill out a card if the service is sub-par at a restaurant. We even pace in front of our microwave, waiting for our snack! And this is truer for today's students than anyone else.

INVOLVED BUT NOT COMMITTED

I describe most students today with this phrase: involved but not committed. It's a Habitude from Book One of our series, *Habitudes: Images That Form Leadership Habits and Attitudes*. It is called, "The Half-Hearted Kamikaze." The syndrome is illustrated by the kamikaze pilot who flew in World War II for the Japanese Air Force. He was still alive after fifty missions! A journalist finally cornered him and asked, "Aren't you an oxymoron? How do you explain the fact that you've been on fifty missions, but you call yourself a kamikaze pilot?"

"Well it's like this," the pilot responded. "I was very involved ... not very committed, but very involved!" I always smile when I think of this story. A true kamikaze flies on one mission. He gives his life for it. There's no such thing as a half-hearted kamikaze. Commitment comes with the territory. The same is true of successful

A TRUE KAMIKAZE FLIES ON ONE MISSION. HE GIVES HIS LIFE FOR IT. THERE'S NO SUCH THING AS A HALF-HEARTED KAMIKAZE.

people today, especially leaders. Sadly, we want one without the other. Students today are active. They are more involved than ever. That's the strange thing about this dilemma. It isn't that they are isolated from each other or from good causes. It's simply that they want to keep all their options open. They want involvement without commitment.

HOW COMMITMENT WORKS

Let me ask you a question. How long did your New Year's Resolution last? Or, based on past failures, did you even make one this year? Most of us fail to keep commitments because we don't realize how commitment works. We want to move from a "wish" to a "lifestyle" overnight—and it usually doesn't work that way. The following are phrases we generally experience as we build commitment into our lives. Remember: students must begin with an idea and move to a conviction.

Ideas: We perceive an issue by the way we think about it—this involves our minds.
Opinions: We begin to express our preferences on the issue—this involves emotion.
Beliefs: We conclude where we stand on the issue—this involves both mind and emotion.
Commitments: We begin to act on our belief—this involves mind, emotion and will.
Convictions: We are ready to die for our commitment—it's now a passion in our lives.

Let me try to summarize how this generation often thinks. They are sometimes called the Mosaics. They don't think in a linear manner but rather like a computer would store information. It is a mosaic menu in their minds. They can live with contradictions; they are overloaded with information, and they are making decisions earlier than previous generations. Sometimes they are not emotionally ready to make some of these decisions. The vast majority thinks about their future weekly, trying to figure out their purpose in life. Parents are their greatest influence—over peers, teachers, or youth pastors. Many have been pampered, and their optimism may make you sick. Their number one goal is education, and they believe one person can make a difference in the world. Almost half are the Influencing style on the DISC test. They want to invest their lives in people and change the world.

STEPS YOU CAN TAKE TO HELP STUDENTS WITH COMMITMENT

So, how do we work with this generation who forgets the last commitment they made yesterday and has dozens of options in front of them today? What are some steps we can take to draw a more firm commitment from them? Let me suggest the following ideas.

1. Listen to them and affirm their dreams and goals.
2. Provide them a sense of big-picture purpose as they perform menial tasks.
3. Give them short-term commitments they can keep, and put wins under their belts.
4. Offer them realistic steps to their often over-optimistic goals; help them prioritize.
5. Work with them to focus on one, meaningful objective and pull it off.
6. Encourage them to simplify their life and remove any self-imposed pressure.
7. Discuss personal values with them and help them to become value-driven.

I trust you will model commitment and develop committed students under your leadership! C

Tim Elmore is the Founder and President of Growing Leaders (**www.growingleaders.com**), a non-profit organization created to develop and equip emerging leaders who will transform society. Through Growing Leaders, he and his team are providing leadership training to middle school, high school, and college students on hundreds of campuses in the U.S. Tim has authored numerous books, including *Habitudes: Images that Form Leadership Habits & Attitudes* and *Nurturing the Leader Within Your Child* (Thomas Nelson Publishers). Tim lives in Atlanta with his wife Pam and his two children Bethany and Jonathan.

STUPID THINGS I DO

BY FRANCIS CHAN

I WONDER IF THE INCONSISTENCY IN MY WALK WITH GOD HAS ANY-
THING TO DO WITH THE FACT THAT I CAN LEAD A "SUCCESSFUL" CHURCH
IN AMERICA WITHOUT BEING IN LOVE WITH JESUS. I'M SURE I COULD
BLAME AMERICAN CHURCH CULTURE, MY POSITION, OR A BUSY SCHED-
ULE FOR MY LACK OF REVERENT INTIMACY. THE TRUTH, HOWEVER, IS
THAT MY SIN AND HYPOCRISY IS A RESULT OF ME.

I FORGET TO LOVE GOD

It's not like I don't want to. In fact, when
I'm deeply in prayer, it's clear to me that
there's no place I'd rather be. I know that I
love God. When I sit and think about Him,
I'm filled with intense feelings of adoration. I'm convinced that He means more to
me than my wife, kids, or anyone else on
the planet. I just forget to love Him.

We can argue that we're busy doing ministry, which is how we express our love.
But if that's all God wanted, His words
to the Ephesians in Revelation 2 would
make no sense.

*"I know your deeds, your hard work and
your perseverance. I know that you cannot
tolerate wicked men, that you have tested
those who claim to be apostles but are not,
and have found them false. You have per-
severed and have endured hardships for my
name, and have not grown weary."* (NIV)

God recognizes the Ephesian church for
their wonderful ministry. Yet He makes
it clear in the next verse that they are not
loving Him. He tells them, *"You have for-
saken your first love."*

What has always surprised me about that
passage is God's threat to remove them

if they don't start loving Him again. *"If
you do not repent, I will come to you and
remove your lampstand from its place."*
God tells the hard working, sin hating,
doctrine-loving, persecuted church that
He doesn't want them around unless they
love Him. He's never been interested in
unloving children. His desire has always
been love. It was the great command in
the Old Testament and the New (Deut.
6:5, Matt. 22:37). Love was supposed to
be the catalyst of all godly action.

When is the last time you came alone
before your Father just to enjoy Him?
If it has been a while, don't waste your
time reading this article. Get alone and
adore Him. Pray that you would no longer
merely love Him through your religious
actions, but with the passion befitting a
person in love.

When I first fell in love with my wife, I
never "forgot" to call her or spend time
with her. Rarely, if ever, did she get
crowded out because I was so "busy."

I FAKE PASSION WELL

Leaders make the greatest hypocrites because of their ability to persuade and de-
ceive. Rarely is there a pastor whose character exceeds his reputation. If I were to

ask those closest to you about your relationship with God, what would they say? If I were to ask God the same question, what would He say? If your family, friends, and congregation have better things to say about you than God, it's because you give them that impression. We do this because we can. God gifted us with an ability to communicate. Too often we use this ability not to convey who we are, but who we want others to think we are.

It's similar to the church in Sardis, to whom Jesus says, "*I know your deeds; you have a reputation of being alive, but you are dead.*" (Rev. 3:1 NIV) Others believed the façade, but Jesus knew the truth. He reminded them that He knew of their spiritual deadness. The hope was that it would jolt them toward true life. God's desire for all believers, especially leaders, is "*life that is truly life.*" (1 Timothy 6:19 NIV) You've all had times, hopefully, when you experienced this "life." But when you aren't experiencing it, you fake it. Why? What's the point in faking it when you can *have* it?

I once heard a Christian leader say, "I refuse to let my public passion exceed my private devotion." As a leader, have you made that commitment? It could make for some pretty boring sermons.

It burdens me when I think we may have missed it. I ache when I consider how we are missing out. Remember, being obsessed with Jesus is a good thing. Trading the truth for a lie doesn't benefit you or any person you are leading. This isn't coming from a writer saying, "You must repent." It's coming from a fellow sinful leader saying, "We're so stupid if we don't." You can have genuine intimacy with Almighty God today. Why not?

I FOLLOW THE PEOPLE I LEAD

It is hard to be rejected. I hated it in junior high, and I still hate it today. It didn't take long to learn how to fit in, in order to avoid the pain of rejection. That ability has stayed with me and begs me to use it.

I know how to keep people from rejecting me and leaving the church. I know what words to say and which actions to take to keep people around. But when I do that, I'm no longer leading. I'm being led by the right or wrong desires of the people.

God calls us to give people what they need, based on His word, regardless of whether they stick around. Jesus led. Few followed, but He kept leading.

Last summer I came to a shocking realization that I had to share with my wife: If Jesus had a church in Simi Valley, mine would be bigger. People would leave His church to attend mine because I call for an easier commitment. I know better how to cater to people's desires so they stick around. Jesus was never really good at that. He was the one who said, "*He who loves father or mother … son or daughter more than Me is not worthy of Me.*" (Matt. 10:37 NIV) I'm much more popular than Jesus.

Having come to that conclusion, I came back to the church with resolve to call people to the same commitment Christ called them to. I knew that people would leave, and they have. I found comfort in that because, "*Woe to you when all men speak well of you, for that is how their fathers treated the false prophets.*" (Luke 6:26 NIV) Over time though, the conviction can fade, and it gets tiresome seeing people leave. There is a constant pull to try to keep people around rather than truly lead the faithful who remain. When my church was started, I used to tell my wife that I didn't care if we only had ten people, as long as they *really* loved God and desired to worship Him with all of their hearts. Where is that conviction now?

I sometimes wonder what I would have done if I were the pastor of the church in Laodicea. We're all familiar with that church in Revelation 3:14-22. It's the "lukewarm" church that Jesus said He would "spit out" of His mouth. Would I have been strong enough to overcome

IF JESUS HAD A CHURCH IN SIMI VALLEY, MINE WOULD BE BIGGER. PEOPLE WOULD LEAVE HIS CHURCH TO ATTEND MINE BECAUSE I CALL FOR AN EASIER COMMITMENT.

the prevailing attitude of the entire church? Or would I have eventually been sucked into its flow and fate? I like to think I could have stood alone, but I'm not so sure.

My youth pastor had a saying that I still remember twenty-five years later, "Leaders lead." It's what we do. It's what God has called us to do. Of course there's sadness when people refuse to follow you, but it's better than the sadness that would come if you stopped leading. Paul said boldly, *"Imitate me as I imitate Christ."* Don't be led by your people. Lead them. It's what you were made to do, equipped to do, called to do. It won't be long before we'll see that it was all worth it.

Galatians 6:9 *"Let us not become weary in doing good, for at the proper time we will reap a harvest if we do not give up."* (NIV)

Jeremiah 1:17 *"Get yourself ready! Stand up and say to them whatever I command*

you. Do not be terrified by them, or I will terrify you before them." (NIV)

Revelation 3:21 *"To him who overcomes, I will give the right to sit with Me on My throne, just as I overcame and sat down with My Father on His throne."* (NIV)

1 Timothy 6:11-12 *"But you, man of God, flee from all this, and pursue righteousness, godliness, faith, love, endurance and gentleness. Fight the good fight of the faith. Take hold of the eternal life to which you were called when you made your good confession in the presence of many witnesses."* (NIV) **C**

Francis Chan is the pastor of Cornerstone Church and the president of Eternity Bible College in Simi Valley. In addition to being a pastor, Francis speaks to thousands of youth throughout the U.S., challenging them to deeper commitment. He can be heard on his radio program "Truth Be Known." Francis has a great sense of humor, a genuine love for Christ and a commitment to teach straight from the Word of God. Francis and his wife Lisa have been married for 12 years and have three daughters and one son: Rachel, Mercy, Eliana and Ezekiel. He is a graduate of the Master's College and Seminary.

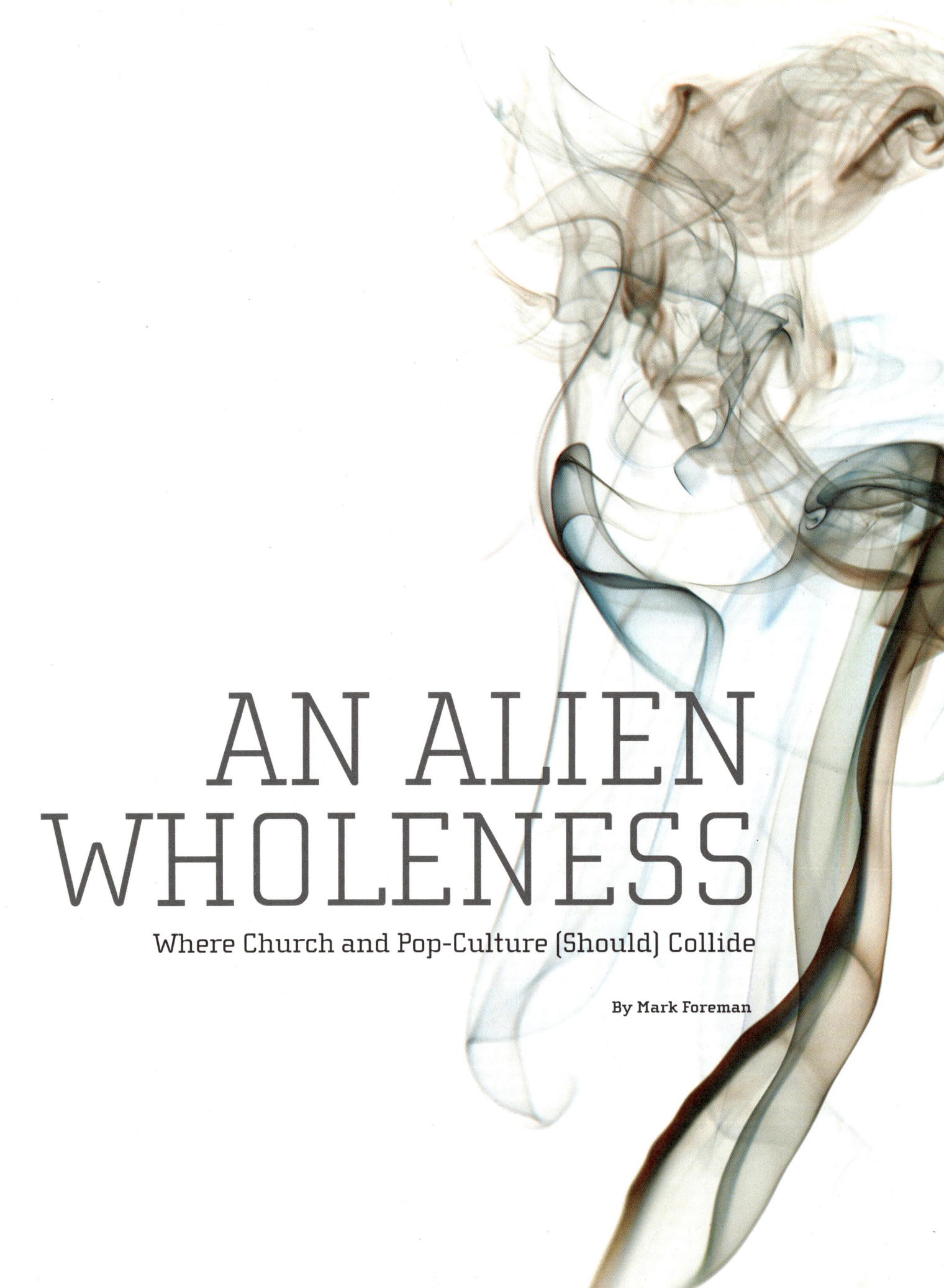

AN ALIEN WHOLENESS

Where Church and Pop-Culture (Should) Collide

By Mark Foreman

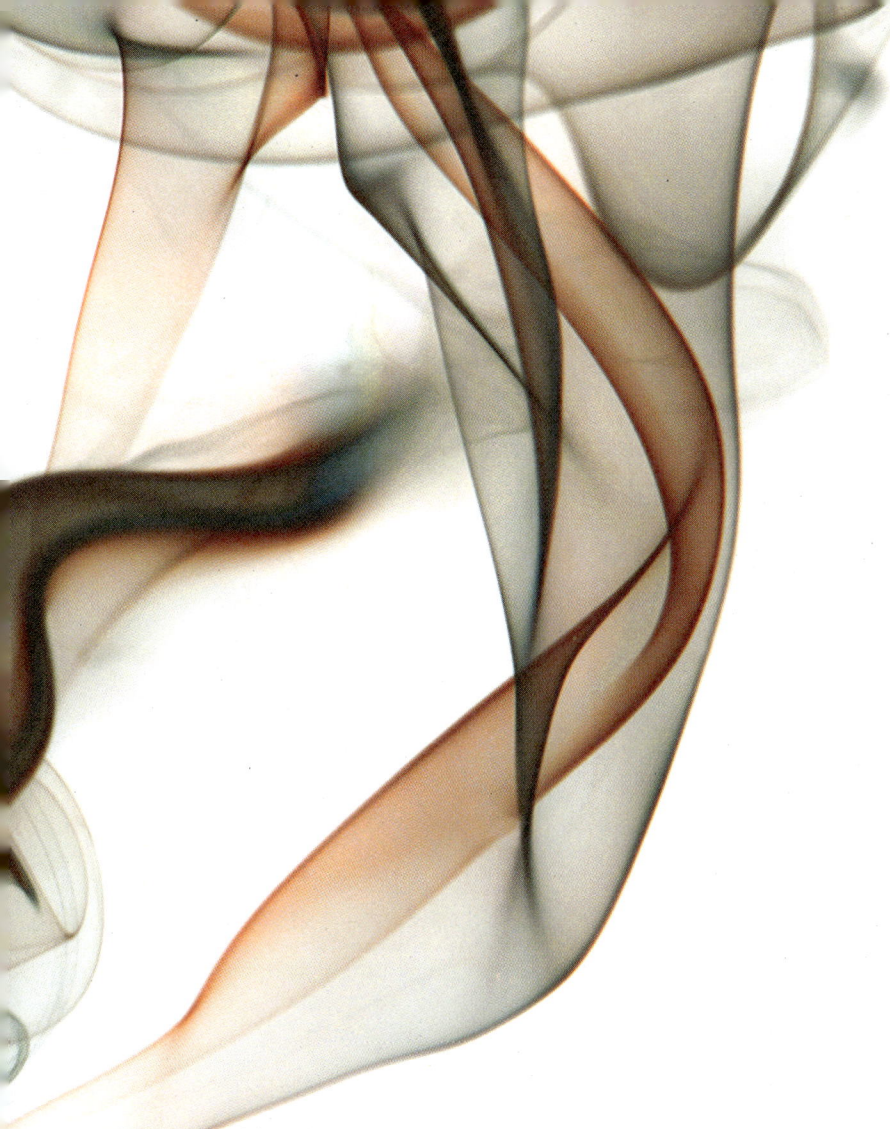

BETWEEN THE SURF COMMUNITIES OF CARLSBAD AND SOLANA BEACH, A LUSH MEDITATION GARDEN SPREADS ATOP OCEANFRONT CLIFFS. ITS IRON GATE OPENS TO A MEANDERING BRICK AND FLAGSTONE PATH FLANKED BY TROPICAL TREES, KOI-FILLED PONDS AND NOOKS OF SMOOTH BOULDERS AND MOSSY BANKS. I ARRIVED AT 7:00 A.M. FOR A DAYBREAK TRADITION.

Bluejean light illuminated the Pacific before the sun crowned the eastern horizon behind me. The garden looked empty. Whispering green space, swaying palm umbrellas, trickling brooks and pools—I had my pick of havens. I followed the path to a favorite on the west end, a bench nestled on the edge of a grass island facing a spectacular view of the reefbreak below. Locals call the break Swami's, after the garden's founder and longtime resident, the Swami Paramahansa Yogananda. He penned his renowned 1946 book *The Autobiography of a Yogi* while watching the same ebbs and flows.

I approached my familiar perch and noticed a grayed, middle-aged man reclining on the bench swallowed by blooming snapdragons. I slid quietly to another bench and watched patiently for him to leave.

Legs outstretched and crossed at the ankles, a plump gold pillow beneath him, the man alternated between closed-eyed meditation and open-eyed trance. Thirty minutes passed like seconds while my eyes ping-ponged between the bench and the surfers below. Eventually, I realized the only meditating I'd done was on my desire to go surfing and my need to drink coffee. I pushed myself up, left the garden and walked to the café across the street. As I waited in line, I read the corkboard's local advertisements:

"Ion Therapy—Living energy medicine"

"Living Prana—Enhancing your well-being holistically"

"Bon—The indigenous practice of Tibet"

"The Shaman's Work-Healing Spirit—The way of original medicine"

"Life Force Connection—A coaching and wellness center"

My turn to order came and the young lady behind the counter handed me a tall white cup. I pumped it full and headed back to the garden. The middle-aged man was climbing the steps to leave as I arrived ...

I'd thought a lot about spirituality in that garden, about themes for Sunday's sermon or topics from recent conversations. Lately, I'd been thinking and talking about the term wholeness. It comes up a lot nowadays. From yoga to Thai chi to meditation and naturopathic medicine, millions of Westerners are adopting Eastern philosophies centered on improving the whole person—body, mind and spirit. The café corkboard is Exhibit A.

Eastern-minded wholeness is no short-term fad either. Americans spend an estimated $3 billion a year on yoga alone, and more than $27 billion on naturopathic treatments in general. Wholeness is a booming industry. And so crowds flock to places like the meditation garden and its property-mate, the world-renowned Self Realization Fellowship. Every summer, I watch buses spill out wide-eyed hopefuls. They hope for the same thing.

I decided years ago that if opportunity presented itself, I would talk to those I met in the garden. Most are wonderful people and their stories are fascinating. Unless they ask, I rarely tell them I'm a pastor. It tends to muddle their perceptions and our subsequent conversation. I focus on listening and learning from them. The middle-aged man on the blooming bench was no exception. Before he passed, I struck up a conversation.

Richard is his name, he said, and he'd been visiting the garden nearly every day

for twenty years. We've probably crossed paths before, I said. He agreed.

"Can I ask you a personal question, Richard?"

"Sure."

"How does coming here help you?"

"Well," he replied, "I believe we're all on a path. Our paths are different and this kind of place isn't for everyone—but this is my path."

"What do you mean by 'path'?"

"Well, regardless of how we come to it, I think we're all searching for wholeness. I'm not saying it's right for everyone, but my path to wholeness goes through this garden."

The Whole World Has Gone Whole
We are proud, ambitious and brilliant. But whether or not we admit it, we are also porous beings, fundamentally shaped by outside forces: people, philosophies, trends, chemicals and the Divine. It seems we are predisposed to find our identity in something outside ourselves. Self-made is ultimately an illusion. Still, we live in a culture that largely believes we can fix ourselves.

Visit Barnes & Noble and you'll find an entire aisle dedicated to the enterprise of "self-help"—a book category that did not exist fifteen years ago. Its enormous ap-

peal today epitomizes a colossal trend. The-pursuit-of-wholeness is the current American self-help remedy.

While many begin their pursuit through the physical door—yoga, Thai chi, meditation—most want more than better health. Most hope also to find healing for their minds and enrichment for their souls—greater meaning to their existence, a fuller humanity. If only the Church were better at illuminating Jesus' offer.

The Savior offers nothing short of restoration to wholeness, complete humanity in unbroken relationship with Divinity, as it was in the first Garden. Only, His offer does not rely on self-restoration. We are not capable, He said. Instead, it is only through His-Spirit-in-us that wholeness can be attained. A wholeness that is wholly outside us, what German theologian Helmut Thieleke called an "alien wholeness." Full humanity from indwelling Divinity. And it is through this alien wholeness that God intends to make "all things new."

That we, the Christian Church, have largely missed the present significance of this offer is a critical consideration. For instance: Why, amidst a culture that seeks wholeness so intently—to the tune of $27 billion a year—do we still present a shrunken, otherworldly view of salvation? Additionally, given Jesus' offer of whole-

ness, could the infusion of Eastern philosophy into Western pursuits be good, something of a lesson from God? If so, should the Church then listen to the infusion and learn from it? Ultimately: Do the holistic pursuits of Western pop-culture speak to us about Christ's message of restoration in ways the Church has forgotten? Could we be guilty of limiting Jesus' full offer?

For certain, there are lines that have to be drawn as followers of Christ, but there are also lines that limit God's purpose. There are churches (and individuals) that already recognize the evangelical significance of Westerners' fascination with health and wholeness. They are, however, the minority.

A Wholly Posture
The prevailing Christian posture is still anti-Eastern philosophy and therefore distrusting (or at least ignorant) of the immense popularity of naturopathic treatment in general. A few in my own church still sneak to yoga class each week for fear of being cast as heretics. It's a sometimes humorous, sometimes embarrassing, all-times significant posture that we need to clarify and modify according to Scripture. We haven't done this for a while—but if there was ever a time, it is now.

Ultimately, when we clarify Jesus' offer and then place it in the context of mainstream spiritual conversation, we find many com-

mon threads. Knowing which threads form a tapestry of truth is a key to presenting people with the true redemptive wholeness they crave and need—people like Richard in the garden. It is also a key to knowing what elements about prevailing holistic philosophy we should embrace and what we should not. When he was in Athens, the Apostle Paul took stock of the city's culture. He learned the context of what the people were seeking, and on Mars Hill, he placed Jesus' message into the mainstream conversation—and it stuck.

As our conversation continued that early morning, Richard talked about how he came to his path to wholeness.

"I grew up in a Presbyterian church," he admitted with some discomfort.

"It wasn't for you?"

"Don't get me wrong. I know some people are on that path and that kind of place is where they need to be. I don't want to leave the impression I'm against Christianity because I'm not. But as I got older I started to realize that what I was looking for was life and I wasn't finding it at church. For

me, the church was all about dogma. All it wanted to do was argue and be right."

I intersect with life-seekers like Richard nearly every day where I live and nearly every time I travel. They are not shy to talk about what they seek. They want better health, a sounder mind and a soul at peace. They want a more whole life, a more meaningful life, and they look for it where it seems most likely to be found: in Eastern literature, in Buddhist temples, in yoga and Thai chi classes and in lush meditation gardens along the southern California coast next door to places called the Self Realization Fellowship.

Like Richard, many life-seekers see in the Christian church something we churchgoers don't: What we offer is not what Jesus offered. We have somehow reduced His promise of perfect wholeness to "forgiveness for now and hope for later." We *live* half-lives while the Spirit of whole-life dwells in us. We *offer* half-life with the promise of wholeness in our hearts and hands. It's a pattern we have to change. That begins when we comprehend Jesus' full message and then place it in today's spiritual dialogue. The combination has eternal implications. ◼

Mark Foreman is the surfer-pastor of North Coast Calvary Chapel in Carlsbad, CA where his suggestions have been playing out for years. He is currently writing a book on the same subject, of which this article is an excerpt.

Used by permission. Copyright © 2007 Mark Forman. All rights reserved.

END SLAVERY—PERIOD.
THE CALL OF A GENERATION

GARY HAUGEN

MORE THAN 25 MILLION HUMAN BEINGS ARE SLAVES IN 2007. THEY ARE NOT SLAVES IN A METAPHORICAL SENSE. THEY ARE HELD IN FORCED SERVITUDE BY OTHER HUMAN BEINGS. THE STATISTICS MAY SEEM INCOMPREHENSIBLE, BUT MY COLLEAGUES AND I HAVE KNOWN THOUSANDS OF THEM BY NAME.

When William Wilberforce sought to abolish the slave trade in the British Empire in 1807, about 50,000 new slaves a year were being boarded onto British ships. While that was a nightmarishly large number for its day, there are far more *children* sold into sex slavery every year in the 21st century—to say nothing of the millions of adults held in other forms of slavery in the mines, rock quarries, brick factories, plantations, and rice mills of our world.

What a tragedy it would be if amidst all the movies and memorials celebrating the life of Wilberforce, Christians missed out on the chance to actually do what Wilberforce did—to be used of God to set slaves free, to bring an end to slavery in this generation, and to bring honor to the mission of Christ in the world.

What follows are, in my opinion, the fundamental challenges.

WILL OUR SENSE OF MISSION REFLECT GOD'S PASSION FOR THE WORLD BEYOND OUR BORDERS?

The vast majority of modern-day slaves live in countries that are far away and unfamiliar to North Americans. But the slaves of the British Empire were infinitely more remote for the millions of common English Christians who nevertheless joined the abolitionist movement—all without the benefit of CNN, anti-slavery websites, television documentaries, or jet air travel. "Am I not a man and a brother?" pleaded the slave figure etched on campaign paraphernalia of Christian abolitionists 200 years ago. Indeed, with a leap of moral solidarity that still baffles historians to this day, common Christians of Wilberforce's England determined that these slaves, suffering in remote lands they would never even see a picture of, actually were their neighbors—and that Christ's command of "do-unto-others" kind of love extended to them as well.

This will be the most fundamental challenge for many American congregations. We hear "for God so loved the world," but often we don't think much about the world He loves.

WILL OUR SENSE OF MISSION RECOGNIZE THE VIOLENCE IN TODAY'S SLAVERY?

Today, many North American Christians who have entered the joy of God's passionate global mission embrace evangelism and compassion ministries that bring food, housing, micro-loans, and medicine to the poor. Yet many are also beginning to see the true basis of slavery, which is another source of suffering for the poor—aggressive violence. That is the core reality of forced labor: coercion and terror. Poverty, ignorance, and spiritual darkness are all part of a complex set of social factors that exacerbate slaves' original vulnerability. But once enslaved, they need someone to rescue them from the brutal hand of their oppressor.

For Nagaraj and his family, there was no mystery about what kept them and 80 other slaves inside the four walls of their compound. They worked 16 hours a day, six days a week, making bricks, to avoid the vicious beatings unleashed upon those who tried to run away. For Elisabeth, a 16-year-old girl held inside a brothel in Thailand, it was money for Bible college that lured her into the hands of a sex trafficker who lied about a job across the border. Once inside the brothel, however, it was sheer violent terror that forced her to submit to multiple rapes by the brothel's paying customers.

To love these neighbors—and the millions of slaves they represent—the people of God must be biblically and spiritually prepared to confront this violence. But how do we do that?

WILL OUR SENSE OF MISSION RECOVER THE WORK OF JUSTICE?
Wilberforce could have done many things to show Christian love to the slaves of his era. He could have sent them Bibles, food, teachers, or paid for their freedom. He could have "transformed the cultural worldview" of slave owners and traders. But he didn't. Instead, he gave them, of all things, a law that made the buying and selling of slaves illegal.

Why? Because he knew that the core ingredient of slavery was violence. He also understood that the problem of violence was properly dealt with in human society by law—bringing to bear the power of government to protect the weak.

You can give all kinds of goods and services to the poor in the name of Christ—but if you have not restrained the hand of the oppressor from simply taking these things away, you have not done much that is significant or sustainable.

WILL OUR SENSE OF MISSION REFLECT THE GOD OF JUSTICE?
It is the Lord who commands us to "seek justice, rescue the oppressed, defend the orphan, and plead for the widow" (Isa. 1:17), and it is Almighty God who promises to go with us as we declare to the Pharaohs of this world, "Let my people go." (Ex. 5:1)

Unlike Wilberforce's era, today's struggle to love the victims of slavery in our world will not be a battle to pass laws, but to enforce them. The problem is that poor people, ethnic minorities, low-caste laborers, and children simply don't get the benefit of law enforcement. Fortunately, there are four steps that every American Christian can take to begin to change that:

1. Learn the facts about modern-day slavery. Pray with others about what you are learning, and help your faith community become aware of the problem.
2. Petition your representatives in the U.S. government to make enforcement of anti-slavery laws a priority in relations with countries that tolerate high levels of forced labor.
3. Help pay for the investigative and legal advocates that slaves need to secure freedom and protection under the law.
4. Help pay to secure aftercare and rehabilitation services for the long-term restoration of former slaves.

I imagine it would be quite a disappointment to Wilberforce if we looked past the millions of slaves in our world and found in his life only a metaphor for the zealous pursuit of what we should be doing. May we not only rediscover the story of Wilberforce, but also the joy of living it. 🅲

For more from the Christian Vision Project and Gary Haugen, visit **www.christianvisionproject.com**.

CHRISTY NOCKELS
SINGER, SONGWRITER, WORSHIP LEADER
Age 33, Franklin, Tennessee, www.christynockels.com

CHRISTY NOCKELS WAS BORN IN FORT WORTH, TEXAS, A SEMINARY BABY. SHE GREW UP IN OKLAHOMA AS THE DAUGHTER OF A PASTOR AND A PIANO TEACHER, WHICH INFUSED HER HEART EARLY WITH A LOVE FOR BOTH MUSIC AND GOD'S WORD.

WATERMARK ORIGINS
I met my husband Nathan in 1993 at the Christian Artists Seminar in Estes Park, Colorado. It was love at first sight! We married two years later and began serving as worship leaders in our local church in Oklahoma City while Nathan finished college and I taught preschool. It was during those early years that many future Watermark songs were written in our little one bedroom apartment.

Soon after Nathan's graduation, we were invited to move to Texas where we led worship at Metro Bible Study, a weekly gathering of 3000 young adults at Houston's First Baptist Church. It was there that we were "discovered" by the folks at Rocketown Records. Eventually we signed a recording contract and moved to Nashville in 1998. Around this time we also became involved with the Passion Conferences.

With the release of our fifth recording, *A Grateful People*, in the Spring of 2006, Nathan and I laid down our Watermark journey to pursue other areas of ministry, allowing the family to stay home a little more throughout the year.

A MINISTRY SHIFT
Now that things have shifted for us ministry-wise, I'm beginning to focus my efforts on ministering to women. My deep desire is to encourage young women through worship and teaching, as well as to encourage women of all ages to pursue mentoring relationships. I'm currently mentoring some young women in my hometown who are called to worship ministry. Ultimately, my heartbeat is to see young women open up their lives fully to God and to leave a legacy with the young church to proclaim the name of Jesus over this generation.

COURAGE IN COMMUNITY
If we want to influence this culture and this generation for Christ then I believe it's important that we speak a language the culture understands, and that we, as Christians, remain accessible to people. I believe the Spirit of God within us can powerfully use us within our culture if we seek out ways to live and work among the lost—shining a glorious light.

One way we can be that light is by pursuing community. It takes courage to pursue community, but the experience can be life changing. It's been especially significant to me being in ministry. For years I neglected it—excusing myself due to my travel schedule. But making the commitment to pursue true community with fellow believers has taught me how precious accountability is—and how much courage it takes to commit to "walk life" with others. C

No More Heroes

By Priscilla Shirer

It was Jackson's fourth birthday. Anticipating a fun-filled day of celebration, he dressed quickly for church. I fitted him with a birthday hat and secured a dollar bill to his shirt. I knew this would encourage others to assist me in celebrating. By the end of the church service my little man had almost $30 attached to his sweater.

Taking the opportunity to teach a spiritual lesson on tithing, I explained we must give the first portion to God and asked Jackson to choose a few dollars we could give to the Lord. He carefully selected several. As I guided him to the offering container in the lobby, I felt his hand go limp and noticed his eyes widen with emotion. He scanned the lobby anxiously. "Jackson," I asked, "What are you looking for?" Without hesitation, he responded in childlike simplicity, "Didn't you say we were bringing money to the Lord? Is He here in the lobby somewhere?"

I laughed and tried to explain the finer points of tithing. My explanation was cut short when Jackson stopped dead in his tracks and gasped deeply. Looking across the lobby he beheld the man who leads worship during our services. With an outgoing, expressive personality, this man who holds the microphone on stage each week seemed larger than life to my child. With his eyes widened and mouth agape, Jackson exclaimed, "Mom, is that THE LORD?" The Psalmist posed a similar question in the 24th chapter, "Who is this King of Glory?" His simple response must resonate in the hearts of the whole earth, "The Lord God who is strong and mighty, the Lord who is mighty in battle." He, alone, is the Lord.

With eyes widened and mouths agape like seeking children, we have pointed at the human celebrities of our faith and set them on a pedestal with God. We read their commentaries on the Bible more than the Bible itself. When they minister, we applaud in their faces instead of at worshipping at His feet. We have unashamedly dished out adoration reserved for the Most High. How often have we subconsciously placed mere humans in the position reserved only for the Great One?

The more visible the gift and the more celebrated the ministry, the more we subconsciously align a human with the Almighty. It is alarming how frequently the Church has glorified the ones for whom Christ died. We have begun to worship our "heroes."

Our tendency to place others in the position reserved for God must end. The Lord alone is the One to whom we are to turn our gaze and attention. It is He who deserves our utmost respect and celebration. When we sing, we do so to the glory of the Lord. When we give, we do so out of the abundance that He has allowed us to enjoy. In all of these things, our object of affection must be clearly pinpointed. We must not allow the veil of humans to stand in the way of our clear view of God.

No more heroes. No more Christian celebrities. Seek the Lord alone. He is the One worthy of your everything. Today, ask yourself, "Who is my Lord?" See where your search leads. **C**

Priscilla Shirer is a Bible teacher whose ministry is focused on the expository teaching of the Word of God to women. Her desire is to see believers not only know the uncompromising truths of Scripture intellectually but experience them practically by the power of the Holy Spirit. Priscilla is now in full-time ministry to women across the country. Find out more at **www.goingbeyond.com**. She is married to her best friend, Jerry, and they live in Dallas, Texas with their two sons.

PASSIONATE ABOUT GOD

Make God personal, starting now. Take a prayer walk or steal away to a private place—a place only the two of you know about. Spend time praising Him for who He is, not just for what He's given you. Write down His attributes and how they bring you hope. After you spend time praising Him, just listen to His still, small voice. When we take time to listen, we don't have to guess at His calling on our lives.

VI. INTENTIONAL ABOUT COMMUNITY

People are in my life at all levels. Close personal friends that keep me accountable, question my deepest motives, and help me stay true to the wisdom God has imprinted on my heart. I value the people that work for and alongside me, recognizing that I am fulfilling a leadership role with people God has entrusted to my care. I value the wisdom of those more experienced than me and seek out council in all things of importance.

The Driftwood Chronicles

Why Nothing Matters Except Pursuing Others
The Way God Pursues Us

By Chris Seay

VISIONS OF THE CHURCH OFTEN SPRING UP IN THE STRANGEST PLACES. I SPENT A YEAR IN HIGH SCHOOL WORKING EVENINGS AND WEEKENDS FOR A SMALL COMPANY THAT RECORDED ALCOHOLICS ANONYMOUS MEETINGS AND SOLD THE TAPES TO ALCOHOLICS WHO WERE LONGING FOR CONSTANT ENCOURAGEMENT IN THEIR STRUGGLE TO STAY SOBER. AT THIS POINT IN MY JOURNEY I HAD BECOME PRETTY DISILLUSIONED WITH WHAT I SAW IN THE CHURCH.

Our Sunday gatherings were the place where we got cleaned up to sing the great hymns, read the scriptures, and come together with all of God's people—at least the people of God that agreed with us. But the make-up and perfume were masking more than a foul odor or emerging acne. We were hiding the truth about who we were. Sin was what other people did, and the really bad sins were the ones that we believed we, or those we loved, would never struggle with. So we put our best foot forward, bragged about our good deeds, and hid all the rest.

So you can imagine my surprise when I went to an AA meeting and saw the people in these meetings, who were mostly Christians, speak with an honesty I had never heard before. They stated their names, confirmed they were alcoholics, and then circumspectly confessed their sins and struggles:

"I am gay."

"I am fat, and I eat to relax."

"I masturbate habitually."

"I am diabetic, and I eat sugar all the time despite the reality that it is killing me."

"I lose my temper and yell at my kids."

"I spend money that I don't have."

"I live in fear of not being accepted."

"I use violence to intimidate the people I love the most."

"I pay people for sex."

Once, I even heard a man acknowledge that he killed his cousin in a drunken rage. These people were broken, but the beauty was that their lives were changing; things were getting better. It was amazing! I had never seen anything like it before. From my earliest years in church I heard stories of people that had sex, did drugs, and drank beer before they met Jesus and then never sinned again—or so I thought. But I never knew anyone struggling with sin, confessing it to brothers and sisters, and finding freedom from the bondage that was destroying them in a loving and redemptive community.

I had a passing thought that I should become an alcoholic so that I could know community in this way, but then I remembered that the book of Acts records that the first emerging church was better than any AA meeting on the planet. That's what I wanted to devote my life to: shaping the church to be a place of safety, beauty, and hope.

A Healthy Community

In recent weeks I have been reminded of the important New Testament principles of healthy community. These reminders have come through new and fresh experiences. Like going on a sailing trip with some friends from our church to the British Virgin Islands—yes, I know, a painful voyage for most, but I was willing to sacrifice. So despite the risk of sounding like a third-rate Bill Hybels, who uses the metaphors of sailing with skill and beauty, I would like to tell you how my week sailing the Caribbean offered amazing insight into life as a missional community.

There were seven of us that signed on from my home church Ecclesia. Seven stout men crammed into the galley of a sailboat—forced to climb out of ourselves so that we could live with one another. This is one of the greatest challenges we face as humans: the challenge to love, trust, give, and receive with each other. I wasn't prepared for the profound understanding I would gain from this sailing trip—the painful beauty of community and redemption. But is my "Aha!" moment really so surprising? After all, the word *ecclesia* means "gathering, church: those called out to live life together." We are called to this kind of life.

The parting words of my friend's wife were, "The interesting thing about this trip is that these guys are going to either come back loving one another or hating one another." I thought this was a bizarre statement; we were just taking a vacation together. But the beauty of being thrown into a small space with six other brothers came down to what we decided this particular community would look like. It reminded me of what my brother and I dreamed and prayed over during the birth of Ecclesia:

How will we live together in community?

How will we treat one another?

Will we get beyond ourselves and be part of something much more significant in the world?

What will that look like?

Will we sail into a storm and die?

And there we were, thrown together on a boat with this to figure out: *How will we relate to one another?* And even as I reflect on this journey, I realize there is so much for us, as "the called," to hear. The close community we developed on the vast ocean, where I got to talk about my real world obstacles, was accepted, loved, and understood—that community that helped me bounce back from flat-lining from all I was up against to feeling great again. Truly, how we relate to one another is unbelievably important.

In this thought, I found a few key things to share from my journey that I believe if we would really live, as the ecclesia, would be life changing. So, tear out this page or write these things down, because it's rare that I ever give bullet points, but here I go ...

1. Pursue One Another

Take the time to genuinely seek one another. Each night on the boat, instead of playing poker like we planned (I'm convinced they were afraid I'd take them to the cleaners) it was suggested we share our life stories with one another—it just felt right. So each night in this group spanning from thirtysomethings to sixtysomethings we shared a meal, sat together, and listened as someone shared their story. A beautiful thing happens when someone gets to the broken parts of their story, and all of us have broken parts in our story. Some of us haven't come to grips with all of them, but they're there.

I often get a phone call the night before someone opens up their life, asking me if they really have to tell their whole story or if they can give the PG version (because truthfully, we are deeply afraid that "if they really knew me, if they really knew all of my story, there's no way they would love me." Right?). But, without exception, every time people begin to share their story—it happens in these groups, it happened on this boat—you could watch those in the circle literally move closer to them as they entered times of brokenness in their story.

The truth is most of us aren't bonded together around our perfection. James says the person who's mastered his tongue is perfect. (James 3:2) I don't know about you, but I don't know anyone who has mastered the art of even stubbing their toe without losing it. But on the boat you

In the act of pursuing one another, a space was created to be real, open, and honest.

could see us bonding together because of our imperfections, with people crowding in, closing the circle, physically agreeing, *"I am with you. I am broken like you are. I love you, and I am not going anywhere."*

In the act of pursuing one another a space was created to be real, open, and honest.

If you are isolated, you need to be thrown into a boat with someone, to have to live in close proximity with others so you will have to figure out how to live in togetherness, and I pray that when you do, it happens for you like it happened for us this week. As we chose to be honest and real with one another and to pursue one another, liberation showed up.

So ask yourself: What does it mean to pursue others in relationships? When was the last time you were pursued beyond just the standard A+B=C conversation: *Hey, how are you doing? What do you do?* but honestly pursued—*Who are you? I would like to know you.* I desperately pray that in community we can honestly say we are seeking to truly know one another, to get beyond the surface, into a place of honesty and reality.

2. Empower

Even more surprising for me is that power structures often rock the boat. On a boat, someone has to be in charge—someone who knows how to sail. I found that what is true in business is also true on a boat—how hierarchy plays out will dictate the entire ride. For example, if you have a captain who knows how to sail but is a dictator, odds are you'll have a mutiny.

But on this boat, our friend and captain shared his power in a way that was beautiful, even allowing his son-in-law to act as captain even though he didn't have as much sailing experience. *When you live in a space where power is shared and not hoarded, beautiful things begin to happen.*

On that boat we were going nowhere if each of us didn't work together as a team. It was imperative that we served one another—working in concert to perform our tasks for the greater good—while operating the ship. The same is true in the redemptive narrative of the Christian life.

3. Destroy Walls

Recently, my friend Greg Holder shared a sermon here at Ecclesia. He remarked, "Wherever we are, we draw lines, and whatever lines are drawn, it's our job to erase them. It's our job to break down the walls to bring people together." As I reflected on his words throughout our trip, they struck me even more.

On the high seas we discovered there were two classes of people:

The Sailors - who sit on their boats and sip cabernet and eat Gouda cheese.

The Fishermen - who throw back Old Milwaukee while crunching pork rinds.

Between these two classes was animosity. The sailors hate the fishermen because they cut across in front of their boats and steal "their" wind. But we weren't really sailors, and out of ignorance in regards to the divisions on the high seas, we brought along our fishing poles (not that we caught any fish, so I guess we're not fishermen either). So the picture is us on our sailboat, towing our lines behind us, clearly misfits to both groups of people. The sailors didn't really like us and nei-

ther did the fishermen, but because we blurred the line between the two groups we could go and strike up a conversation with any of them.

That's what the Gospel is about. Beauty is invited in when we pursue one another and wake up to find there's no Jew. There's no Gentile. Where people of totally different ethnic classes, cultures, and races come together in community and say, "I want to walk alongside you." We desperately need to be part of a community where fences are being torn down, where we're drawn together with people

This is what the Gospel calls us to be, a gathering of people intentionally choosing to live well together.

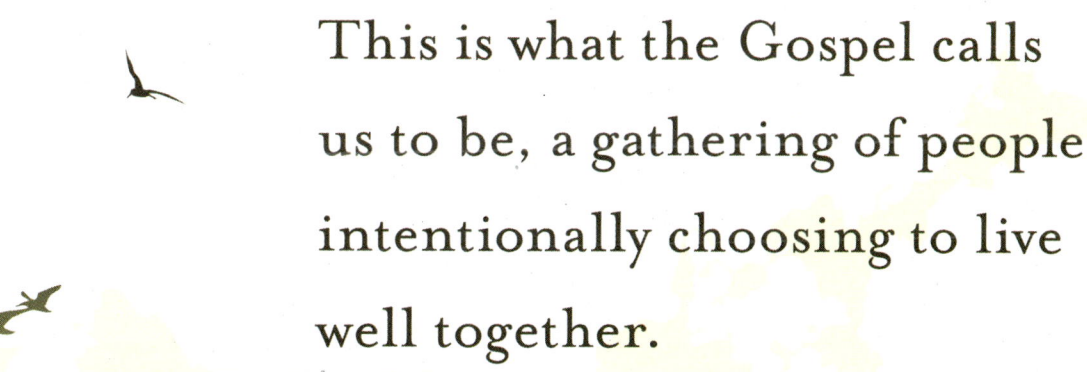

who aren't like us, where we get to learn from one another, where beautiful things can begin to happen.

4. Suck The Marrow Out of Life

Most of us live at an unbelievable pace—we rarely stop. While sailing, we'd stop everything to witness the sun sink out of the sky into the water, to watch the colors blow up and then snuff out—there was nothing else to do but sit and watch it. We met beauty face to face.

Back in the real world, with a phone that's constantly ringing and emails pouring in, we fail to see the beauty in one another, in nature, and in creation. I want to be part of a community where people are constantly taking the time to soak in beauty, where people will take the chance to laugh: Laugh at one another, laugh at ourselves. If the Gospel makes us so serious that we can't enjoy ourselves, what good are we? We need to fully embrace beauty and laughter when it is before us.

5. Recognize Love

But even through the jesting and the fun, we'd state often and clearly that love was present among us. It was a goofy little thing, a bunch of men on a boat ... sleeping in extremely close quarters ... packed in like sardines. There could have easily been sparks, but we decided at some point—I don't remember when, maybe God decided it—that we were going to speak lovingly to one another and choose to declare that love.

So when problems arose, it was in this foundation that the air we were breathing was one of love and care for one another. The hardest thing to do is not only to be loving toward someone, but to speak lovingly (James 3). If you can begin to deal with the words that come out of your mouth, then community will build and strengthen. People are attracted to those who chose to live and speak from love. I find great hope in a community committed to living like this. This is what the Gospel calls us to be, a gathering of people intentionally choosing to live well together.

The truth is that our lives are not always sailing on smooth water. At any time we may be struggling to survive. Like Paul the Apostle who survived a shipwreck by holding onto a small piece of the ship, we are simply hoping to make it. Our lifeline is the Church and we are called to care for one another. So if your plans to create tremendous programs do not include finding people to live with—up close and personal—then abandon them. Our first priority is each other; everything else is driftwood.

It never fails to amaze me the miracles that happen at Ecclesia when people live together in the love of Christ and abandon all other pretense. **C**

Chris Seay leads a unique congregation at Ecclesia – Houston that is living out the Gospel faithfully in an urban environment. He is also the author of seven books. Learn more at **www.ecclesiahouston.com**.

1. What keeps you from sharing your true self with fellow believers?

2. In your small group, take time right now to share your story—unedited and unencumbered by pretense. Then reflect on how this transparency affects your group.

3. What does it look like for you to "share power" in your ministry context?

4. We must be intentional about destroying societal walls. Are you a barrier builder or a wall destroyer? Make a list of action steps that will promote a culture of inclusion.

5. Next time your group meets, do so at a lake, park, beach, or garden. Discuss how you can soak in beauty in your own lives.

6. Words can cut or inspire. Take inventory on your verbal impact: What can you change to promote a community built on speaking love to others?

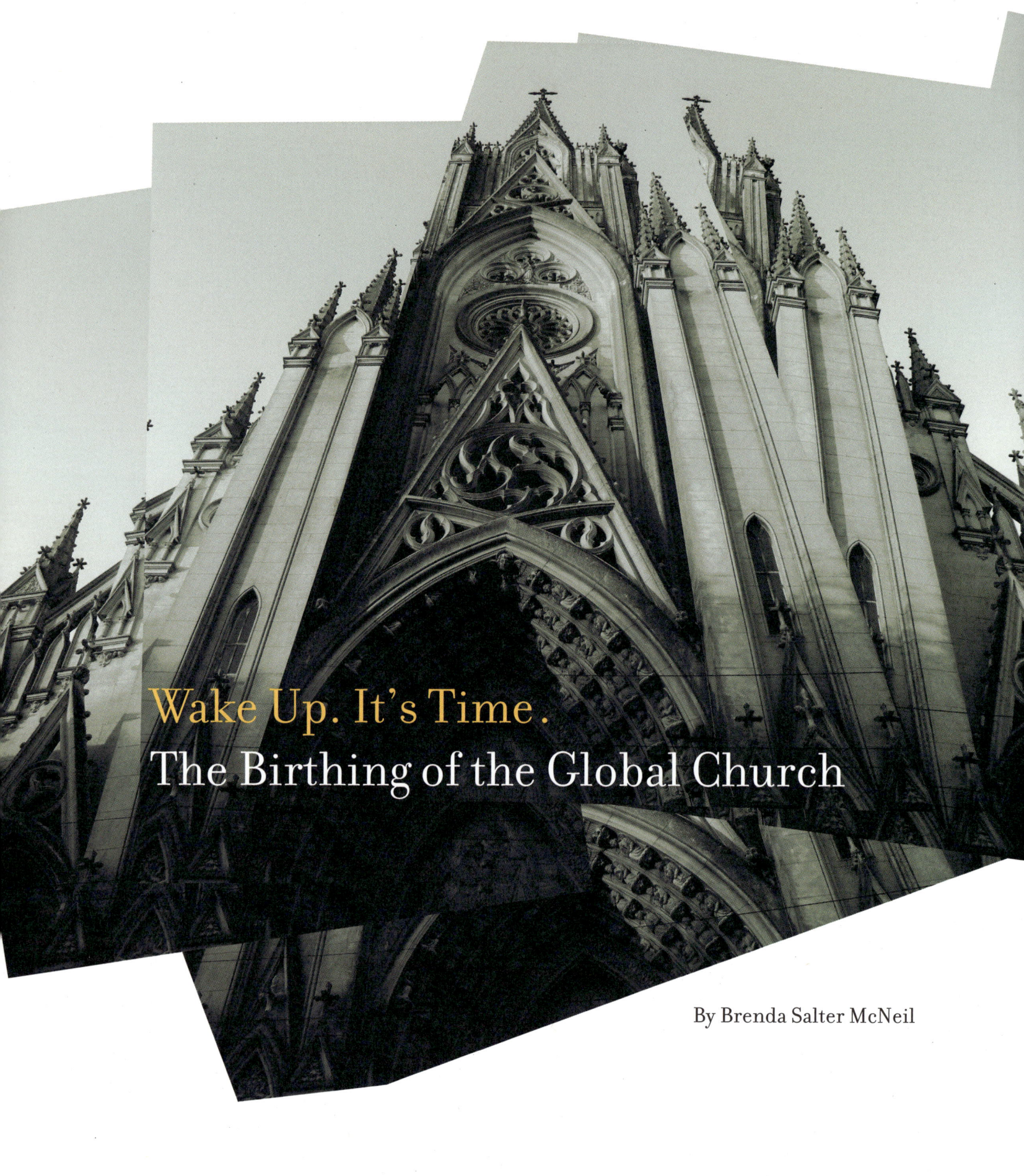

Wake Up. It's Time.

The Birthing of the Global Church

By Brenda Salter McNeil

IN 1986, I DISCOVERED THAT THE WORLD WAS CHANGING. THAT YEAR MY HUSBAND AND I TRAVELED TO ENGLAND, ALONG WITH A TEAM OF SEMINARY STUDENTS AND PASTORS FROM FULLER THEOLOGICAL SEMINARY, TO LECTURE AT THE OXFORD CENTRE FOR MISSION STUDIES ON THE HISTORY OF THE BLACK CHURCH IN AMERICA.

Then, as now, the Church of England was facing unprecedented institutional challenges and numerical decline. Beautiful gothic churches were closing their doors as places of worship and being used as office spaces, or libraries, or they were simply left vacant. The staff of the Oxford Centre was convinced that these changes were occurring in part because of urbanization. They wanted to learn from churches that thrived in these conditions. They discovered that the black church in America excelled at dealing with the challenges of the urban environment. They were growing strong, vibrant churches in the midst of the city.

So they invited us to come to teach on everything we knew about the black church. The students took copious notes. It was the first time in my life that anyone had expressed a sincere interest in understanding my experience as an African American Christian. I had no idea that my life as a black, Pentecostal female had any relevance to anyone else. No one had ever asked.

I left that trip convinced that God was getting ready to do something extraordi-

nary, and that this "new thing" was going to unite people from all over the world who didn't look like one another. For the first time it occurred to me that this "new thing" was going to uniquely and strategically include people of color. People who had previously been marginalized and minimized would now be used by God to provide prophetic leadership as agents of reconciliation and renewal.

There are times in history when people must accurately recognize what God is doing. These times are not determined or controlled by human beings. In the New Testament, Paul uses the word *kairos*, which means the right time, the set time, the opportune time, the strategic time, or the decisive time. If you will allow me the analogy, it is the "pregnant" time.

When a man and woman conceive a child, they wait for months in anticipation of their child's birth. Even in the age of ultrasound, when they're able to determine the gender of the child and cherish grainy photos from the womb, they can only guess at what their child will look like. So they wait, hope, and pray in eager expectation, and perhaps also some

anxiety. Then one night, usually when she least expects it, the woman starts to feel something different in her body. She turns to her husband, nudges him gently but firmly and says, "Honey, wake up. It's time!" She doesn't want him to tell her the time on his watch. She wants him to get up and spring into action, because "*kairos* time" is a decisive time that demands a response.

BIRTH PANGS

What are the decisive signs of the times for us as North American Christians? Is it possible that we are at a *kairos* moment, a time when God is moving, and we must choose how to respond? There are signs that we are, indeed, at such a moment. Like the initial birth pangs that lead to delivery, the signs of a *kairos* moment can prompt anxiety or nurture anticipation. But what cannot be doubted is that a time of radical change is approaching.

The population of our nation is changing. Ethnic minorities have doubled their share of the U.S. population since 1950, and according to the U.S. Census Bureau's latest projections, almost all the growth in U.S. population over the next 50 years—

from 282 million in 2000 to 420 million in 2050—will come from ethnic minorities, primarily Asians and Hispanics. On those projections, sometime shortly after 2050 non-Hispanic whites will become a minority in the United States.

This unprecedented shift in the demographics of the United States will be a serious challenge—and not just for whites, who will have to reassess their assumption of what counts as an ethnic "minority." African Americans, who had been the largest minority group since the nation's founding, saw that role pass to Hispanics in 2003. We already have evidence that this shift is producing birth pangs, from the streets of South Central Los Angeles to the poultry farms of the southeastern United States. Not long ago, British television presenter David Frost asked Billy Graham what he saw as the most important issue facing the Church in the 21st century. Graham answered, "Racial and ethnic hostility is the foremost social problem facing our world today."

Our economy is changing. For many decades middle-class, majority-culture Americans assumed that graduating from college would secure them a good job, a decent house, and a safe place to live. Yet not long ago, I was in an Enterprise Rent-A-Car office on my way to a speaking engagement with college students. The young man waiting on me asked what I was planning to speak about. "Make sure you tell them that when they graduate, they're not going to a get a job," he said. The cynicism in his voice was plain. "What was your major?" I asked. He had majored in computer science—a field he had thought would surely secure his future. Instead, he was renting cars.

Our economy has continued to be, by many measures, astonishingly productive. But as the benefits of that productivity flow to fewer and fewer people, the rest of the country struggles to keep even, let alone get ahead. "In our multiethnic society," writer Anthony Walton observes, "this conflict

over resources and profits has tended to be 'racialized.' ... Issues that are not racial in and of themselves come to be seen in racial terms because of our tendency to be tribal in allocating opportunity and blame."

Economic uncertainty causes people to become self-protective, fearful, and ethnocentric. We have seen how deep tribal divisions go when resources are stretched to their limit in Iraq, the Balkans, and the horn of Africa. In America, too, there is the real risk that we will increasingly see people from different races as a threat to our opportunity and economic security.

Our worldview is changing. The previous American century was one of supreme confidence in the power of science and technology to improve the world. Now we are entering a postmodern era marked, among other things, by a loss of confidence in the Western, scientific worldview. This trend is clearest in medicine. In the third decade of the AIDS epidemic, we are no longer so sure that diseases will readily yield to our technical prowess. Alternative medicine, holistic therapies, and traditional medicine from other cultures are all rising in popularity.

Faced with these dramatic changes, we can choose one of two basic responses. The first is to retreat defensively into the assumed security of people "just like us," protecting the narrow interests of our tribe. The truth is that many American Christians have chosen this path. Lacking any deep sense that God has invested some of His image in every culture and people group, we have stayed ethnically and racially segregated in our churches, our communities, and our institutions. Why not? We had no sense that we had anything to learn from people who were ethnically different from us. Sadly, our self-sufficiency blinds us to the myriad of international perspectives all around us and limits our global understanding.

In a world where none of us will be a member of the majority, where we will

face persistent economic insecurity, and where the limits of our technological mastery will be palpable, we may find that retreating is no longer a viable option.

'WAIT UP FOR US'

One day during our time in Oxford, my husband, Derek, found himself saying candidly that after centuries of trying to be included in the white church, black people had developed a vibrant church life and no longer wanted or needed to be accepted by white Christians. While he was expounding forcefully on this topic, an Anglican priest named John Mockford interrupted and said, "Wait a minute, lad. Your church is young and agile. Our church has become old and arthritic. We need you to wait up for us." A single tear fell from his eye. He turned to a man sitting next to him and said, "This is embarrassing, eh?" There was a moment of total silence.

Then Derek said, with a new level of empathy in his voice, "By asking me to wait up for you, you have just empowered me to be in relationship with you." That day we experienced an authentic moment of racial reconciliation—because one man had the courage to acknowledge his need for someone who was ethnically different from him.

In England, I began to understand that African Americans are uniquely positioned to be reconcilers all around the world. The tragedy of our past has uniquely qualified us to speak on issues of reconciliation, forgiveness, healing, and restoration— with the authority that is born of experience. If African Americans ever gained a sense of our global significance, we would view racial and ethnic hostilities around the world as opportunities for prophetic leadership. There are people all around the world who are waiting for us to come and share our unique perspective.

But we African Americans, too, need others as much as they need us. I once met a brother from Ghana, West Africa, who was completing his Ph.D. in the School of World Missions at Fuller Theological Seminary. During one of his trips home, he attempted to share the Gospel with several people who lived in his community. Although they listened respectfully, no one turned to Jesus Christ. He later learned that they were intimidated by a witch doctor who lived nearby. The witch doctor kept a symbol of his authority hanging outside his home: a lattice basket, filled with water, that never leaked.

My friend decided to pray that God would empty the basket.

He stayed outside the home of the witch doctor and prayed all night that God would demonstrate His power. At some point he fell asleep. The next morning he was awakened by a commotion. The basket was empty. That town saw a mass revival as people learned about the God who caused the water to come out of the basket. There had been a power encounter—and God had won.

We who were raised in the West, with the West's rational worldview, can try to explain that story away. But I believe we need African Christians to teach us how to preach the Gospel in power. The West is overwhelmed with information for information's sake and wary of truth that is rational yet impotent. The next major evangelist may well emerge from Africa or Latin America or China or Singapore.

We will need them, and simply saying that we will need them is a big step for many of us. The culture of America, of American Christianity both white and black, has been one of self-sufficiency and independence. But what God may be doing in this dramatic, perilous *kairos* moment is calling us to something different—a culture of interdependency, where we depend on one another across racial, ethnic, and national boundaries.

It is not easy to risk the vulnerability and uncertainty that such a time requires. We need to proceed with faith, believing that God is at work in the global Church, and He has something for us in the unfamiliar faces of our brothers and sisters. But since God is in control of this *kairos* moment, not us, what we most need to do is what the expectant mother asks her husband to do at that crucial moment: Wake up. It's time. **C**

Rev. Dr. Brenda Salter McNeil founded Overflow Ministries, Inc., a nonprofit, faith-based organization devoted to her growing passion for authentic reconciliation. She continues this work through Salter McNeil & Associates, LLC, a racial and ethnic reconciliation training, consulting, and leadership-development firm based in Chicago. Together with her husband and their two children, she stands at the forefront of an international movement to advance God's Kingdom of peace, justice, and reconciliation. To learn more, visit **www.saltermcneil.com**.

A CHRISTMAS CONSPIRACY

BY RICK MCKINLEY

EVERY CHRISTMAS, IT HAPPENS. I GET EXCITED FOR THE CELEBRATION OF JESUS' BIRTH—THAT MOMENT IN HISTORY WHEN ALL OF SCRIPTURE CAME TO LIFE! GOD BECAME FLESH. THE CHRIST-CHILD MOVED INTO OUR NEIGHBORHOODS AND REVEALED TO US ANOTHER KINGDOM: PREGNANT MARY, EVIL EMPIRES, AND THAT MOMENT WHEN THE WORLD STOOD STILL TO WORSHIP WITH THE ANGELS. IT WAS THE PINNACLE MOMENT OF THE REDEMPTIVE HISTORY!

And then I get depressed; inundated with commercials of what new gadget to buy, people in mad rushes to get more stuff, credit cards opening up sink holes that people will be climbing out of for months to come, and newscasters telling us that fights are breaking out at Wal-Mart over the last Xbox 360.

It isn't just THEM! It's us too! We're missing out on this powerful moment of worship that changed the world because we are spending every spare moment buying meaningless sweaters for uncle so and so. Can you name two presents you got last Christmas? I can! For the first time, I can tell you what I got for Christmas, six months after Christmas is over.

We preach of His greatness, we sing the songs, and for that sacred hour on Sunday we get pulled back into what matters most. With little warning, we are soon thrust back into the mayhem when we are hit in the head by an elbow of a competing shopper who assures us that what matters most is not what *really* matters most.

PULLING THE PLUG

Last Christmas, some pastor-friends and I pulled the plug on Christmas. What started out as an experiment ended up transforming us, our people and a whole bunch of other people with whom we shared the love of Christ. We worshipped the Baby as though it was for the first time. Because God gave us His Son—the world has never been the same.

So here's the story, and I am praying that as you read it you will want to join us. It's so simple, it's scary; so revolutionary, it's world changing.

We decided that we would ask our people to *live* the advent story—not just talk and sing about it or dress up like shepherds. We asked them to live counter-culture lives that modeled our celebration after His incarnation.

Christ resisted the empire of Herod by coming in weakness as a baby, making Herod so insecure that he murdered hundreds of toddlers. We decided we would resist the empire of consumerism and spend a lot less.

Because God gave us a relational gift, his Son, we decided to give meaningful and relational gifts too. We didn't want to focus on just buying stuff, but rather to concentrate on things we could make, trips to take, poems to write—the kind of things you keep forever and will recall a year from now when someone asks you what you got for Christmas last year.

Since Christ re-distributed His wealth by becoming poor to make us rich, we re-distributed our wealth also. We took all the money we saved by giving relational gifts, and we gave an offering with the money that was left over. We brought in close to half a million dollars between five churches. Crazy! We adopted low-income schools and hundreds of people were blessed, both locally and globally, with the monies we raised. We also decided that we would use a large portion of the money to bring clean water to people around the world whose very lives are at risk because they don't have clean drinking water. Just this week I received pictures of four wells we are sponsoring in Liberia. People are drinking clean water because God gave us the Water of Life.

Because Christ was worshipped through our meaningful giving, we worshipped the Baby in a way we never had before. The kids led the way. Everyone feared they would hate it, but it turned out that they understood it better than the adults. Some children emptied their whole piggy banks the day we took the offering. The Imago Dei Kids bought alpacas for some families in South America. (We had a llama at church that day to show them something close to an alpaca.) Our worship started on Sunday and went throughout the week. Instead of rushing to the malls, families were hanging out at home making gifts. Because God gave us His Son, we in turn were giving of ourselves to others.

There were so many stories it was, and continues to be, somewhat overwhelming. It had a viral effect. The main factor was not the offering, or the meaningful gifts, or the hundreds of people who were helped, it was that everything we were doing pointed us back to The Story— God gave us His Son, and we have never been the same.

After an amazing last year, churches started asking us about what we did. So, we began to dream. What if the church created a conspiracy of kindness at Christmas? What if every church in America celebrated Christmas this way? What impact could that have on the proclamation of Christ in our communities and our world?

So we created the Advent Conspiracy, and we are inviting you to join the revolution. Now, every year we anticipate the coming of Christ at Christmas. We can't wait to worship Him and to see how He changes the world *again*!

The statistics can't be ignored. Ten billion dollars gets clean water to everyone in the world. Fifteen billion dollars feeds everyone. In America, we spend $450 billion at Christmas. Get the picture? The world is watching for the star to rise again and for the people of God to gather around the Baby. Will you join us?

WHAT IS THE ADVENT CONSPIRACY?
The Advent Conspiracy is a catalyst to help churches and organizations equip their people to engage in the Christmas story in a way that will transform their people and as a result bring transformation to the world through their people, as they worship Christ at Christmas.

THE FIVE THEMES
1. Worship:
The central theme of the Advent Conspiracy is that Jesus is worshipped in such a way that His followers experience the power of Christ coming into the world. This powerful story brings with it the promise of transformation in His followers as they celebrate His birth with faithfulness and integrity. People being led in this journey will not be competing with the consumerist impulses of our culture, but instead they will be aligning themselves with Christ, thereby worshipping Him in a holistic way.

2. Resisting the Empire:
When Christ was born, the empire was threatened and as a result Herod, who was one of the more powerful kings of the day, ordered the killing of all the children two years old and under who lived in Bethlehem. The reason for this was that he hoped to take out the child-King that posed a threat to his kingdom.

CHRIST RESISTED THE EMPIRE OF HEROD BY COMING IN WEAKNESS AS A BABY, MAKING HEROD SO INSECURE THAT HE MURDERED HUNDREDS OF TODDLERS. WE DECIDED WE WOULD RESIST THE EMPIRE OF CONSUMERISM AND SPEND A LOT LESS.

While we are not living under Herod's reign, there is another empire of consumerism and materialism that threatens our faithfulness to Jesus. Jesus brought with Him an extraordinary Kingdom that is counter-culture to the kingdoms of this world.

A part of saying "yes" to Jesus means that we say "no" to over-spending. We say "no" to over-consumption. We say "no" to these things so we can create space to say "yes" to Jesus and His reign in our lives. The National Retail Federation was forecasting that Americans would spend approximately $457.4 billion at Christmas in 2006. [1] The American Research group estimated an average of $907.00 per family to be spent at Christmas in 2006. [2] After the Holiday season, we work for months to get out of debt, only to find that the presents we bought in the name of Christ furthered a consumerist mentality in our children and us. Our focus on shopping took our focus off of the greatness of Jesus. As Christ-followers, the Advent Conspiracy starts with us resisting a culture that tells us what to buy, wear and spend with no regard to bringing glory to Jesus.

3. Relational Giving:
In saying "no" to over-spending, we are then invited to say "yes" to give in relational ways. We do this because we worship a God who gave us a relational gift; God gave us His Son. This is an incredible opportunity to reclaim the heart of what matters most as we learn together to give gifts of meaning instead of simple material gifts. Pictures, poems, pieces of art, a baseball bat and a trip with dad to the ballpark all become relational alternatives that foster what matters most in life. In thinking in a new way about what it means to give ourselves to each other, we are transformed by the story of Advent, knowing that we give relationally because God gave relationally.

Some organizations have done do-it-yourself workshops to help their people learn the art of relational giving. Whatever you decide to do, the key is that you spend less and give relationally of yourself.

4. Re-Distribution:
Christ, though He was rich, became poor to make many rich. It was in the Advent that Jesus entered our poverty so we would no longer be poor. With the money we save by giving relationally and resisting the empire we, in turn, re-distribute the money we saved to the least of these in our communities and world.

We recommend that, before Christmas, each organization take an offering made up of the money that was saved through relational giving and resisting the empire. With these funds each church and organization decides how to re-distribute the money. It is an amazing picture when you see how much money is collected and how much good it can do in the world. In 2006, only five churches participated, and they collected just under half of a million dollars. Through this kind of radical giving, we are transformed by the advent story as we worship Jesus more faithfully.

5. Water:
Advent Conspiracy exists to be a catalyst for the church to help us worship Jesus more fully at Christmas and therefore be transformed by the God of Advent. We believe that we are better together than we are apart. Each year the Advent of Christ should be an opportunity to declare to the world that God has given us the greatest gift.

We are asking that each church and organization that participates designate at least 25 percent of the offering for clean water projects around the world. The vision is that in the next decade Christ-followers, acting as one people, can blot out the water crisis in the world. The estimated cost to solve the water problem is $10 billion. This is doable, given the number of churches and the amount of money that is spent on Christmas each year.

According to the World Water Council, 1.1 billion people live without clean drinking water; 2.6 billion people lack adequate sanitation. 1.8 million people die every year from diarrhea diseases and 3,900 children die every day from waterborne diseases. [3]

It is truly a declaration to the world that Jesus cares and that is why He came and created the Church to act on His behalf. How you go about spending the money for clean water is up to how God leads you. We will let Him be in the CEO on this, and just faithfully respond to His direction. **C**

Rick McKinley is the lead pastor at Imago Dei Community Church in Portland, Oregon. (**www.imagodeicommunity.com**) He is the author of *This Beautiful Mess: Practicing the Presence of the Kingdom of God* (Multnomah, 2006) and *Jesus in the Margins* (Multnomah, 2005).

*To get involved in the Advent Conspiracy sign up at their website: **www.adventconspiracy.org**. The site provides stories, resources (the Co-Conspirator newsletter), and recommends agencies that you can work with. Participants are encouraged to blog their results after the holidays, sharing how much money was re-distributed and what creative methods they used. For additional information email Jeanne McKinley, Director of Advent Conspiracy at **Jeans@imagodeicommunity.com**.*

The Color of Responsibility

By Tri Robinson

I HAVE ALWAYS CONSIDERED MYSELF FULLY PLANTED IN THE CONSERVATIVE CAMP. OVER THE YEARS, ON MOST ISSUES, I HAVE GENERALLY VOTED FOR THE REPUBLICAN PLATFORM. I'VE BEEN A FAN OF FOCUS ON THE FAMILY AND OTHER CHRISTIAN GROUPS THAT HAVE BEEN ADVOCATES FOR THE SANCTITY OF LIFE AND WHO CHAMPION THE MANY VALUES I'VE ALWAYS HELD DEAR. BUT WHEN I STARTED TEACHING ABOUT WHAT I BELIEVED TO BE A BIBLICAL MANDATE—TO CARE FOR CREATION—I FOUND MYSELF IN A NEW AND SOMEWHAT DIFFERENT POSITION.

After I taught this value to my church through a series of messages and gave it time to become entrenched as a Biblical responsibility in our congregation, I began to write *Saving God's Green Earth* (Ampelon, 2006). It's the story of what happened in our church in Boise. It was a call for Christians everywhere to embrace the idea of environmental stewardship. There was no question; it was controversial. Right away, the book became a magnet for criticism from conservative leaders who had developed the mindset that the environment was a liberal agenda, and if Christians were to become advocates of the environmental cause, it would weaken the Republican front.

Controversy isn't always bad. In fact, if you're trying to draw attention to a book of this nature, the debate itself motivates people to take a look at it. Our publicist saw the opportunity and seized the moment by scheduling me to be interviewed by dozens of talk radio and television hosts across the country.

Even though I had resolved in my own mind that environmental stewardship ("creation's care" as we began to call it) was not only Biblically correct but an actual commission from God, I still felt that I was walking on shaky ground. I knew I was no match for some of the hard-core conservative talk show hosts who pushed their agenda day after day and had the ability to intimidate people with conflicting views. Needless to say, I was a bit nervous for these first interviews.

THE SHAKY VOICE OF CLARITY

The very first interview was such a bad experience I wanted to give up before I even got started. It was scheduled with a hard hitting radio talk show host out of Detroit; I'll call him Bob. It was a phone interview that I took at home in my study. My wife Nancy knew I was unsettled and said she would be praying for me in the other room. Ironically, the week before this interview I had been conducting a leadership seminar just outside of Ann Arbor, Michigan. A number of the younger leaders who were familiar with Bob's show had warned me to be on my toes—Bob would have both barrels loaded. As it turned out, the interview was everything they promised and more.

The phone rang and a very business-like radio production manager put me on hold during a commercial break. In minutes I would be on the air, and my heart started to pound. My head became light, and everything I had rehearsed in my mind seemed to immediately dissipate. I couldn't remember a thing; my deep convictions and passion to call Christians everywhere to this cause seemed to be gone.

Bob came on and introduced me as the author of *Saving God's Green Earth*. Im-

IT IS THE RESPONSIBILITY OF EVERY CHRISTIAN NOT ONLY TO CARE ABOUT THE CREATION, BUT ALSO TAKE AN ACTIVE ROLE IN DOING SOMETHING ABOUT IT.

mediately, he began to share with his audience why environmentalists were extremists, anti-pro-life and promoters of gay marriage. When I finally had the chance to make some comments, I was undone and humiliated by my inability to communicate in such a hostile forum. My words and arguments seemed to dribble out of my mouth as I stuttered and stammered, searching for a starting place.

But all of a sudden, everything began to change. I believe the prayers of my wife must have kicked in and taken effect. There was a calm that came over me and clarity filtered my mind as a righteous anger welled up in my heart. Something screamed inside of me that this was wrong, and everything God had put in me was right.

I remember saying in a very collected way, "Bob, I understand what you're saying; there have been a lot of extreme anti-Biblical agendas driving the environmental movement that have offended us all. They have been wrong in thinking that things like abortion are the answer to a declining global environmental condition, but I just want to say one thing."

He gave me a moment to continue, and I said, "You know, Bob, it's people like you that intimidate solid Bible-believing evangelical leaders like me from promoting and leading the way in something as Biblical as this. God has clearly commis-

sioned His people to be stewards of His creation, but because we're afraid of criticism from people like you, we've given our responsibility over to a liberal non-Biblical society to do it for us. We should be the leaders in this area, but instead we've given up our leadership. Consequently, the stewardship of the environment is being led in directions that often offend us. If you think that's a good idea, then keep it up because you're doing a really great job of it." Bob paused, then thanked me for coming on the program and announced that we were out of time and the interview ended.

I hung up the phone and told my wife I never wanted to go through that again. Ironically, over the course of the next several months, I was interviewed on about forty programs around the country. Each time it became a little easier as my conviction grew stronger. After that first interview, I received a call from my publicist who told me that what I'd said to Bob impacted him, causing him to reconsider his stance on caring for the environment.

OUR RESPONSIBILITY
We are not called to a lifestyle of waste and neglect. Rather, it is the responsibility of every Christian not only to care about the creation, but also take an active role in

doing something about it. The global environmental condition is in rapid decline. As a result, humanity is suffering and the first to feel it are the poor, especially in developing nations.

Glaciers are melting; the ocean is rising and already affecting the agriculture of low-lying countries such as Bangladesh. The quality of fresh water is now resulting in the deaths of children around the world, especially in places like Africa. The world's most fertile soil is being covered over by metropolitan sprawl, washed away by the erosion of deforestation and polluted by excessive chemical application. Soon the world population of 6.6 billion people will be in desperate want for the very resources that sustain life itself. Those in desperate living conditions are crying out for the Church to rise up and address the problems that are causing an escalating global crisis.

The hour is growing late, but caring for creation can bring significant global impact. We can make a difference if we embrace this Biblical mandate, unify, and together express the love of God in practical ways by taking action against the injustices and practices that are hurting the very people we were called to serve. **C**

Tri Robinson is Senior Pastor of Vineyard Christian Fellowship in Boise, Idaho. Learn more at **www.vineyardboise.com**.

PRACTICAL CREATION CARE FOR CHURCHES

Consider employing these creation-conserving ways to make your church more eco-friendly.

ALTERNATIVE TRANSPORTATION

Minimize emissions while strengthening community by offering creation-friendly ways to get to your building.

- Offer a shuttle bus or van for your weekend church services.
- Set up walking or bike riding groups.
- Incorporate carpooling or vanpooling into your community group strategy.

REDUCE, REUSE, AND REDUCE MORE

Recycling is good, but eliminating is better. Reducing the amount of waste you create is the "ounce of prevention" that makes the biggest impact in creation care.

- Reduce paper cup waste at your church's coffee bar by bringing your own coffee mugs.
- End junk mail by entering your address at **www.optoutprescreen.com**.
- Keep recycling drives a constant in your church—cell phones, old sneakers, ink cartridges, and milk jugs can all be repurposed into different forms.
- Visit **www.earth911.org** for a listing of what you can recycle and how to start a program.
- Print only one worship guide per month, and reuse them from week to week.
- Replace trash cans with recycling collection bins in your church. Make people go out of their way to not recycle.

GET DIRTY

Members of Vineyard Boise maintain a one-third acre community garden that serves church members as well as the church's Barnabas Food Pantry. Last year, the garden produced over 13,000 pounds of fruits, vegetables, and herbs. Use the soil around your church to sow and reap in the most literal sense. Weekly volunteer days will help take care of plowing, planting, watering, weeding, and harvesting.

Architectural Evangelism

By Mel McGowan

AUTHOR AND SOCIOLOGIST RAY OLDENBURG, IN HIS BOOK, *THE GREAT, GOOD PLACE,* DESCRIBED HOW PEOPLE THROUGHOUT HISTORY HAVE LIVED IN THREE REALMS, DEFINED BY PHYSICAL AND SOCIAL RELATIONSHIPS. THE *FIRST PLACE* IS THE ENVIRONMENT INHABITED BY THE FAMILY UNIT, WHETHER NUCLEAR OR EXTENDED (I.E. THE HOME). THE *SECOND PLACE* IS TYPICALLY UNDERSTOOD AS THE PLACE WHERE ONE MUST GO TO PAY FOR – OR TO PREPARE TO PAY FOR – THE FIRST PLACE (I.E. THE WORKPLACE OR SCHOOL). THROUGHOUT HUMAN HISTORY, INDIVIDUALS HAVE ALSO HAD AN ADDITIONAL OPTION, A PLACE TO GATHER. THE *THIRD PLACE*.

Perhaps the earliest example of a Third Place in Western history was the Greek agora – basically an outdoor community living room, where people "did life together." On one side, merchants would set up shop in the marketplace stalls. Within shouting distance was the birthplace of democracy, free speech, Western philosophy and education, and last, but not least, the temple. This arrangement was not unique to Greek culture. For millennia, communal space was typically anchored by sacred space. From the Roman Forum, Italian piazzas and Spanish plazas to (across the Atlantic) New England Village Greens and Midwestern Town Squares, this "Big Idea" of making room

in public places for authentic community went unquestioned.

However, with the rise of Modern culture, architecture, and urban planning, an odd thing happened. After World War II, America not only forgot how to create Third Places, we actually outlawed them. You see, Modern architects and urbanists saw cities as functional machines that needed to be organized by separating the land uses. "Form follows function" became Modernism's dogma. City planning then "devolved" into the separation and classification of industrial, commercial, recreational, and residential uses. Land use zones were linked by roads and highways and were largely inaccessible to the pedestrian. The intent was honorable (after all, who wants to live next to a slaughterhouse?), but the outcome has not been quite what was planned: commercial "strips," homogeneous malls, suburban sprawl, and social isolation.

MACHINES OF WORSHIP

Today, vacant land is rarely designated as a "church zone" because of property tax

I believe that the Church has a unique opportunity to provide authentic community in the form of relational environments …

devaluation and perceived land use conflicts. Churches have to "beg for forgiveness" to exist at hidden locations within industrial parks or in the "boondocks" through a "Conditional Use Permit" process. This has left modern churches with two basic site plan options:

- Place the building closest to the intersection with the backside to the community, and the front door facing the rear parking. (The non-technical term for this is "mooning the community.")
- Set the building back to the rear of the property (strip-mall style) with an "ocean" of parking separating the community and the church.

Modern church architecture is based on the idea that buildings are "machines." Houses are "machines for living," and presumably churches are "machines for worship." Once a church is designed, the modern assump-

tion is that, like a toaster, the design should work just as well in Anchorage, Alaska, as it would in Orlando, Florida.

But how well is the modern church-building machine working? According to Barna Research, from 1993 to 2000 the amount of dollars spent on church construction more than doubled, presumably in the name of "expanding the Kingdom." Yet during that same seven-year period, the U.S. population increased by eight percent and church attendance decreased by eight percent. A statistician would call that a directly inverse correlation.

In Postmodern society, there is an increasing recognition of the pent-up market demand for Third Places. From Starbucks, to *Truman Show*-styled New Urbanist housing developments, to regional shopping malls that attempt to recreate Main Street USA, the marketplace has tried to

respond to our natural hunger for community. However, the reality is that many of these attempts to provide a neighborhood that emulates Mayberry often leave us feeling hollow. In the sea of an anonymous consumer crowd, we feel welcome only so long as the private commercial owner feels that we are paying customers. In these private developments masquerading as public spaces, there are often rules of behavior posted which in fact do not allow true free public speech and debate, much less worship.

A NEW COMMUNITY

I was convicted of the need for genuine, Christ-centered community during my tenure at the Walt Disney Company, as we drew inspiration for the layout of California's Downtown from a European village. With meandering streets that expand and contract, Downtown Disney reaches an experiential climax at a central gathering place. Of course, in any old-world village, the piazza would have been anchored by the church. No matter how lost you ever got wandering through the narrow streets and alleys, you could always look up and see the spire keyed to the heart of the community. As the team of Disney "Imagineers" substituted entertainment and commercial uses for this spiritual anchor, I recognized that we were attempting to fill the *God-shaped hole* in our master plan with the same thing that many lost people use to fill the God-shaped hole in their lives!

Churches across the country are adding coffee bars to replace the old folding table with a box of doughnuts. However, many are missing the point. They are trapped in the modern planning mindset which says that a church facility should be a machine for worship that can accommodate so many cars and attendees for a few hours one day a week and then sit empty of all other uses on the other six days of the week. In other words, "get 'em in, get 'em out." But I believe that the Church has a unique opportunity—and a responsibility—to provide authentic community in the form of relational environments, for horizontal (person-to-person) and vertical (person-to-Creator) connections.

The narrative of the Bible begins with God creating this perfect relational environment in a garden, and ends with Him restoring it in a city. If we define the Postmodern Church as *a culturally relevant, Christ-centered community,* and if we look back to the Book of Acts and the first century Christian Church, we find that 3,000—and later 5,000—were added in one day in the Third Places of the time!

VISIONEERING THE FUTURE ASSEMBLY

Across the country, maverick pastors and emerging leaders are responding to a Nehemiah-like calling to rebuild an authentic community centered on God. Rather than simply applying secular planning paradigms and design approaches to the Church, emerging master plans for Postmodern churches are being "visioneered" to include a powerful conceptual overlay (or "Big Idea") which informs everything from the site plan, the architectural direction, the spaces between the buildings, the graphic tone, and the interior experience.

In Northern California, Dale Borgen, a church planter and pastor, is negotiating with the master developer of a 9,000-acre "New Town" to integrate three megachurch sites into the planned "downtowns" as alternative types of anchor tenants— sharing parking and capitalizing on the cross-flow of people. Outside of Chicago, Darren Sloniger (a former concert promoter, successful developer, and pastor who holds a masters in urban planning) has opened a "Lightclub" housing Christian concerts on Friday and Saturday nights, church on Sunday, and coffee / community uses the rest of the week. Nearby, Dave Ferguson and the Institute for Community are practicing social architecture as they covertly integrate church into a master-planned community center where they run the social recreation programs.

At The Crossing, a Christian church outside of Las Vegas, the journey of God's people through the wilderness is illustrated with an "architecture of impermanence": fabric, metal, and desert-toned stucco. Visitors enter underneath a town "gate" with ancient writing noting that "The Journey begins at the Crossing." In Beloit, Wisconsin, a town economically ravaged by the effects of the rustbelt, Central Christian Church uses its lobby as the community food bank distribution center and employs architecture in its "Restoration Square" influenced by the look of an industrial plant to proclaim that God is the source of power and light for the community. In Corona, California, Crossroads Church is developing CandleWalk, where the church auditorium serves as a performing arts center and thousands are drawn onto campus by secular concerts, a restaurant, and the Londen Institute for Evangelism. The church is the anchor tenant, fronted by the "Circle of Light" piazza with pop-jet fountains and a polycarbonate cross-tower / campanile.

This approach, which seeks to tear down the walls and re-connect the Postmodern community to Christ, is what I call "architectural evangelism." Whereas modern churches focus on getting cars parked, bodies seated, and an effective "product" delivered for a few hours one day a week, architectural evangelism seeks to shape culture through Christ centered evangelistic environments that are not only safe to seekers, but attract them.

The Samaritan woman at Jacob's Well would never have made it to the Outer Court or the Inner Court (much less the Holy of Holies), but the God of the Universe came to her and offered her relationship. He did not allow a church building to get in the way. Neither should we. ▣

Mel McGowan is founder and president of Visioneering Studios, America's leading master planner and architect of "Christ-centered communities." Mel left a background in alternative music, film, and a decade-long stint at the Walt Disney Company to emerge as one of the youngest leaders of a national architecture firm, with studios in California, Colorado, and Georgia. Learn more at **www.visioneeringstudios.com**.

COME, LEARN WITH US
AN INTERVIEW WITH OSCAR MURIU

IN THE 1950s A GROUP OF WHITE EXPATRIATES STARTED A CHURCH IN KENYA—NAIROBI UNDENOMINATIONAL CHAPEL. THE CHURCH WAS LOCATED WITHIN A SECURED AREA WHERE AFRICANS WERE NOT ALLOWED.

AFTER THE MAU-MAU REBELLION, AS WHITES LEFT KENYA, THE CHURCH DWINDLED. IN THE MEANTIME, THE UNIVERSITY OF NAIROBI BEGAN GROWING AND OCCUPYING THE LAND AROUND THE CHAPEL. BUT UNTIL 1989, THE CHURCH HAD NO UNIVERSITY STUDENTS, AND ONLY ONE AFRICAN FAMILY AMONG THE REMAINING TWENTY MEMBERS IN THE CONGREGATION. THAT'S WHEN THE CONGREGATION APPROACHED AN INDIGENOUS AFRICAN CHURCH TO TAKE OVER. A YOUNG GRADUATE STUDENT NAMED OSCAR MURIU BECAME THE PASTOR OF NAIROBI CHAPEL.

TODAY THE CHURCH HAS PLANTED 25 CONGREGATIONS IN NAIROBI, WITH THOUSANDS OF MEMBERS. ANDY CROUCH OF THE **CHRISTIAN VISION PROJECT** RECENTLY INTERVIEWED OSCAR.

CVP: *What happened to change Nairobi Chapel from a dwindling group of discouraged whites to a vibrant, international, church-planting fellowship?*

MURIU: They began to pray that God would show them what to do, and they sought new leadership to help them reach the African students around them. That's how I got to come to the Chapel. I was finishing my studies at Nairobi Evangelical Graduate School of Theology.

CVP: *Did you have a plan?*

MURIU: I knew nothing about church leadership. My core prayer was, "Lord, give me 30 university students." One of the first students who came along is now an associate pastor with us. Last year we divided the main church up into five different congregations. I'm now pastoring one of the new church plants.

Since about 65 percent of Nairobians live in the slums, we made a commitment that for every church we plant that reaches out to an educated elite, like the Chapel, we would intentionally plant two churches that were unlike us, in the slum areas. So of the churches we have planted, seven or eight are like the Chapel, and the others are in the slums.

CVP: *Is church leadership different in slum areas than it is in educated areas?*

MURIU: For me, planting churches among the university educated is easy. They are like me. The challenge comes when I cross the social divide of status and wealth. That's been hard.

My hope had been that we could be a multi-economic church. But it's not turning out that way. Partly because of the location, partly because of what the different groups understand. When I deal with university students and the educated elite, I'm using statistical evidence, quoting historic figures and world leaders, citing books and movies.

That doesn't work with the poor. They don't understand statistical references; they don't know who Einstein was; they don't understand a reference to a movie. So the language of the educated elite excludes them. What they understand are real-life stories and parables like Jesus told.

CVP: *So how does the Chapel plant churches in poor areas?*

MURIU: Our task is to take from the wealthy and give to the poor. We find leaders who can speak the language of the poor and link the poorer churches with a richer, more educated church.

I have the responsibility to resource and enable the churches in the slums and to help my members have a real presence there. We recognize that we are going to work together. It's not in the same gathering, but there is a relationship.

That's not an ideal answer, but it is the real answer.

CVP: *What must Americans learn, and unlearn, to be effective agents of God's mission in the world?*

MURIU: Paul's model of missions is very different from the model of Western missions in the last 100 years. The West has designed a model of missions that only works for the West.

Americans enter the economically depressed communities of the world with a lot of resources. They come and stay in hotels. Paul's model says, "Stay with whomever opens their door to you."

We are a very hospitable people. But we've found that Americans want their space. They want to be picked up from a hotel in the morning and be dropped back in the evening. They can, in a sense, travel with a little bubble of America around them.

CVP: *Your church has a huge vision. How can churches in the West help? Do short-term mission trips help?*

MURIU: They work for the West; they don't work for us very well. We don't call them "short-term missions." We call them "short-term learning opportunities." The problem with calling it a mission is that it implies an agenda. There's something I need to come and do for you, to better your life. In reality, that doesn't happen in two weeks. Life is far too complex for that.

The greatest benefit is that you come and learn.

CVP: *So what happens when there is an interchange?*

MURIU: Americans know almost nothing about Kenya so the culture shock when they come is very deep. Some of them see destitute poverty for the first time ever. When you see poverty in America, on your television, it is sanitized. But the first marker of poverty is that it smells. That's how you know real poverty: the smell. I have watched short-term missioners come in, and I've realized, We need to go and debrief quickly because they're weeping; they're broken; they have an immense sense of guilt.

CVP: *Your church has developed some deep partnerships with churches in the United States. What have been the key ingredients of those partnerships?*

MURIU: In each of these churches it's been important to find a bridging relationship—someone who comes in quietly, speaks slowly, is a good listener, and is trying to learn.

CVP: *Are there enough such churches in Africa to handle this level of partnership? I'm afraid you'll be overwhelmed with churches wanting to do this with you.*

MURIU: In the whole continent of Africa there are increasingly more. The task we at the Chapel have is to say to other churches, "Wake up. There's a golden opportunity here to craft a new model of missions. So come, learn with us." There is enormous potential for us all to learn together. **C**

For more from the Christian Vision Project and Oscar Muriu, visit **www.christianvisionproject.com**.

© 2007 Christianity Today International. All rights reserved. Used by permission. Photo courtesy of Andrew Silk.

TOMMY KYLLONEN
LEAD PASTOR, CROSSOVER CHURCH
Age 34, Tampa, Florida, www.urband.org

TOMMY KYLLONEN (A.K.A. URBAN D) GREW UP IN PHILLY AS A PASTOR'S KID, SO CHURCH WAS A BIG INFLUENCE ON HIS LIFE—BUT SO WAS THIS NEW EMERGING CULTURE CALLED HIP-HOP. THROUGH HIS TEEN YEARS TOMMY STRAYED FROM HIS FAITH ROOTS. IT WASN'T UNTIL HE DECIDED TO GO TO A CHRISTIAN COLLEGE THAT GOD SHOWED TOMMY THAT HE WANTED HIM TO GO BACK AND REACH THE HIP-HOP CULTURE.

THE CALL

My calling is to see people from my generation get truly connected to God. Most people influenced by Hip-Hop believe in God, but they don't have a real relationship with Him—they aren't plugged into a faith community. My life's calling is to get that people group connected to God and connected to a church. It's a whole movement that is starting across the country.

SCOPE AND STYLE

Our environment is definitely unorthodox in a lot of ways—except the doctrine. It's a multi-cultural crowd of singles and young families mostly in their 20s and 30s. In the crowd you see people with hats, braids, and baggy pants all the way to someone rocking khaki pants with a polo shirt. About 70 percent of the Hip-Hop crowd is unchurched.

Our style is transparent. Although we don't call ourselves a Hip-Hop church, we target that culture, so you'll see Hip-Hop elements throughout our worship experience. The service itself is visually driven. We have a great creative team that helps produce short films for messages, along with occasional dramas and live songs to illustrate the Scripture we're teaching.

THE STRENGTH OF OPTIMISM

In urban ministry money is often in short supply. It's always a faith walk—personally, for the church, and for the staff serving each week. We have seven full-time staff members that sacrifice a lot to work here—it takes courage to trust that God will provide. And He always does.

Typically the crowd that we work with has serious life baggage, issues that Bible College doesn't teach you how to deal with. There's a lot of encouragement, pushing, and accountability that has to happen on a regular basis. As the lead pastor, I have to be strong for my team and the congregation. It's important to stay positive and optimistic in the face of adversity and trials.

REDEEMING RESULTS

Most conversations are incredibly positive and encouraging. We've had a lot of great favor with the media, local and national, which has been encouraging. We thank God that every article has been positive. However, the real reward comes in seeing changed lives. That's the real fruit. We've seen many people—drug dealers, addicts, the lonely—turn their lives around because of what God is doing through our ministry.

THE UNORTHODOX

Be unorthodox. That's my theme right now. Break from convention and tradition and be who you were created to be. If you're trying to be something you're not, our culture will realize you aren't being authentic. Your influence will suffer. God made you a unique person, so just be yourself. **C**

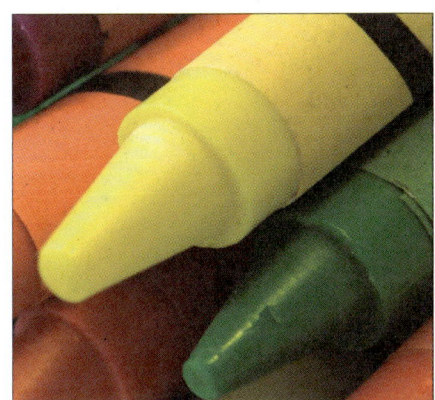

Crayons and Community

By Erwin R. McManus

One of the questions I am asked the most is concerning Mosaic's diversity. Usually when a person refers to diversity, it means dealing with ethnic or racial differences. I understand why this is such an important focus in our culture. The need to deal with the ever growing segmentation and the tensions that ensue have made diversity one of our culture's most significant issues.

Mosaic represents somewhere around 70 different ethnic groups. Just this past week we baptized someone from Finland, had a first time guest who was a Russian-Jew, and once again faced the challenge of how to integrate them into a community where we also have to deal with transplants from Michigan. Ironically, the tremendous success we've had in bringing the world together hasn't happened as a result of what you'd expect. I haven't spent the last 15 years preaching, teaching, or even focusing on racial reconciliation. My experience and observation tells me that those churches that actually raise the banner of reconciliation and diversity rarely accomplish it. Whatever measure of success we have experienced in this arena comes from a very different focus. We have spent an endless amount of time and energy identifying, nurturing, developing, and maximizing the uniqueness of every person.

Rather than trying to create a rainbow coalition of white, black, brown, and whatever other colors our eyes might see, we have instead taken on a far more complex challenge. Racial reconciliation is like trying to fill a box of crayons with blue, red, and yellow. Granted, they're beautiful and every other color is derived from them, but you're still dealing in primary colors. Imagine expanding from the three-pack of crayons to the 64 pack filled with a seemingly endless array of color and opportunity. Reach in and pick a color—turquoise, indigo, silver, coral, magenta, tangerine. To the casual artist, some colors seem redundant. Many of us are incapable of identifying the nuanced differences. But to the skilled artisan, those nuances are absolutely critical for their full creative expression.

It's the same when building human community. If all you see are the primary colors, you'll always be limited, even though all the potential in the world is there. When you begin to see people beyond the surface and excavate the real uniqueness that resides within them, you'll wonderfully discover that the diversity you hoped for was just a starting point. What you'll come to realize is far more than you could have imagined. **C**

Erwin R. McManus is the lead pastor at Mosaic—a remarkably diverse ethnic and cultural congregation in Los Angeles, California. (**www.mosaic.org**) He is the author of several books including *Soul Cravings* (Thomas Nelson, 2006). For more information visit **www.soulcravings.com**.

To read more about diversity, I recommend Eric Bryant's book, Peppermint-Filled Piñatas.
Visit **www.ericbryant.org**

© 2006 Awaken. Used by permission.

INTENTIONAL ABOUT COMMUNITY

So often we attempt to force community by attending group meetings, while those closest to us remain the most isolated. Take time to evaluate those in your immediate community. List their names—pray for them. How can you begin to lay a foundation of trust and love in your neighborhood and in your church family?

CLEAN WATER | COMING TO RWANDA SOON

BY JEFF SHINABARGER

IT WAS A NIGHTMARE. I DREAMT OF A BOY, ABOUT 8 YEARS OLD, 4 FEET TALL, NO SHIRT, ONLY RIPPED UP, MUD- STAINED PANTS, WITH A BIG LITTLE BELLY. I STILL CAN'T REMEMBER WHAT HIS FACE LOOKED LIKE. IT WAS LIKE A HYPE WILLIAMS MUSIC VIDEO WHERE HE FOCUSES ON THE SUN GLEAMING AROUND THE PRODUCT HE WANTS YOU TO SEE. SUDDENLY THE ANGLE OF THE SUN MOVED AND AN EMPTY GLASS OF WATER APPEARED. THE BOY LEANED DOWN TO FILL THE GLASS AGAIN, AND THE SHOT PANNED BACK IN A CINEMATIC STYLE. I WATCHED THE BOY DIP THE GLASS INTO A FILTHY PUDDLE ON A MUD STREET. HE TOOK ANOTHER DRINK. I WOKE UP.

It was 3:27 in the morning. I was sweating. I went to the kitchen, filled up a glass of ice water from my refrigerator door, and took a drink. I woke up my wife Andre. I had dreamt of injustice. Rwanda Clean Water Project began.

That nightmare birthed in me a real world dream to bring clean water to Rwanda. I shared the idea with my good friend, Gabe Lyons, who gave it legs. He located a foundation partner to help us receive money and send it on to our implementation partners in Rwanda.

We decided to launch the idea of bringing clean water to Rwanda at an event called Catalyst in October 2005. On one particular morning, when approximately 8,000 church leaders entered the conference center, every person was given a bottle of water—no explanation, no tag, no branding, no cost, just pure clean water. Then we shared the story of the need for clean water in Africa. We take clean water for granted in America. The reality is, if there were clean water in developing countries today, the number of sicknesses literally would be cut in half. In a span of ten minutes, the leaders responded by giving $105,000!

In the spring of 2006, a group of 15 of us went to Rwanda to assess the progress of the first wells that had been dug since that 10-minute offering. The following account is what I wrote the day we met the families that were benefiting from the existence of these new wells:

Wells. We all saw the child that pumped the well and balanced the tin of water on his head and posed for us to take pictures. He was only one of many that gained from the well. From that one well alone, there are 2,999 others that smile just like him every day. That was one of the proudest and most humbling moments of my life. We saw how the simplest modern convenience can change the health and hope of an entire village. This is such a simple act, yet it could change humanity today. What if we worked to give everyone in the entire world an opportunity to have access to clean water? Can you imagine the smile on that child's face multiplied by millions of smiles from all over the world? Now that would be priceless. A small offering has the ability to change a society.

We came home and were humbled by how many lives were changed and how little we did to make such a substantial difference for thousands of people in Rwanda. Yet millions more still don't have the luxury that I have of clean water every day. What if we could do more? What if more families had access to clean water? Those were the questions we asked as we left Rwanda.

Since that trip to Rwanda, we have collaborated with individuals and churches all over the nation that have grasped the importance of clean water. Together, we have raised $440,000 toward clean water in Rwanda. Our goal is to raise $1 million. As this dream becomes a reality, I continually reflect on three powerful concepts I have learned along the journey:

COMMON GOOD
PROJECTS UNIFY PEOPLE

Thirty kids made beautiful artwork on ceramic pitchers that they sold on Ebay. In Alabama, the Cove United Methodist Church collected a free will offering on a Sunday morning that totaled $70,000. A coffee shop in Orlando found a matching donor for a fundraiser at their business and raised $12,000. We are partnering with high-profile celebrities and executives on a film that will be released in 2008 about the global need for clean water. We recently connected with an entrepreneur from Boulder, Colorado committed to the teaching of Gandhi, who was extremely excited about the project.

N.T. Wright explains in *Simply Christian*, "We all share not just a sense that there is such a thing as justice, but a passion for it, a deep longing that things should be put to rights." [1] The story of Rwanda Clean Water is shared

WE SAW HOW THE SIMPLEST MODERN CONVENIENCE CAN CHANGE THE HEALTH AND HOPE OF AN ENTIRE VILLAGE. WHAT IF WE WORKED TO GIVE EVERYONE IN THE ENTIRE WORLD AN OPPORTUNITY TO HAVE ACCESS TO CLEAN WATER?

by the gifts from thousands of individuals. Rwanda Clean Water is comprised of people of different convictions theology, age, religion, and location working together to better humanity. Clean water is an essential to life. All people agree. Justin Dillon, creator of "The Concert to End Slavery," refers to this form of solution as an "open-source project." Humanity is suffering. This is a global concern that all can agree on and work together to meet the needs. Unifying for the common good is a great lead-in for Christians in our day-to-day conversations.

CLEAN WATER CREATES SUSTAINABLE COMMUNITIES

We are all aware of the genocide that resulted in millions of deaths in Rwanda. Thirteen years later, they are restoring friendships through conversations and grace. In his book *Fabric of Faithfulness*, Steven Garber says, "Community is the context for the growth of convictions and character." If this is true, then we need to help create simple, community-driven environments, where convictions and character can be reclaimed.' [2] When I visited one of the new wells in Rwanda, I noticed hundreds of people walking for up to three miles with these unforgettable yellow jugs. Every day, a person from every family will walk or ride a bike to the well to get water for the day. In the book that Starbucks uses as mandatory reading, *The Great, Good Place*, Ray Oldenburg refers to this idea as "The Third Place." It is a social environment separate from home and work that is important for "civil society, democracy, civic engagement, and establishing feelings of a sense of place."

In the hills of Rwanda, the well is "the third place," where everyone gathers. It is the hub of the social network. Through clean water locations, healing to individuals is happening daily. Conviction and character is being restored. In his brilliant book, *Deep Economy*, Bill McKibben thinks growth in developing countries, "should concentrate on creating and sustaining strong communities, not creating a culture of economic individualism." Clean water will forever be an essential in the lives of not only individuals, but it also offers a place for developing deeper relationships in the Rwandan community.

INFLUENCE IS GAINED BY DOING SOMETHING

The most difficult element of moving an idea into motion is starting. Yet, when a great idea is launched, influence quickly follows. The dream that woke me up that night was about one little boy, yet thousands of people have joined in the initiative and thousands of Rwandans have benefited from one boy. Rwanda Clean Water has gained attention from media, churches, and cultural leaders because we did something. Everyone has an idea, but few people move that idea into reality. When creators move from idea to action, people will follow. Don't search for influence. Don't care who gets the credit. Search yourself. Find what moves you. Discover a place of need. Authentically pursue a vision that helps humanity. Use the gifts you have been given. Influence will follow at the moment when you can handle the responsibility.

JOIN RWANDA CLEAN WATER PROJECT

As encouraging as this project has been to me, most people in rural Rwanda still do not have access to clean water. Women and young children walk for miles to fetch water from swamps and dirty rivers with buckets and canisters. It is amazing that with a simple gift of money we can literally save lives, decrease illnesses, and create sustainable communities.

We are looking for 300 churches to join a growing community in raising funds to bring clean water to Rwanda. Give $3000 to Rwanda Clean Water and 750 people will receive the simple gift of drinking clean water for the rest of their life. Your community, your family, your neighborhood, and your friends can work together to raise the funds that will forever change lives. Please join us in providing clean water to Rwanda. **C**

www.fermiproject.com/rwanda

Jeff Shinabarger is a big idea guy, acting as creative director and experience designer for all Fermi Project initiatives, and editor of Fermi Words, a digital media magazine educating leaders on shaping culture. Jeff was also a creative mind behind the Catalyst Conference where he was the lead experience designer for three years and Executive Editor of the Catalyst GroupZine. He recently started **giftcardgiver.com** to shape a new form of giving to those in need. Jeff lives in East Atlanta, Georgia with his wife, Andre, and dog Max.

FOOTNOTES

Driving on Ice

[1] Warren Bennis and Burt Nanus, *Leaders* (New York: Doubleday, 1992), 144.

[2] Peter M. Senge, *The Fifth Discipline* (New York: Currency/Doubleday, 1990), 155.

[3] Jim Collins, *Good to Great* (New York: Harper-Collins, 2001), 89.

[4] Stephen Covey, *The 7 Habits of Highly Effective People* (New York: Simon and Schuster, 1989), 99.

SESSION 1
COURAGEOUS IN CALLING

The Last Two Cents
Real Stories of Calling

[1] Matthew 16:17

[2] Genesis 12:1-3

You Can Be an Abolitionist

[1] Kevin Bales, *Disposable People* (Los Angeles: University of California Press, 1999), 3-4.

A Mind Ablaze
The Vanguard of Christian Thinking

[1] George Weigel, *Letters to a Young Catholic* (New York: Basic Books, 2004), 43-44.

[2] Robert Louis Wilken, *The Spirit of Early Christian Thought* (New Haven: Yale University Press, 2003), xiv.

[3] Henri Nouwen, *Reaching Out: The Three Movements of the Spiritual Life* (New York: Doubleday, 1976), 50-51.

[4] Richard Hofstadter, *Anti-Intellectualism in American Life* (New York: Alfred A. Knopf, 1963), 24-25.

[5] Micah 6:8 NIV

[6] Dennis Hollinger, *Head, Heart and Hands: Bringing Together Christian Thought, Passion and Action* (Downers Grove: InterVarsity Press, 2005), 44.

SESSION 2
ENGAGED IN CULTURE

The Outside View
Why Outsiders View Us as unChristian

[1] David Kinnaman and Gabe Lyons, *unChristian* (Grand Rapids: Baker Publishing, 2007), 245-246.

[2] ibid., 227.

True Story
Steve Beard

[1] C.S. Lewis, *God in the Dock* (Grand Rapids: William B. Eerdmans Publishing Co., 1970), 93.

SESSION 3
AUTHENTIC IN INFLUENCE

Mavericks
The Path of the Uncommon

[1] Alexander Roberts and James Donaldson, *The Anti-Nicene Fathers* (Buffalo: The Christian Literature Publishing Company, 1885), 41.

[2] C.S. Lewis, *The Lion, the Witch, and the Wardrobe* (New York: Harper Collins, 1950), 81.

[3] Kenneth Scott Latourette, *A History of Christianity, Vol. 2: Reformation to the Present* (Massachusetts: Prince Press, 2005), 717.

[4] Garth Rosell, "America's Hour Has Struck" (*Christian History and Biography*, No. 92, 2007), 16.

Momentum Theorem

[1] James 1:8

[2] Matthew 19:26, Mark 10:27

SESSION 5
PASSIONATE ABOUT GOD

Beyond Our Walls

[1] www.theamericanchurch.org

[2] Rebecca Barnes and Lindy Lowry, "The American Church in Crisis" (*Outreach* magazine, May/June 2006).

[3] Jeff Sharlet, "Soldiers of Christ: Inside America's Most Powerful Megachurch" (*Harper's Magazine*, May 2005).

[4] Cathy Lynn Grossman, "Evangelical: Can the E-Word be saved?" (*USA TODAY*, 23 January, 2007).

[5] Isaiah 6:8 NIV

SESSION 6
INTENTIONAL ABOUT COMMUNITY

A Christmas Conspiracy

[1] The National Retail Federation, "NRF Sees Subdued Holiday Gains in 2006" (September 19, 2006). www.nrf.com

[2] American Research Group, Inc., "2006 Christmas Spending Plans Hold Steady" (November 22, 2006). www.americanresearchgroup.com/holiday

[3] D. Zimmer & D. Renault, "Water Crisis Facts and Figures" (World Water Council, 2003). www.worldwatercouncil.org/index

Clean Water | Coming to Rwanda Soon

[1] N.T. Wright, *Simply Christian* (New York: Harper Collins, 2006), 6.

[2] Stephen Garber, *Fabric of Faithfulness* (Downers Grove: Inter Varsity Press, 1996), 159.

YOUR SMALL GROUP WILL NEVER BE THE SAME... LIQUID...GOD'S WORD FLOWING THROUGH OUR LIVES.

CREATED BY **JOHN WARD** AND **JEFF PRIES** OF MARINERS CHURCH— ONE OF THE TOP 100 LARGEST AND TOP 100 FASTEST-GROWING CHURCHES!

Designed specifically for your small group, Liquid is a DVD-based experience featuring five 10-minute episodes in each series and a 112-page Reflection Guide with questions and leader's tips.

Each episode introduces present-day characters whose problems and struggles mirror biblical stories, illustrating that God's word is as true today as it was when it was written.

With emotionally provoking videos, introspective questions, and tips for leading a small group, **Liquid** is the perfect experience for individual growth or small group study.

Your small group can experience **Liquid** for only $19.99 per series!

   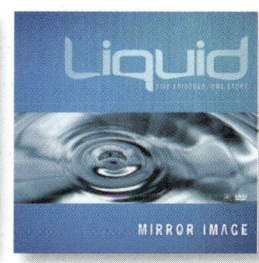

LIVE AT FIVE, based on the book of James, follows the story of Natalie Neff and her struggles just out of college to discover purpose and direction in her life as she's faced with daunting personal and professional challenges. $19.99

CROSSING features five stand-alone episodes based on stories from the book of Joshua. Each story illustrates a situation that could either be controlled by fear and insecurity, or where God can reach out and help His people cross to a better place. $19.99

FORK IN THE ROAD is a modern retelling of the life of David. From his legendary triumph over Goliath to his greatest downfall with Bathsheba, Fork in the Road portrays one man's crucial moments of decision that either lead him to victory or defeat. $19.99

MIRROR IMAGE, based on some of the most famous biblical parables, is the story of a family from Orange County who faces dramatic events and must choose how to respond, reminding us how to be salt and light in the world. $19.99

Experience **Liquid** for yourself at www.experienceliquid.com or contact Nelson Ministry Services at 1-800-933-9673 for a **FREE PREVIEW DVD.**

Thomas Nelson
Since 1798

For other products and live events, visit us at: **thomasnelson.com**

CATALYST™

The Catalyst Conference is a leadership experience unlike any other! Learn how to be courageous in calling, engaged in culture, authentic in influence, uncompromising in integrity, passionate about God, and intentional in community.

'08

OCTOBER 8-10
ATLANTA, GA

CATALYST: The Leadership Filter for What's Next in the Church

WWW.CATALYSTSPACE.COM
888.334.6569

www.catalystspace.com

THE LEADERSHIP FILTER FOR WHAT'S NEXT IN THE CHURCH

CONTENT

FILTER

Filter is a brand new offering from Catalyst featuring exclusive content not available anywhere else. Your one-year Filter membership includes unlimited access to a unique online community, never before released writings and talks from leading communicators, invitations to intimate events, private webcasts, pre-release mailings of new resources, discounts on offerings from Catalyst partners, and much, much more.

CATALYST PODCAST

Get behind the scenes with the speakers, writers and personalities of Catalyst. Delivering practical leadership, cultural insights, and profiles of next-generation leaders, you'll hear our guests answering the questions that no one else is asking! Download what's next. Subscribe for free.

CATALYST GROUPZINE™ SERIES

Catalyst brings you what's next in small group studies. A collection of writings with an innovative magazine design, GroupZines are a tool to help facilitate engaging discussion and powerful teaching opportunities. These studies are for individuals and teams who are ready to step up to the challenge of engaging and equipping the next generation of leaders.

CATALYST MONTHLY

A FREE online magazine with no ads, Catalyst Monthly connects with the pulse of the next-generation leader's desire to engage culture with both significance and relevance through articles, stories, and cultural commentary. You'll crave this up-close dose of pure leadership, delivered directly to your inbox. Subscribe now.

filter

CATALYST MONTHLY